Madcap Military Mayhem

200 years of the bizarre, barmy, bungled, brave and bloody brilliant

BENEDICT LE VAY

After the First World War, some British infantry officers thought one-man tankettes would be a brilliant idea. Eccentric Lieutenant-General Sir Giffard Le Quesne Martel adapted his own car to make the first Morris-Martel tankette. One is pictured under test, but never found official favour. He kept inventing things such as a quickly unfoldable bridge, and was known simply as 'Q'

Cover picture: Not a giant tuba regiment about to play, as it appears, but a Japanese acoustic aircraft detection unit, intended to direct the anti-aircraft guns in the background, pictured between the wars, before the advent of radar. They are being inspected by the Emperor

Copyright © 2017 | Benedict le Vay

Fourth edition

All rights reserved.

ISBN: 1537784471
ISBN-13: 978-1537784472

ONE PARTICULAR HOUSE ('Easier to find than Random House'),
LONDON, AMAZON and KINDLE

The Sizaire-Berwick Wind Wagon armoured car of 1915. Enthusiastic officers thought aircraft engines on the ground would be a great idea. It wasn't

At Gallipoli, in 1916, the fire was so dense that two bullets hit each other in mid-flight, making a souvenir for a survivor of the doomed expedition

DEDICATION

For all the courageous men in uniform who twice in the past century stood up, faced horrors and gave their all so we, the luckiest generation in history, could grow up in peace, make a life, make a career, make babies, make merry, make mistakes – but not have to make war. And the men and women who stand ever ready to do so again. Thank you. It's a debt we can never repay.

ACKNOWLEDGMENTS

Kelvin Wynne, Andy Simpson, Robin Popham, Lawrence Webb, Jeff Shaw, Bill Smith, Canadian Aviation and Space Museum, Australian War Memorial, Colin Smith, War History Online, Dr Richard Harvey, The Economist, Imperial War Museum, Frank Coldrick, Daily Mail, Wikimedia, Maine Department of Agriculture, Conservation and Forestry, United States Navy History and Heritage Command. Any comments, conclusions or mistakes are, however, utterly my own, so contact me on benlevay@aol.com with any brickbats, brainwaves or bouquets, as readers have very kindly about my other books

FOREWORD

THE first thing that *must* be said, despite this book being crammed with the funny peculiar, the funny hilarious and the funny unbelievable, is that war isn't funny. The suffering of those involved, and their families, is huge and deserves some respect, as do their sacrifice and courage.

And *all* war is mad, in a way. It shouldn't be happening. I remember as a young reporter watching the British fleet sail for the 1982 Falklands War, and thinking: 'This *can't* be a sensible way to settle a diplomatic or political dispute in the modern world.' Hundreds of brave young men going to tear apart the bodies of other young men – in the enemy's case because some lying political swine had conned them – until one side is too hurt to carry on.

It seemed like something in an old newsreel, the weapons being loaded aboard, girlfriends proudly waving, flags flying, ships' sirens tooting, etc. And then when they came back, the bands playing, the weeping families, the Argentine guns strapped to the back of the ship as trophies. Several hundred men didn't come back, many more were maimed. It must have been hideous – and that was a relatively clean war – military against military, right against wrong. The suffering on the other side must have been worse. Those boys had mothers too.

But with full respect for all that, I recall the black humour of the servicemen, and the odd characters that kept them going. The late, great Spike Milligan, when a comrade complained at the din of the biggest artillery barrage since World War I at the start of the Battle of El Alamein in 1942, retorted: 'If you don't like a laugh, you shouldn't have joined up.'

And if war isn't funny haha, it *is* often funny peculiar. In this book, I have tried to check the accounts of the frankly rather incredible by several methods. And where pictures are not of the

relevant event, I make this clear. So with those caveats out of the way, strap on the old leather flying helmet, snap on those goggles, start the engine, and we're clear for take-off into strange, silly skies!

CONTENTS

	Acknowledgments	i
1	Unlikely wars	7
2	Long and Short Wars	19
3	Disastrously Stupid Wars	23
4	War of Elephants and Chandeliers	29
5	Weird War I, II, and III…	50
6	Bizarre Battles	76
7	Flying in the Face of Reason	98
8	How obsolete 'Stringbags' doomed Hitler's most powerful and modern war machine	168
9	Animals at War	175
10	Nutty or Naughty Nauticals	205
11	Barmy Army: Eccentric Soldiers	259
12	The Brutal War of Brainboxes	281
13	Almost True: Brilliant fakes, hoaxes and conspiracy theories	285
14	The Shameful Hidden War of France v Britain, 1940-42	307
15	Mesopotamian Mayhem	323
	About the author	337

1 UNLIKELY WARS

THE GREAT EMU WAR: This happened back in the 1930s, when the military might of the Australian state – in the form of Major G.P.W. Meredith of the Seventh Heavy Battery of the Royal Australian Artillery – took on an apparently easy-to-defeat enemy: the emu, an ostrich-like bird.

Given that the emu cannot fly, is generally unarmed and untrained, and is an easy target at six feet tall, and that the soldiers were armed with Lewis guns and 10,000 rounds of ammunition, it should have been a walk-over. In fact, the emu was the clear victor.

I say *the* emu, but there were lots of them – about 20,000 – and to be (briefly) fair to the authorities for a moment, the emus made a mass attack on farms in Western Australia. The birds ravaged the crops and tore holes in fencing so whole regiments of rabbits could join in on their side. The farmers – mostly veterans of the First World War who had been encouraged to settle there, just in time for the Great Depression to slash prices for their crops – were desperate and pleaded for drastic government action.

In October 1932, the military expedition arrived in the Campion district. Hostilities were delayed by heavy rain, which had the effect of breaking up the emu army into small detachments. On November 2, the campaign started with farmers attempting to herd the emus towards the waiting guns. However stupid emus may be, they weren't having any of this (unlike, one must sadly say, the poor soldiers in the recently finished war). The emu ranks broke up into small groups running off in all directions. The Lewis guns opened fire, but the range was too great and hardly a bird was hit.

Australian troops with a Lewis gun (on a later occasion)

Another skirmish later in the day resulted in only a few dozen emu fatalities.

On November 4, Meredith tried to be more cunning. He set an ambush at a local dam with one of the Lewis guns. A force of 1,000 emus was seen approaching, and the gunner held his fire until he could see the critters' beady eyes. He opened fire, but soon the gun jammed and only 12 of 'the enemy' were accounted for.

In the following days, Meredith moved his forces south towards the apparent emu HQ, or rather where they seemed more docile. He made the mistake of mounting one of the guns on a truck. This bumped and lurched over the rough ground so it could not keep up with the emus or aim accurately. The bullets flew everywhere – endangering nearby farmers – but hit very few emus.

By November 8, emu forces (a humorous mock-up picture is shown of one emu participant, left) were embarrassingly outflanking the military force. Local ornithologist Dominic Serventy commented:

> *The machine-gunners' dreams of point blank fire into serried masses of Emus were soon dissipated. The Emu command had evidently ordered guerrilla tactics, and its unwieldy army soon split up into innumerable small units that made use of the military equipment uneconomic. A crestfallen field force therefore withdrew from the combat area after about a month.*

Major Meredith was forced to explain his force's humiliation to the Defence Minister, and he paid this unlikely tribute to the emu 'enemy', who carried on even after being hit several times:

> *If we had a military division with the bullet-carrying capacity of these birds it would face any army in the world... They can face machine guns with the*

invulnerability of tanks. They are like Zulus whom even dum-dum bullets could not stop.

The unimpressed and obstinate Minister of Defence, Sir George Pearce, seemed to stick his head in the sand like an, erm, ostrich. He ordered a second campaign which started in late November and lasted into December. Instead of tens of thousands of emus being killed as hoped, the numbers were about a 40 a day. Soon, all the ammo – which the farmers were forced to pay for – was expended, and the Army withdrew, leaving the triumphant emu ranks to be reformed. It was a national humiliation for the mighty Australian military – defeated by a bunch of overgrown chickens!

Emu War	
Part of The Great Depression	
Date	1932
Location	Campion, Western Australia
Result	Decisive Emu Victory
Belligerents	
Commonwealth of Australia	Emus
Commanders	
Major Meredith	none
Strength	
2 machine guns	20 000 birds
Casualties and losses	
10 000 rounds of ammo. Dignity.	12 birds+

**How one internet page summed up the Emu War.
Note the caustic comment on losses!**

PS: If you read anywhere of co-ordinated emus converging on London from all directions, don't panic! It happens every day. It's a railwayman's acronym for electric multiple units – commuter trains.

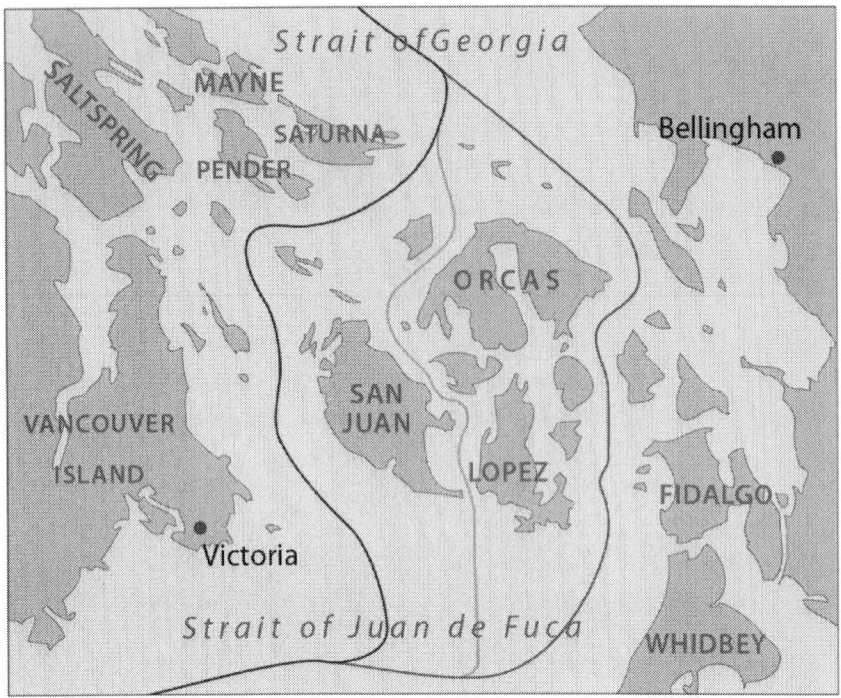

THE PIG WAR OF 1859: This war on the U.S./Canadian border involved hundreds of men from the United States and British forces, three warships, colonels and captains, a rear admiral, dozens of cannon, tons of ammunition and other stores, the Kaiser of Germany, top diplomats, international conferences around the world … and a pig. Only one shot was fired … at the pig. Only one casualty was recorded …the pig.

The trouble had started because of a treaty between the United States and Great Britain about where the boundary between Oregon and Columbia district (today part of Canada) would run. The treaty said the boundary would run along the 49th parallel 'to the middle of the channel which separates the continent from Vancouver Island and thence southerly through the middle of the said channel … to the Pacific Ocean.' Fine, except no one had taken a look.

There was no middle of the channel – it split in half around some islands, San Juan in particular (see map, above). Not too much of a problem until a chap called Lyman Cutlar, a American who was a failed gold prospector, arrived on the island to claim the land as his farm and grow potatoes. On the morning of June 15, 1859, it all started to go wrong. Cutlar found a pig snaffling his potatoes – digging them up half-grown, no less – and took umbrage, took out his rifle, took aim and took a pot shot. He killed the pig.

It turned out the pig belonged to a local Irishman, Charles Griffin, who thought he was in a part of the British Empire, not the USA. This almost started a full-scale border war (the two countries had been belligerents several times in the previous hundred years, the British famously having burned down the White House in Washington about 40 years earlier).

Both men appealed to their authorities for protection from the pig and potato debacle. In a ludicrous over-reaction, the Americans sent 66 men to stop the piggery jokery, and the British sent three warships. Cannon were shipped in to either end of the island, and flags raised. Would there soon be a crackling of gunfire? Or something rasher?

Fortunately a bit of common sense saved their bacon. The military occupation and stand-off went on for an insane 12 years. During all that time the two camps fraternised, celebrating national holidays with each other, the British laying out a formal garden next to their warship, and both sides consuming much alcohol and competing on sports days. Orders from London and Washington to take a sterner line were studiously ignored and not one more shot was fired. Local commanders expressed the view it would be ludicrous to spill blood over pork and potatoes.

In the end of the boundary question was referred to Kaiser Wilhelm I of Germany, who had never heard of the place, let alone visited it. He set up a commission to investigate. It ran for a whole year in Geneva, Switzerland, and its members also never visited the place. It ruled in favour of the Americans, who were losing interest because of their Civil War (their local commander quit his post to fight against the government he had just been standing up for).

Today, the island is a tourist attraction. The pig that nearly started a full-scale war is forgotten. But every day, U.S. government employees raise a flag at the spot known as English Camp. A Union Jack.

THE WAR OF THE STRAY DOG: This started in 1925 with a trivial cause, like the War of the Pig (above) and in this case the dog wasn't even killed. But the result was far from trivial, with at least 50 and possibly more than 100 people – mostly civilians – killed in the one week before it was over. And it included an early and effective intervention by the League of Nations, the peace-keeping precursor of the United Nations set up after the First World War.

On October 25, 1925, a Greek soldier's dog strayed across the border with Bulgaria at a place called the Pass of Demirkapia, near the Bulgarian border town of Petrich. The soldier nipped across the border to grab the errant animal – at which point a Bulgarian sentry shot him (the Greek soldier, not the dog) dead.

Oddly enough, considering what happened later, the Bulgarians were quick to express regret, to say it was due to a misunderstanding, and to offer to set up a joint commission to investigate why the shooting happened.

The Greek government, under dictator Theodoros Pangalos, was having none of this. It issued a three-point ultimatum to Bulgaria:

1. Punishment of those responsible.
2. An official apology by the Bulgarian state.
3. Two million French francs in compensation.

Failing to wait for this to take effect, it also sent its soldiers to attack and occupy the town of Petrich. This led to the deaths of 50 Bulgarians, mostly civilians. The accounts differ, however, with the Bulgars claiming 121 Greeks killed.

The League of Nations was involved very rapidly, and ordered a ceasefire by telegraph. It judged Greece's actions needlessly aggressive, and ordered:

1. An immediate ceasefire.
2. All Greek troops to withdraw from Bulgaria.
3. Compensation of £45,000 to be paid by the Greeks, and

British, French and Italian observers to monitor this whole process. Both sides complied, but the Greeks were humiliated and complained of double standards – when Italian aggression started the Corfu Incident only two years earlier, Italy (which launched a major attack on that island causing about 20 deaths and 30 injuries) was not punished and the League of Nations ordered Italy to be compensated by Greece. The Greeks felt there was one rule for the great powers – in that case the bullying Italy – and one for the minor countries.

But in the War of the Stray Dog, why did one passportless pet pooch cause such mayhem? Well, for something so minor to trigger a major explosion, the situation has to be loaded with stress beforehand. The background to the War of the Stray Dog was a period of tension, border war, territorial dispute, guerrilla action and assassination between the neighbouring countries since the start of the 20th century. It is not known what became of the stray dog – the picture, although appealing, is not of the particular animal, and the flag shown below left is that of Greece – but this short war left a legacy of local bitterness that took decades to dissipate.

THE WAR OF PORK AND BEANS: Was a similar U.S./Canadian barney to the 1859 Pig War (above), at the other end of their land border. This 'war' in the U.S. state of Maine (then a part of Massachusetts), was similar in that no one was killed by direct military action, although forces were called out to confront each other. But different in that the two sides somehow managed to lose 38 men through accidents and disease (the grave shown, below, was erected much later, and engraved in error – it is of a man who was died later and run over by one of his own U.S. Army wagons, and not in an Indian War but this one. The wagon may well have been carrying pork and beans – certainly that's what the Maine troops complained of eating all the way through the months of confrontation).

It took place in 1839-42, 20 years earlier than the Pig War, so the Americans' potential enemy was British North America, rather than Canada, and the border was far from clear, which is what it was all about. It's also called the Aroostook War after a river valley involved, but either way, it had consequences for both countries.

The trouble was that the 1783 Treaty of Paris which ended the American Revolutionary War failed to mark the boundary between British North America and the USA. In what is now northern Maine, then beginning to be settled by Americans, conflict arose with what they considered to be invading, thieving lumberjacks from New Brunswick in Canada.

The brouhaha started with posses being sent out to confront each other, escalated with locals arming themselves by breaking into an armoury, an attempt by the British to arrest some of the leaders trying to form an American township, the calling out of militias, and the building of forts, barracks and blockhouses. Regular Army regiments were also called to the confrontation.

It was complicated by the involvement of one black bear and potentially of French settlers – the bear joined in the Battle of Caribou on December 29, 1838. This was a skirmish between Maine and New Brunswick lumbermen in which the Americans accused the northerners of stealing timber. As armed parties confronted each other, a black bear attacked, causing shots to be fired at it and general firing to break out by men who assumed the other side fired first. Luckily, they all missed and went home.

The French Canadians were Acadians – left over from failed

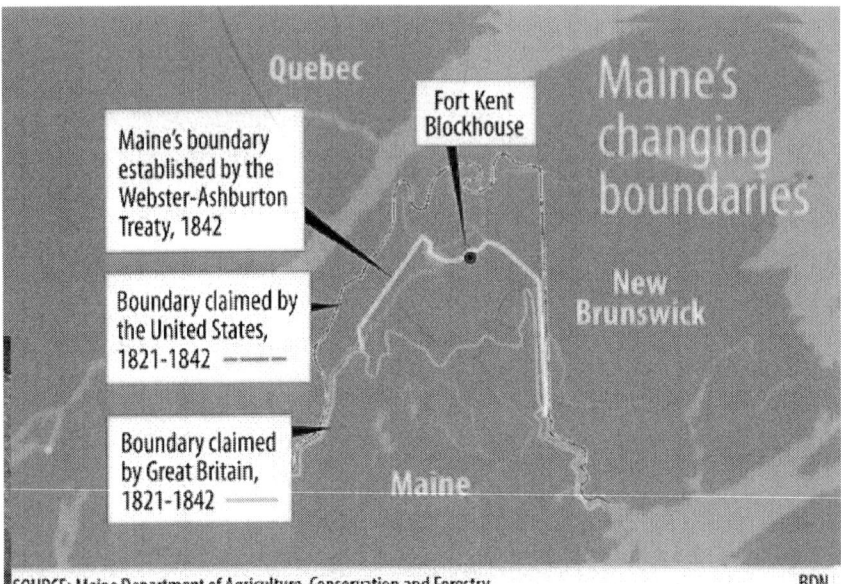

French attempts to colonise Canada and Louisiana – who were nominally British Crown subjects but in fact claimed to be freemen and in a republic of their own. They were too small in number to make any difference, but their sympathies were with the Americans, not Queen Victoria.

In the end, two politicians, American Daniel Webster and British Lord Ashburton, saw sense, but not until after King William I of the Netherlands had been called in to arbitrate – and been ignored – and maps had been produced by both sides and then hidden or faked, according to whom you believe.

With the Webster-Ashburton Treaty in 1842 fixing the current-day border, the British achieved what they wanted most – to keep military access to New Brunswick from Quebec and keep the Americans away from the seaway to the north. The Americans got most of the land they thought was theirs. Locals on both sides claimed that their respective governments let them down.

Left: Fort Kent, complete with gun slits, built during the Pork and Beans War, has guarded the U.S. border ever since

* * * * *

THE SOCCER WAR: This sounds like the most trivial of the wars in this chapter – as it started with a defeat on a soccer pitch – but was in fact the most serious so far, with air forces conducting bombing raids, armour and artillery getting involved, and 3,000 people killed – all for no purpose or long-term effect.

And of course the bitterness and anger between Honduras and neighbour El Salvador was already strong before the football competition that provided the final trigger for military conflict. The immediate setting was a set of qualifying matches for the 1970 World Cup. The two Central American countries met for the first game in the Honduran capital of Tegucigalpa on June 8, 1969, which Honduras won 1–0. Fighting between rival fans took place. The second match, on June 15, 1969 in the Salvadoran capital of San Salvador, was won 3–0 by El Salvador. This was followed by even greater rioting.

This made a decider necessary which took place on neutral ground in Mexico City on June 26, 1969. El Salvador won the third game 3–2 after extra time.

Despite this, later that day a furious Salvadoran government angrily broke off all diplomatic ties with Honduras, but the mood created by the football against a hated neighbour was just the trigger, and the Salvadoran statement for its reasons for taking such drastic action made this clear.

The dispute was about migration, poverty and land. For much of the 20th century, hungry Salvadorans had been migrating to much less overpopulated Honduras and settling as peasant farmers. Now they were

being evicted as refugees to an already over-crowded El Salvador, so the Honduran government could give their unofficially occupied land to people born in Honduras. The Salvadoran government and people were furious at the way this was being carried out. Some youngsters had been born in Honduras, and there were many marriages between the nationalities.

When the diplomatic ties were broken off, El Salvador said: 'The government of Honduras has not taken any effective measures to punish these crimes which constitute genocide, nor has it given assurances of indemnification or reparations for the damages caused to Salvadorans'.

So the war wasn't entirely caused by soccer, as legend has it, nor did it erupt immediately after the game, as is also claimed. It wasn't until July 14 that serious military conflict started.

San Salvador was put on full black-out while bomber aircraft –in fact passenger planes with packets of explosives tied to the side which could be released – attacked Toncontin International Airport, which left the Honduran Air Force (pictured above with troops on parade) unable to respond.

The Salvadoran army invaded Honduras along two routes, and artillery and armour were involved. It seemed to threaten the capital, **Tegucigalpa**. Meanwhile the Honduran air force finally hit back on July 16, bombing an air base and oil depots. It was, by the way, the last war in which piston-engined (ie not jet) fighters fought each other, including some World War II vintage aircraft, such as Corsairs and Mustangs.

Intense diplomatic pressure from the Organisation of American States brought a cease-fire on July 18, but refugee problem got only worse, and the poverty this caused contributed directly to the El Salvador Civil War, about ten years later.

The immediate cost of the Soccer War was about 300,000 refugees, some 900 killed on the El Salvador side, and about 2,250 on the Honduran, including 250 troops. The Soccer War solved nothing, achieved nothing, and made the suffering and poverty at the root of the conflict worse.

THE 30-YEAR RHODODENDRON WAR: In February 2017, an Irish politician gave an impassioned speech about out-of-control shrubbery. 'The rhododendron situation in Killarney National Park has gotten so bad, minister,' Michael Healy-Rae declared from the floor of the Irish parliament, 'nothing short of calling in the army is going to put it right.'

It turned out that the Irish state had been waging war – using horses, tractors, chains, poison spray, flame-throwers – for 30 years on *Rhododendron ponticum*, a plant that was relatively restrained in the Himalayan uplands but just went bonkers when introduced to the humid climate and acidic soils of western Britain and Ireland, where the dense shrub has few natural predators or serious competitors. Its leaves are, after all, poisonous to animals, so why would they eat it?

Its foliage is so thick that nothing can grow underneath. In 2014, two experienced hillwalkers had to be rescued when they became trapped in a thicket of it. Well, frankly, one has a feeling of doom about this whole thing – like the Great Emu War at the start of this chapter. One wag even suggested telling the redundant IRA terrorists that the pesky shrubs came from England. They'd be blowing them up in no time.

2 LONG AND SHORT WARS

THE 38-MINUTE WAR: Was between Great Britain and Zanzibar on August 27, 1896, and as well as being remarkably quick, epitomized gunboat diplomacy – literally – and British Imperial power at its zenith. Thus as well as high-handed regime change, it brought an end to slavery in that island Sultanate off East Africa. It also illustrated the massive resources the Royal Navy – the biggest the world had ever seen – could call on all round the globe.

The immediate cause was the death of the pro-British Sultan, Hamad bin Thuwaini on August 25 and the succession of Sultan Khalid bin Barghash who was more hostile to Britain and possibly pro-German. The trouble was that a Treaty signed between the two countries a few years before required the

British Consul to approve the new Sultan. The Consul issued an ultimatum to Khalid to leave the palace by 9am on the 27th. He didn't.

Meanwhile the Consul gathered a formidable fleet – three cruisers, two gunboats, 1,590 Marines, and 900 pro-British Zanzibarian troops. Defending the Palace were about 2,800 troops, two artillery pieces and some machine guns. Oddly enough the Zanzibarian Navy – an armed royal yacht called *HHS Glasgow* (pictured) – was anchored amidst the British fleet. Firing started as promised after the 9am ultimatum expired, and the Palace was soon on fire, the Sultan's flag shot down and the royal yacht, which was firing a few cannon, sunk. The Sultan's harem (pictured right) took a

particular hammering. It was all over by 9.40 as the surviving defenders fled, the Sultan to the German consulate. Casualties on the defending side were heavy – 500 killed or wounded – but only one British sailor was wounded. The shortest war in history was over in 38 minutes.

The sailors of the *Glasgow* clambered up the masts as she sat on the bottom of the harbour, and were quickly rescued by the British. For many years afterwards the masts poking out of the water were a familiar navigation feature to look out for (below).

The British even made Sultan Khalid's supporters pay for the ammunition they had expended.

The Sultan escaped from the German consulate by bringing a German warship alongside and using a plank between the two so he never had to leave German territory, and a new Sultan – a semi-colonial puppet government – was installed. But things improved, slavery was abolished, and peace reigned for 67 years. Eventually after independence, Tanganyika and Zanzibar merged to form the modern independent country of Tanzania in 1964.

Press reports from the time. The top picture shows the sunken Zanzibarian royal yacht *HHS Glasgow*. Two other small launches were also sunk in the unequal battle

LONG AND SHORT WARS

THE LONGEST WAR IN HISTORY: Also involved the British. But, unlike the shortest war, above, it caused fewer casualties. In fact, none.

For 335 years this war was fought – or rather, not fought as everyone had forgotten about it – between the Isles of Scilly (southwest of Cornwall, aerial photograph above) and the Netherlands.

It was an official war, however. It happened because of the English Civil War (1642-52), of the parliamentary Roundheads versus the royalist Cavaliers. The Royalists were losing, so were eventually driven out of the mainland Cornwall to the Scilly Isles, taking a small navy with them.

The Dutch, who had escaped Spanish domination with English help over the previous century, sided with the English parliamentarians. This meant they were the enemy to the Scilly garrison, who used their small navy to raid passing Dutch ships and get much-needed supplies.

In March 1651, the Dutch Admiral Maarten Tromp arrived in the Scillies to demand reparation for these shipping raids and an end to

them. He was sent away without a satisfactory answer.

Tromp was recorded in April 1651, on landing in Cornwall, as having declared war on the Scillies. This was not a light-hearted matter – the Dutch had a formidable and aggressive navy (above) which had fought the English recently and would so do again soon. No mere bombardment with Edam cheeses!

However in June that year the English Navy, under parliamentary control, arrived under Admiral Robert Blake and took possession of the islands. The Dutch sailed home, problem solved.

No one ever bothered to make a peace treaty as the Scillies were no longer a separate country.

Move on to 1985, and the chairman of the Scilly Isles Council, Roy Duncan (pictured), was fed up with hearing the 'myth' that they were still at war with the Dutch. He wrote to the Netherlands Embassy in London to debunk the idea.

They found they *were* still at war, technically. The Dutch ambassador Jonkheer Rein Heydecoper was asked to visit and sign a peace treaty, which he gamely did on April 17, 1986. He joked that it must have been rather harrowing for the Scillonians all those years 'to know that we could have attacked at any moment.' At last the islanders could sleep soundly. What a Scilly state of affairs!

3 DISASTROUSLY STUPID WARS

THE POINTLESS PARAGUAYAN WAR: This war of 1864 was one of the most staggeringly stupid and horribly costly of all those in this book. In fact the worst war in South American history – with an estimated 400,000 deaths – was completely pointless.

The war of 1864-70 started with Paraguay's needless aggression against its bigger neighbours, Brazil, Uruguay and Argentina, who formed a triple alliance against it. The cited cause was some imagined border dispute, but it was the delusional, vainglorious leadership of President Solano Lopez that was the real cause.

Even when roundly defeated in the field, the Paraguayans carried on a costly guerrilla war for years. In scenes to be recreated in the Soviet Union in World War II, soldiers were asked to charge into battle unarmed, with the chance of picking up weapons from the fallen. They were also urged to kill any comrades, even officers, who talked of surrender. Cavalry had to eat their own horses to stay alive. And retreat involved destroying the locals, crops, foodstuffs and anything of value.

When their lunatic President Solano Lopez (pictured) was finally cornered and killed on March 1, 1870, he died shouting: '¡Muero con mi patria!' ('I die with my homeland!'), which was nearly true, as probably most of his countrymen had perished in the war. Estimates vary but suggest up to 69 per cent of the population was lost, and up to 90 per cent of the young males. These are the higher end estimates, but even so the slaughter seemed even more appalling than the then recent U.S. Civil War which was terrible enough.

Photos exist of piles of bodies at some of the 21 battles – we won't share them here – but diseases such as cholera and sepsis seemed to have made huge impacts on the various armies involved.

For example a whole battalion of thirsty Brazilian troops died after drinking from an infected river.

However vague the figures for Paraguayan losses, the triple alliance certainly lost 140,000. The survivors in Paraguay were thrown into abject poverty for decades. All for nothing.

THE PASTRY WAR: Yes, really! Known in Spanish as the *Guerra de los pasteles*, or in French – and it involved them too – as *Guerre des Pâtisseries*. In fact no fewer than six nations had a slice of this pointless 1830s war, which started over a complaint about just one bakery, and never seemed to be about much else.

Neverthless, it cost 127 lives and left 189 wounded, so it was far from half-baked. It soured relations between France and Mexico for decades – the war flared up again for a second helping in 1861, and normal relations did not resume until 1880.

The original complaint was over a small bakery shop run by a Frenchman at Tacubaya, near Mexico City. Many other properties had been damaged in civil unrest at about this time but the owner of the shop, a Frenchman named Remontel, decided to complain to the King of France, Louis Philippe.

Far away in Paris, if he had had a *soupçon* of common sense, the king would have declined to get involved in such a petty complaint so far away.

French forces in the Pastry War bombard a Mexican fort at Veracruz (Vernet)

But then pastries, and bread, are pretty important to the French, – even if the late Marie Antoinette hadn't really said: 'let them eat cake' a few years before. Now the French monarchy had been restored, it seemed – absurdly – a matter of national honour.

Reparations for the supposed damage to the shop were demanded. In fact quite a lot of dough, as it were, was sought – 600,000 pesos, at a time when a Mexican workman's daily wage was one peso. After the French king failed to get any answer from the Mexicans, he decided to send a war fleet.

One wants a Pastry War ordered by the French upper crust to be one involving *croissant* catapults and charging with fixed *baguettes*, the odd chocolate *bombe* rolling across a deck – but this was to be a real shooting war.

A French fleet arrived in November 1838 and blockaded the Mexican coast, and bombarded a fortress off Veracruz. By December the French had captured the whole city, so the Mexicans had reluctantly to declare war.

Now it gets more complicated – the United States, which logic suggests would be on the side of residents of America against a colonial European power – side with France *against* the Mexicans.

The British, oddly, join the Mexican cause. And Texas, still an independent republic, wades in against Mexico. None of these powers actually do any fighting at this point, but the U.S. sends a warship to help the French blockade the Mexican coast.

The Mexicans try to get round the blockade by smuggling in supplies from the Republic of Texas. Authorities there clamp down on the contraband, and in one raid discover 100 barrels of white powder left on the shoreline by fleeing smugglers. It is flour, for bakeries. That bit of the Texan city of Corpus Christi is known as Flour Bluff today as a result.

Enter a larger-than-life character by the name of (take a deep breath) Antonio de Padua María Severino López de Santa Anna y Pérez de Lebrón (pictured). Called Tony by his friends, one almost wants to add after such a florid title, but in fact he was known as Santa Anna and was a huge character in this era of Mexico's war of independence against Spain, and later the war to keep its rebelling provinces, one of which had become Texas (where as you know, nothing secedes like success).

Santa Anna had been President of Mexico a few times – three times, briefly, in 1833, for example, each time swapping with the same politician – but was known better as a strong military leader against the new nation's enemies. He was called 'Saviour of the Nation' and 'Napoleon of the West' – mainly by himself, it must be said, but the titles caught on. He had fought both *against* and *for* Mexican independence, and had been a conservative, a liberal, a republican and a royalist at different stages, so he was consistent only in one thing – about being a self-proclaimed national hero.

At this point he was in retirement and in semi-disgrace for having lost Texas but was still the most famous fighter/politician the country had ever had. If he joined in, even a Pastry War, it's a recipe for drama, and Santa Anna is soon leading the army from the front. He has his leg wounded by French grapeshot, and has to have it amputated in the field.

Like Britain's Lord Uxbridge a few years earlier at Waterloo, Santa Anna has his leg buried with full military honours. And also like Uxbridge – who became Marquis of Anglesey – he has several false legs made and fights on, militarily and politically, for many years.

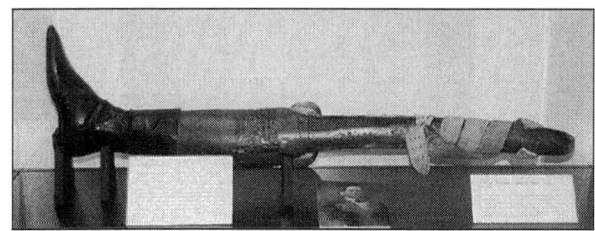

One of his legs (pictured) even gets captured by the Americans and used, somewhat disrespectfully, as a baseball bat. The 4th Illinois Infantry never did return it and it can be seen in their museum today. His replacement leg is also on show in Mexico, so just like the Marquis of Anglesey, there are three monuments to the same leg. Like Uxbridge, Santa Anna had the dubious option of attending part of his own funeral. (Recall the wonderful exchange at Waterloo while Wellington was on his horse observing the French with a telescope. Uxbridge, who had been standing alongside: 'By Gord, Sir, I've lorst a leg.' Wellington glances down and says: 'So you have, Uxbridge' and calmly resumes looking through his telescope). Both men became known - sorry about this – as leg ends in their own life time!

You might have thought Santa Anna would be hopping mad (sorry, not taking this too seriously) about losing his leg to the French, but in fact they did him a massive favour and it gave him a leg to stand on, as it were, to regain power. He never lost an opportunity to remind the Mexican people that he'd already laid down at least part of his body in their defence.

At this point the British intervene, diplomatically, to restore some kind of sanity. The French withdraw after being promised 600,000 pesos by the Mexicans, although this can have been only a fraction of the cost of the whole absurd expedition, which collapsed like a half-baked soufflé.

The Mexicans never pay it so the French (by now led by another vainglorious royal, Emperor Napoleon III) go for a second helping of Pastry War, launching another attack on Mexico in 1861, waging a huge campaign involving an invading army, installing their own man as Emperor Maximilian I. The French are eventually beaten back, and after a rising, their man Maximilian (above) is soon toast – he was shot by firing squad in 1867.

Which all goes to show that you cannot shrug off the importance of French *pâtisserie*. The Pastry War was no mere *hors d'oeuvre* of history, but ended up being the *entrée* to a wider conflict. And that vainglorious leaders, sometimes, get their just deserts.

The execution of Emperor Maximilian, as depicted by Manet

4 THE WAR OF ELEPHANTS AND CHANDELIERS

THE ANGLO-ETHIOPIAN WAR OF 1867-68: The war between Queen Victoria's British Empire and that of Emperor Theodore II of Ethiopia in the late 1860s is simply and spectacularly one of the strangest ever fought. Theodore (pictured, the name is anglicised a bit) was handsome, often fabulously dressed, courageous, proud, bombastic, madly cruel yet also well-mannered, courteous to the point of courtly, and indeed often kind and thoughtful. Like his people, he was an avowed Christian, unlike his Muslim enemies all around his seemingly impenetrable mountainous kingdom.

To put his contradictions in more modern terms, his personality veered between that of Idi Amin (the cruel, vainglorious paranoid, megalomaniac Ugandan dictator of 1970s) and that of Chris Eubank, the dandyish British boxer of recent years, who acted, talked and dressed like an English gentleman of the old days, but could fight like a tiger too.

For the British, it was a startlingly huge endeavour using all the imperial logistics of the age to take on an African tyrant hundreds of miles from the boiling hot, arid coast across deep ravines and gorges, in his mountain fortress of Magdala. It involved the latest Victorian technology of steamships, railway building and rifled guns (with grooves inside the barrels), yet it was still in the era of ranks of red-coated infantrymen – as at the Battle of Waterloo. These scarlet uniforms made them such an easy target before khaki was adopted. It even had elements of ancient history – elephants marching across the mountains like Hannibal – and echoes of medieval chivalry, with Emperor Theodore's gorgeous pavilions with silk carpets, rich incense, exotic fruit, caskets of jewels, gifts of leopard cubs or indeed chandeliers.

In outline, it sounds like a typical colonial war, part of the 'Scramble for Africa' by which bullying European rival powers –

massively outgunning the natives – greedily grabbed vast swathes of the continent.

In fact, it was nothing of the sort. It was undertaken very reluctantly, to rescue British and European hostages from the tyrant's towering fortress, and at all stages the British made it clear they sought to conquer no lands, to harm no Ethiopians if it could be avoided, and they paid for their supplies en route instead of seizing them as most armies did. They maintained a polite but firm correspondence with constant offers to withdraw without a shot being fired if the prisoners were released.

To see Ethiopia suffering a brutal colonial war, you had to wait until the fascist Italians arrived in the 1930s, using poison gas and machine-guns against the tribesmen in a blatant, ruthless land-grab (it was the Second Italo-Ethiopian War, the Ethiopians having humiliated Italy once by beating them off in the 1890s).

This Anglo-Ethiopian War back in the 1860s was not like that.

Looking from our vantage point in history it seems the kind of over-reaching military thrust deep into hostile, unmapped country that could have gone horribly wrong. Like the First Anglo-Afghan war of just 20 years before, where from a huge British army, just one man returned alive. Or the later Boer War with its massacres of British at Spion Kop, or the Maori War where the New Zealand natives proved far tougher than the Brits expected.

Or perhaps, as it was a hostage rescue operation, it could be compared with the U.S. attempt to free hostages from Teheran in 1980 when – having taken over from Britain the self-appointed role as the world's great power policeman – the U.S. and President Carter were deeply humiliated by their failure, leaving their hostages still detained and their aircraft wrecked in the desert.

And yet the British hostage release campaign of 120 years before did *not* go wrong. It worked amazingly well – for the British side, that is. Yet, perhaps because we are far more fascinated by defeat and disaster – at Gallipoli, Dunkirk, or Balaclava for example – we have almost totally forgotten all about this odd Anglo-Ethiopian War.

WHAT WAS THE CAUSE? One of the best guides to the detail of the run-up to the war and the war itself is Alan Moorehead's excellent history, *The Blue Nile* (one of a pair with his book *The White Nile*). The problems in relations between Britain and Ethiopia started when

Britain's representative to Theodore's court needed replacing in 1861. The old one, Walter Plowden, had been a favourite of the Emperor, while another Briton, a Mr Bell, even ran the court as his Grand Chamberlain. So when Plowden was killed by a local tribe while travelling through the country, Theodore's vengeance was swift. He led an army to that area, and tortured, mutilated and killed at least 2,000 people in his anger. Bell was killed in the fighting, trying to protect the Emperor.

The British sent a new representative to his court, a Captain Charles Cameron. Initially, he was well received – Cameron arrived in 1862 and gave the Emperor a brace of fine pistols, each inscribed in silver with the message: 'Presented to Theodore, Emperor of Abyssinia [Ethiopia], by Victoria, Queen of Great Britain and Ireland, for his kindness to her servant Plowden, 1861.' We shall see those pistols again at a crucial moment in this story, or rather one of them.

Things then started to go wrong.

Theodore wrote a courtly reply, beginning:

In the name of the Father, of the Son, and of the Holy Ghost, one God in Trinity, Chosen by God, King of Kings, Theodore of Ethiopia, to Her Majesty Victoria, Queen of England.

The letter sounds as if it were from another age:

Mr Plowden, and my late Grand Chamberlain, the Englishman Bell, used to tell me there is a great Christian Queen, who loves all Christians. When they said to me 'We are able to make you known to her and establish friendships between you' then in those times I was very glad...

All men are subject to death, and my enemies, thinking to injure me, killed these my friends [Plowden and Bell]. But by the power of God I have exterminated these enemies, not leaving one alive, though they were of my own family, that I may get, by the power of God, your friendship.

Theodore sent this off with high expectations. He may have thought his letter would make him the focus of attention in London, whereas Britain was dealing with huge matters of war and peace with

Russia and France, and other crises. Against this, a small African chief in a unknown, backward country (we are in a period of imperial, possibly rather racist arrogance, remember) might not have seemed a major issue. The gesture of the pistols was probably just dreamed up by a colonial office wallah.

Theodore's reply did, after many weeks, reach London, where it was read by some functionary and then filed away without any response. Big mistake, as it turns out. For someone as prickly as Theodore this could be seen as a snub – and when the next British move was to order Cameron to travel to Sudan, home of Theodore's Muslim avowed enemies, things got worse.

The paranoid Theodore took this as a grave insult and provocation, though in fact this was far from the British intention – Cameron had been sent to investigate the possibilities of growing cotton by the Nile there (the U.S. Civil War had damaged the British textile industry by making cotton prices soar). Cameron was also to report on the slave trade, flourishing in the Sudan, but banned by Britain, which indeed fought against it throughout the world. Theodore was also supposed to be against slavery, but he ignored that and saw the whole thing as an insult. When Cameron left for the Sudan, Theodore assumed he was going to England to get Queen Victoria to talk to him; when he heard of his real destination – the land of his enemies – he was incandescent with rage.

All the European missionaries in his country were put in chains. He ordered that Cameron should be arrested and tortured. A young Irishman who arrived from England to be Cameron's assistant was immediately put in chains too.

The British authorities in colonial Aden, 100 miles across the sea, heard of all this in April 1864, and urged London to reply to Theodore's original letter. This was done in May, 1864, and a letter sent from Queen Victoria assuring 'Our good friend Theodore, King of Abyssinia' of Britain's friendship and urging him to release Cameron and the others as a gesture of goodwill.

The British envoy taking this message had an extraordinary journey lasting months, waiting outside Theodore's reach in Massawa on the Red Sea coast and communicating with him and the captives by letter. Eventually he decide to go to Cairo and bought chandeliers, mirrors and glassware, two cases of Curacao and other stores, as presents for Theodore. Eventually, in October 1865, the British peace envoy set off from Massawa with the chandeliers and other stores lashed to a great train of camels. They received a letter from the captive Cameron encouraging the rescuers to hurry up. It said: 'The King sent us a cow a-piece sometime back – the first notice he has taken of us since the torturing. He has spoken rather kindly about us lately in public, but we are still bound hand and foot.'

Approaching the Ethiopian capital and court was difficult, as it moved constantly. The British were startled to encounter an escort of 10,000 men sent out to meet them and conduct them to Theodore. They were met by volleys of gunfire in salute.

Cause of a war: Some of hostages in the Ethiopia crisis

This mobile capital – comprising thousands of tents and huts, Theodore's being the biggest and grandest – would decamp sometimes daily – an enormous caterpillar of 90,000 men, women and children, their animals, their supplies of food and shelter, moving on foot all day from dawn to dusk up to 30 miles across a landscape riven by hills and ravines. This vast nomadic complex sustained itself by pillaging the farms and villages along the way. It moved as Theodore's whim took it, towards his imaginary or real enemies whom he thought needed attention.

The torturing and execution of his enemies – those who had committed some supposed offence – was constant. The cruelty involved cutting off hands and feet, or tossing the children – who had committed no harm whatsoever – over a precipice and then sparing the parents so that they suffered all the more.

Once the British mission had arrived, and the chandeliers received with much joy (more clobber to drag across country!), they were kept in gorgeous tents – pavilions, almost – and given charming messages and constant gifts from Theodore – a beast he had shot, a set of firearms.

A long game of cat and mouse ensued, with the British and European hostages eventually joining them – Cameron was haggard after two years in chains – and then promises of release, actual release, re-arrest, mock trials under trumped-up charges, etc, all while they could watch other, Ethiopian, prisoners, being brutally tortured to death.

Sometimes the hostages were treated well, with freedom to walk about the lake shores of wherever the camp was at the time, and even showered with presents – and other times put back in chains and on mock trial.

Theodore sent one of them to England with a message promising that they would all but one be released if Queen Victoria sent him skilled workmen. Then he left them, to launch another murderous campaign across his own country, lasting a year and half.

The forbidding fortress of Magdala, ringed by walls and thorny barricades

The British sent a party of volunteer workmen as requested, arriving on the Red Sea coast, out of Theodore's reach, in December

1866, and replied that he could have them and many gifts. The Emperor was sent a letter which made clear he could have these if he released the hostages first. Theodore refused, the workmen on the coast were sent home, and the prisoners eventually moved to Magdala, a mountain stronghold far into the interior. It was built on a volcanic plug soaring out of the surrounding plain, a bit like Edinburgh castle but steeper and three times higher.

Here they had fetters hammered on to their legs once more. There was only one steep path out of the fortress through two fortified gateways. On all other sides there were sheer cliffs falling a thousand feet into rock and thorny scrub – into which other prisoners were regularly hurled. Soldiers with rifles would pick off those who survived that fall, and then vultures would feast on their spattered remains. Escape was out of the question. Even so, the Europeans retained their own stores and their own servants. They ate well and seemed little affected by the cholera that was raging, killing a hundred a day sometimes.

THE CAMPAIGN AGAINST THEODORE: By 1867, public opinion in Britain was beginning to rise against the imprisonment of its people in this far-off land, and the Press demanded that something be done. The Prime Minister issued an ultimatum, no answer was received, and so orders were given to prepare for war.

But how? The place had never been invaded because the jagged terrain was so difficult; terrible diseases, fierce tribes and dangerous wild animals made it even less inviting. So it had been bypassed by history – Arabs, Napoleon, the British had all ignored it. As Gibbon put it in *The Decline And Fall Of The Roman Empire,*

Encompassed on all sides by enemies of their religion, the Aethiopians slept near a thousand years, forgetful of the world, by whom they were forgotten.

Not any more. The British Government turned to one of the army in India's greatest soldiers, Sir Robert Napier, who had blazed his way through India and China with great efficiency and personal courage. He twice had his horse shot from under him, and never complained about his wounds. And as a former Army engineer, he was good on what we now call logistics. Really good, as this expedition would be as difficult as a modern Moon landing. The planning by Napier (right) was almost on a D-Day scale.

Forty-four specially trained elephants would be brought from India to carry the heavy guns. A staggering 17,934 mules and ponies, 8,075 oxen plus camels were found to carry the other equipment. Plus 2,538 horses were needed. Can you conceive of the fodder and water needed for this lot alone?

A railway, including several locomotives, wagons, and twenty miles of track would be laid across the coastal plain to the mountains. Two large piers, lighthouses and warehouses had to be built. A telegraph line several hundred miles long would maintain communication with the front. (Both of these were new technologies – the first, primitive public railway had been opened only 40 years before, the telegraph was even younger.)

Three hospital ships would be needed, with the new-fangled ice-making machines to help treat heatstroke. Two condenser machines to make fresh water out of seawater. The British intended to pay their way through the country, where oddly enough the only accepted currency was Austrian Maria Theresa dollars, and only the 1780 one at that – the one with the busty empress image on it. Not enough could be found, so the imperial mint in Vienna was contracted to produce 500,000 new ones, of the old design.

Food was difficult, with the different races and religions having different taboos – which had recently caused the Indian Mutiny – but the scale of it can be gathered from the fact that 50,000 tons of salt beef and 50,000 tons of pork were required, plus 50,000 gallons of rum. In the end the force consisted of 52,000 men (mostly support staff, servants, etc, only 13,000 being fighting men of British or 'native' sorts), and 55,000 animals.

Every soldier was issued with a pith helmet and a 'cholera belt' – totally useless against the disease, as it turned out.

The fleet sails in: British ships unloading at Annesley Bay, off Zula

A vast fleet of 75 steam and 205 sailing ships converged on the Red Sea from all quarters of the Empire carrying the above, (which surely out-clobbered the tons of clobber the Emperor Theodore was carting around with his capital). They arrived at Zula, where an advance party had built 900ft long piers and warehouses, and started the railway.

An unknown disease swept the animals, killing most of them, so more had to be sent for while the stinking carcasses floated around the dock. There wasn't enough water in the searing heat, but as most of the army moved inland there was fresh water aplenty and cooler conditions.

To continue the comparison with the Moon landing, where only the small capsule on top of the gigantic rocket actually arrives on the Moon, in this case a huge organisation was needed to get a small fighting force to Magdala.

The fleets, the support staff, storesmen, the whole line of the march inland had to be guarded, those soldiers needed daily food supplies, as did the people running the mule trains, the mules and other animals needed fodder – it was mind boggling. But it worked.

Napier sent an ultimatum to Theodore. It started:

To Theodorus, King of Abyssinia.

I am commanded by Her Majesty the Queen of England to demand that the prisoners whom your Majesty has wrongly detained in captivity shall be immediately released... and ended:

Should they not be delivered safely into my hands, should they suffer a continuance of ill-treatment, or should any injury befall them, your Majesty will be held personally responsible and no hope of further condonation need be entertained.

R. Napier, Lt-General, Commander-in-Chief, Bombay Army.

It never reached Theodore, who probably would have ignored it. Rebels seized it and it was delivered to the hostages at Magdala, who destroyed it lest it infuriate Theodore.

Napier also issued another proclamation, which presaged various other wars (in Iraq, twice) yet to come:

To the Governors, the Chiefs, the Religious Orders, and the People of Abyssinia.

It is known to you that Theodorus King of Abyssinia detains in captivity the British Consul Cameron, the British envoy Rassam, and many others, in violation of the laws of all civilised nations. All friendly persuasion having failed to obtain their release, my Sovereign has commanded me to lead an army to release them.

All those who befriend the prisoners or assist in the liberation shall be rewarded, but those who may injure them shall be severely punished....

The Queen of England has no unfriendly feeling towards you, and no design against your country or your liberty. Your religious establishments, your persons and your property shall be carefully protected. All supplies required for my soldiers shall be paid for: no peaceful inhabitants shall be molested.

The sole object for which the British force has been sent to Abyssinia is the liberation of Her Majesty's servants and others unjustly detained as captives, and as soon as that object is effected, it will be withdrawn...

Up in the mountains, Theodore was told of the approaching British army. He said he was delighted at the prospect. 'I long for the day, when I shall see a disciplined European Army.' He talked of a legend where the future of his country would be settled in battle by a great foreign king and a great Ethiopian king. This was it, he claimed (it wasn't that at all, it was a hostage rescue).

He was ready to fight, and put his faith in a wonder weapon, a great mortar his German engineers had constructed for him. Theodore was not at Magdala but ordered a steep road built up to the gates of the fortress, so 500 men could drag it up on a gun carriage agonising step by step up the steep slope, followed by seven other artillery pieces.

It was shaped like the biggest church bell you could imagine, weighed 70 tons, and it was extraordinary that it had been constructed at all in this remote country. A small replica can still be seen there (pictured). This would save him, he thought – not the last paranoid dictator to trust in a wonder weapon. He and his army also turned towards Magdala.

All the time the vast British army was approaching, with hundreds of miles of difficult country ahead, and what a spectacle it was. You can't better Alan Moorehead's depiction:

It must have been a wonderful sight to see the column go by, nothing but the wild Ethiopian plain around it, the ragged mountains in the distance, and, just occasionally, on the line of march, a tumbledown village where the inhabitants stood like great flocks of birds, chattering, staring and apprehensive.

The cavalry came first, the troopers dressed in crimson caps and uniforms, and the officers with silver helmets on their heads. Among the infantry that followed on, many of the white men in the Irish regiment wore beards, their cheeks burned a deep brown by the Indian sun, and the native soldiers, the Beloochees, marched along in green tunics with red facings and with large green turbans wound around their fezzes. Others were got up in light blue and silver, or the regulation scarlet jackets and white turbans...

The transport train with the guns and stores came last, and it trailed across the country for seven miles, with half the races of India and the Near East marching in its ranks: Turks, Persians, Egyptians, Arabs, Sikhs, Moslems and Hindus. The sight of the elephants with the heavy guns lashed to their backs and the mahouts sitting on their necks filled the Ethiopian villagers with amazement. Here in Africa, the elephant was a wild and savage beast. To see it responding to commands and tamely ambling along almost as if it were a cow or an ox – this was a miracle.

Then somewhere in the midst of the vast procession there would be a brass band playing, a crowd of natives swarming around an overturned cart, or a sick protesting camel, a Moslem contingent prostrating itself towards Mecca, and a little group of Parsees riding along with sharp and sober faces, their saddle bags filled with Maria Theresa dollars with which at every halt they bargained with the villagers for food and fodder.

This discipline and fair treatment of the local people by an invading army was rare then, and is sadly still rare in the Middle East now. The official history of the war, as dry as the dust of the plains mostly, goes a bit flowery on this. 'No swarthy damsel was subjected to any rude gallantry on the part of the redcoats.' Which is a more pleasant way of saying rape was not allowed. Indeed, the village elders at each stop were received by Napier in his tent, and the British Museum expert, together with some officers, would go to examine the paintings and manuscripts in the local church. It was a very British invasion.

The fact was that many Ethiopians hated Theodore, for good reason, and some of the other tribes now joined Napier's cause. Their leaders were received with full honours. The tribes saw this as a chance not just for hostage rescue, but for what we would now call regime change.

By March 28 the advance guard had reached the Takkaze River, only 40 miles as the crow flies from Magdala, approaching from the north. From the south, an equal distance away, Theodore and his army also approached the fortress. The prisoners there heard news of both armies and waited with apprehension to see which would arrive first.

Theodore, nearing Magdala, ordered the chains to be struck off the British envoy Rassam's feet. Rassam recalled: 'Some of the chiefs assisted me in striking off my fetters, while others placed their fingers between the iron and my flesh to prevent my ankles from being hurt.'

When Theodore arrived first, on March 29, he was strangely considerate and polite. He asked Rassam to dress in his blue uniform to meet him and shook his hand heartily, saying: 'Today, we must all be English,' toasting his health. He said of the approaching British Army: 'I hope, Mr Rassam, that when your people arrive they will not despise me because I am black. God has given me the same faculties and heart. But how can I show these ragged soldiers of mine to your well-dressed troops?'

Yet his character was as bipolar as ever. He ordered the 600 Ethiopian prisoners to be released in a general amnesty, but then flew into a rage when it took hours to strike off their chains. He had those unlucky to be at the back of the queue to be freed brought before him, where the supposed crimes (some imagined insult from years, perhaps decades earlier) were read out and Theodore screamed at them in rage, and had them thrown off the precipice, or even killed them himself with a sword or pistols. By the end of that day, 197 bodies lay smashed on the rocks below the cliff, no doubt getting attention from jackals and hyenas before daylight brought vultures.

Theodore then spent the night drinking heavily and praying for forgiveness for the massacre he'd just committed.

The massacre and rage had been witnessed by all the terrified European prisoners, by sound if not by sight. He had them brought down to the plain below, with all their baggage and tents, as if soon to be released, and lodged them in a gorgeous silk pavilion, while he wore white pantaloons and a gorgeous robe of white Lyons silk woven with real gold.

The next day he had them all sent back up to the fortress. It was a horrible cat and mouse game.

THE BATTLE OF MAGDALA: All of this so far has had elements of fantasy, at times medieval or even faintly like tales of Narnia. Even the day of the battle – Good Friday – seemed theatrical. Neither army can have known much about the other side. But now it was to get bloodily real and a price would be exacted for the posturing of the powers involved.

To get up to the three-mile long plateau from which three peaks suddenly soared, including the half-mile long citadel of Magdala, the British had to climb up from the Bascillo river valley. One column just climbed the bare hillside, while the other used the new road.

The climb, in the tremendous heat and humidity of an impending thunderstorm, took most of the day, and some men passed out with exhaustion. As they reached the plateau, they would have to pass the first, smaller peak of Fahla. Here the ambush had been set for them. On its top Theodore had stationed himself with his giant mortar and other cannon. On the forward slopes of Fahla were ranged his 7,000 men, under the command of a loyal chieftain called Gabry. At 4pm, the British columns had just begun to reach the plateau.

From the top of Fahla, a shattering boom rang out, echoing round the mountains, and white smoke erupted. The great mortar, hauled up there with insane efforts, had exploded on first firing, killing those nearby. The other cannon fired wildly, their random shells finding no targets.

But Theodore's army took this as the signal to attack, and they charged down the slopes, some on horses, some running with rifles and some with spears, singing war songs as they rushed towards the British, who were in danger of being overwhelmed, with only a few hundred men up on the plateau at that point. Most of the British troops were out of sight, climbing the far slope.

A depiction of fighting with Magdala in the distance. Note the artillery firing from the other peak

Napier reacted just quickly enough. He ordered the men to drop their burdens and form a defensive line. A battery of rockets was fired at the approaching massed enemy, exploding over their heads, killing some, but failing to stop the onrush. The thunder had now started to add to the din. Still the thousands came on but the British held their fire as they were trained to do. At little over a hundred yards a hail of rifle fire cut down the Ethiopians. With the new Enfield breech-loading rifles, soldiers had trebled their rate of fire, up from three volleys a minute to ten.

Few of the Ethiopians reached the British lines alive, and those that did were dispatched with swords in close combat. All the time British troops were pouring into the battle line. An Indian regiment of riflemen was pouring fire in from one side.

It turned from a chance for a swift victory for Theodore into a horrible massacre. Not that the Ethiopians lacked courage. Each time they were beaten back, the survivors would reform and charge again. But it was futile. As night fell, Napier decide not to give chase in the dark and camp there for the night. They counted 700 dead on the field, with an estimated 1,200 wounded. The gorgeously attired

Gabry, (initially thought to be Theodore by the British troops), was among the dead. The artillery on top of Fahla had turned out to be useless, and their crews were killed by British rockets which soon found the range. Not one British soldier was killed at the Battle of Magdala, although some were wounded and died later.

"THE PUNJAUBEES, AFTER FIRING A VOLLEY, RUSHED DOWN AND CHARGED THEM WITH THE BAYONET" (*p.* 414).

Fighting at Magdala, as later imagined: From a British book

The European hostages, still imprisoned on top of Magdala, had heard the firing two miles away but could not make out what was happening and at nightfall tried to sleep, despite their fears. At 10.30pm Rassam was woken by a messenger from the emperor. The typically polite but strange missive read:

How have you spent the day? Thank God, I am well. I, being a King, could not allow people to come and fight me without attacking them first. I have done so and my troops have been beaten. I thought your people were women but I find they are men. They fought very bravely. Seeing that I am unable to withstand them, I must ask you to reconcile me to them.

At dawn the next day two, of the captive Europeans were sent by Theodore to the British lines, accompanied by Theodore's son-in-law, where the troops greeted them with wild cheering. They told Napier that the Emperor indeed wanted a 'reconciliation'.

Napier drafted a positive reply, starting: 'Your Majesty has fought like a brave man, and has been overcome by the superior power of the British Army. It is my desire that no more blood be shed.' It guaranteed 'honourable treatment' for himself and his family if the captives were immediately released.

Napier took care to show the son-in-law the heavy guns and elephants that had now been brought up. He was assured that the guns used the previous day were mere playthings compared to the power of these guns, and further that if any harm came to the hostages, all the chieftains would be pursued to the ends of Ethiopia and punished. The son-in-law asked for 24 hours delay.

But again Theodore's mood darkened. He sent a long, mad, rambling reply in almost Biblical language.

Out of what I have done of evil towards my people, may God bring good. His will be done. I had intended, if God had so decreed, to conquer the whole world... to lead my army against Jerusalem, and expel from it the Turks. A warrior who has dandled strong men in his arms like infants will never suffer himself to be dandled in the arms of others.

Hardly the clear reply Napier sought.

A panoramic composite showing the approach to Magdala, by Richard Harvey

With his chiefs Theodore ranted and raved, blaming his own people for cowardice in battle (which was hardly fair) and being irreligious, even sticking a pistol in his own mouth and firing it in an apparent suicide attempt. It failed to go off. Some of the chiefs called for all the Europeans to be thrown off the cliff and for the fighting to be resumed. After failing to kill himself, Theodore lay prostrate on the ground with a cloth over his head. It seemed a madman's end was nearing.

Suddenly he allowed all the Europeans to be released, except one sick woman, whose children stayed with her, and by the dusk of the Saturday they reached the cheering British lines.

On the morning of Easter Sunday, Theodore took another tone. He wrote to Napier that Satan had visited him during the night, and got him to try to kill himself. God having intervened and 'signified to me that I should not die', he wrote, he released the hostages. 'Today is Easter; be pleased to let me send a few cows to you.'

All the remaining Europeans were brought down safely from the citadel. This would have seemed the perfect ending, but somehow events contrived to go awry again.

Theodore sent 1,000 cows and 500 sheep across to the British camp – all that he possessed, pretty unwise as he had an army to feed himself. Yet another terrible misunderstanding came about. Napier had been told that if he accepted such largesse, by Ethiopian custom this was a peace settlement, so he sent them all back.

This sent Theodore into a rage. He took what men who would still follow him up the steep path to Magdala, declaring he would continue the fight. The chiefs were now beginning to desert him. On the Monday, April 13, his now tiny force of perhaps 50 men descended again to the plain to try to move his battery of heavy guns up to the gate of fortress by hand. It was hopeless. Theodore then seemed to have finally gone beyond reason. He jumped on his horse, firing his rifle in the air as he rode towards the British lines, challenging them to single combat. No one took any notice. He retired to the gates of Magdala with a few men, declaring his desire to continue the fight.

Death at Easter for a Christian Emperor: Theodore would not be taken alive

By this time Napier had seen the pile of mutilated corpses at the bottom of the cliffs under Magdala, and his attitude to Theodore had hardened considerably.

A British assault force of about 3,000 men now started to attack, some up the path to the gates, carrying crowbars to force an entry, some using scaling ladders up the cliffs, all under rifle fire from high above and under torrents of rain from another thunderstorm. Meanwhile British shells were falling on the fortress above.

The attackers got through the first gate with only seven men down, then rushed a second before the defenders could close it, and shooting some as they scrambled up. They burst through to attack whatever was on the flat top of the mountain – and found the resistance had ceased. Ethiopian troops came from all directions to lay down their arms and surrender.

Looking around, they found one of the bodies by the second gate was Theodore. He had taken one of the ornate pistols Queen Victoria had given him and put it to his mouth – and this time succeeded. Napier marched in like a conqueror, followed by a brass band.

On the following day, the Emperor was buried in Magdala's church (pictured) by a Coptic priest with full royal cermoniies.

Then the British troops departed, leaving explosives to blow up every building except the church. Theodore's guns were also destroyed. As the army marched away, they could see clouds of smoke billowing from the ruins.

Nothing was done to colonise or reorganise Ethiopia – this had never been the aim – so a bit like more recent regime changes, chaos ensued as tribes settled old scores.

One of the most helpful – to the British – chiefs called Kassai was rewarded with weapons and stores, so he became a strong ruler in his part of the country, and eventually Emperor Johannes IV, but Napier's only object, having rescued the hostages and defeated Theodore, was to withdraw the hundreds of miles to the coast with as little loss as possible.

By June nearly all the remaining stores had been withdrawn and Napier sailed for Suez and England.

There Parliament thanked him, he was made Lord Napier of Magdala, and got a statue too, and the lesser ranks were also rewarded. All the participants received the Abyssinian War Medal.

Ethiopia slipped out of sight into obscurity once again.

If the triumph, where not one Briton was shot dead at Magdala, gave the British ideas that their armies were invincible or superior, they were to be horribly disabused of this notion at places like Spion Kop, Gallipoli, and the Somme.

Abyssinian Medal, note lettering on the left. Picture: Richard Harvey

Footnote: It's irrelevant, but interesting – Magdala *did* see one Briton shot dead, on Easter Day too, and a young, blonde British woman killed as a result – but a century later, in 1955.

Intrigued?

It was David Blakely who was shot by Ruth Ellis, who became the last British woman to be hanged for murder. But it was outside the Magdala pub in Hampstead, London, named after Napier's victory, a story which by then nearly everyone had totally forgotten.

5 WEIRD WAR I, II AND III...

TOTAL CRAP: The elite French commando parachutists' unit, the Commando de Renseignement et d'Action Profondeur, were puzzled by the lack of respect they received from foreign armies. This may have been because they had acronym CRAP on their uniforms. It's been changed to Groupement de Commandos Parachutistes.

POMMY WHAT? That grenades are named after pomegranates, which they in some ways resembled inside and out, is obvious from the French word for the fruit: *grenade*. In World War I they were more dangerous to the throwers, because if you were standing in a trench, the throwing hand could catch on the back of the narrow trench then drop it, and it would blow up (which was a bit bananas). The British developed a grenade that also looked like a fruit, but not a pomegranate: the 'pineapple' (below right).

THE RIGHT CALIBRE: With the millions of shots fired across the trenches in the First World War you'd think that someone would have got a bullet down the wrong end of a rifle. Well someone did. A

British soldier was in his trench lining up to fire at a German sniper, and as he pulled the trigger, felt an enormous blow that knocked him off the firing step. The two bullets had met halfway down the barrel (the German one being of a slightly smaller calibre), which blew open at that point, the two projectiles having fused together (the British Army preserved the rifle, below). The soldier picked himself up but had no long-term damage; if the German's heart had beaten just at the wrong time and deflected the shot a jot, the Brit could have been dead. The German went to his grave thinking he *had* killed that man.

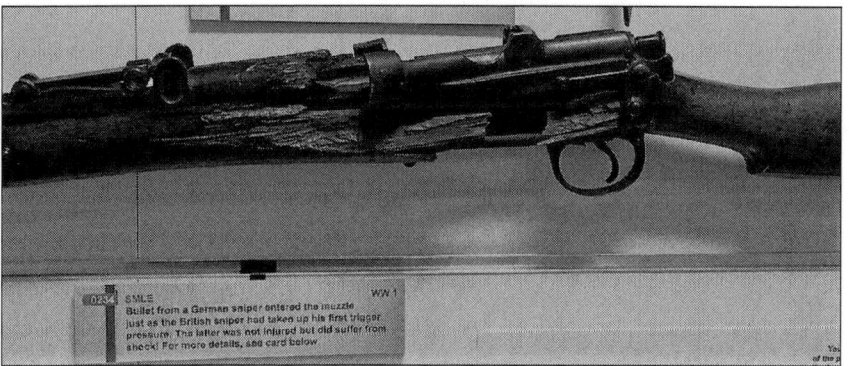

Above: The rifle that got a German bullet down the wrong end. Below: A rare British 1914 trench howitzer. Pictures: SASC Weapons Collection Trust

FAREWELL SALUTE: At the beginning of the American Civil War, in April, 1861, Fort Sumter in Charleston harbour endured a bombardment of 36 hours during which more than 4,000 rounds were fired. No one was killed by all these shells, miraculously, and the fort surrendered. As the flags were hauled down at the surrender ceremony, a salute was fired and a cannon exploded, killing two men and injuring four.

PARATROOPS at the beginning of D-Day were dropped so low that their parachutes failed to open and they thudded into the ground and were killed. Others were dropped at the correct height onto flooded fields and drowned in their heavy kit. One American, John Steele, famously snagged his parachute on a church spire and survived only by feigning death while the battle raged beneath him. Yet others were mini-men dolls, with smaller parachutes, to fool Germans – you can't tell from the ground. They had firecrackers attached that went off when they landed to start apparent firefights.

ATOM BOMBS: Colonel Paul Tibbets who commanded the flight that dropped the first atom bomb on Hiroshima on August 6, 1945, incinerating many men, women and children and mortally wounding hundreds of thousands, had been born to drop things from planes, it seems. At 12, he had hitched his first ride in a plane with a stunt pilot dropping somewhat less dangerous free chocolate bars over Miami Beach. Tibbets had been given the job of chucking the sweets — each with its own little parachute — out of the cockpit of the tiny red-and-white biplane. He died in 2007, having seared his mother's name – Enola Gay – into the world's history because he named his bomber after her. There is no record of her ever objecting to being associated with the atomic mass slaughter. At the time, of course, it was regarded as a necessary thing (outside Japan) and saved millions of lives on both sides by ending the war.

FANCY A MUSHROOM CAKE (mushroom cloud, that is)? Given what atom bombs did to people – making their skin hang off like stripped wallpaper in Hiroshima, for example – you might not think a celebratory cake shaped like a mushroom cloud was in the best possible taste. But this is what Vice Admiral William Blandy enjoyed (pictured) after testing the U.S. H-bomb at Bikini atoll. His wife's hat wasn't that appealing either. In fact Blandy was angered at accusations of trivializing the issue, saying: 'I am not an atomic playboy.'

TANKS A LOT: 'Tanks' as a code-name for the military vehicles was devised to fool the Germans into thinking they were merely containers. The British Landship Committee was behind the project, and they were first used in 1916 (A Mark I is pictured below). After the Germans captured one, they got rather good at using 'landships' by the next war. Or panzers, as they called them.

LANDSHIPS AHOY! The whole landships idea came because of the desperate need to break the murderous stalemate of trench warfare on the Western Front in the First World War. An American magazine's idea rather fancifully included this:

'ARMOURED' QUADRICYCLE: This 1899 British design doesn't look very armoured, and the feeble 1.5hp engine at the back would have not produced much speed. Useless over rough ground, and as the black thing between the legs is the petrol tank, potentially a mobile crematorium. The bowler hat just adds to the slightly loony, Monty Pythonish look.

A RUSSIAN GIANT: A very odd First World War Russian 'tank' design intended to get over barbed wire and trenches was this, the Tsar fighting vehicle. You don't realise the size of it till you see the normal armoured car to the left, and the man standing on one of the gun turrets. Only one was built, and it soon got stuck in a bog and was never put into action.

MARCH OF THE STRANGE TANK: Most people know that the first usable tanks – a British invention, although Leonardo Da Vinci had sketched an idea back in the 15th century – which appeared to great German consternation on the Western Front in 1916 were that funny lozenge shape, a rhomboid or leaning-over rectangle, pictured a couple of pages back. And that by World War II they had evolved to what we think of today as tank-shaped.

But in the meantime, there were some deeply strange oddities. Some of these were complete failures, like the British Independent tank, with five turrets on a very narrow chassis. It was too top heavy, would fall over in ditches and trenches, and was impossible to turn.

Five turrets on one tank: The Vickers A1E1 Independent, designed in 1924

The reason it was still too narrow – if it had been a lot wider it might have had a chance of working – was that tanks needed to be moved about by railway in that era, and the British railway loading gauge was not generous. Bovington Camp, home of the British tank regiments even today, had its own branch line off the Waterloo-Weymouth route for loading armoured vehicles, but they had to fit through bridges and tunnels like any other train.

By the Second World War, various military leaders were wondering if you could make a tank fly. Here is a Russian Antonov design from 1942. It would have delivered a lightweight tank, but this is just a model.

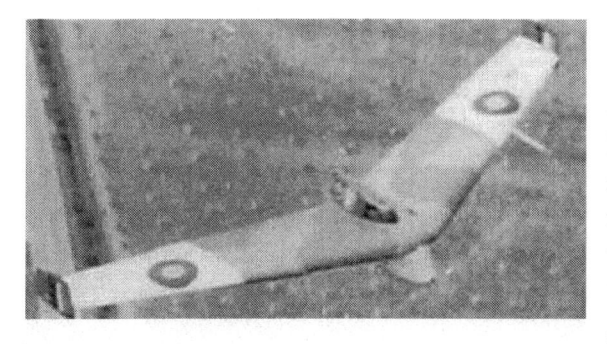

One such contraption that did actually fly was the British Bayne's Bat, named after its inventor. Only one was built, one-third size, but the tailless glider did work, and pictured here is the one very poor quality photograph that survives. The wings would have been left on the battlefield. In the end, gliders that could take a Jeep or light tank inside the fuselage were adopted.

A strange Venezuelan design, the 1932 Tortuga

Not unlike Da Vinci's 1487 design (modern replica)

'HOBART'S FUNNIES' AND OTHER ODDBALL TANKS: The specially modified tanks, developed after the Dieppe Raid disaster, for the invasion of France included this swimming Sherman, where you dropped the skirts and the propellors (right) took over. It could drive off a landing craft ramp and swim ashore. At least, that was the theory. Some were launched so far out, off the Normandy beaches that they sank and are still down there, some with their drowned crews inside. Others were driven down too steep ramps and flipped over, killing the crew. They just had to be bashed out of the way so many others could go ashore, which they did in enough numbers to overcome the Germans.

The modified special purpose tanks (more, see next page) were called Hobart's Funnies after Major General Percy Hobart, commander of the 79th Armoured Brigade. In the late 1930s, Hobart had been pushed out of the Army by hidebound officers for his unconventional ideas. Just in time, Churchill had him brought back.

WEIRD WAR I, II AND III

HOBART'S FUNNIES (Continued): The Flail tank, above, had metal chains on a spindle which lashed the ground to set off any landmines. You had to remember to turn your main gun to the rear, of course! But it could clear a path through a minefield for invading tanks in minutes, which would have taken men on foot hours, under fire and in great peril from the mines.

If you had soft ground, tanks and troops lorries could sink in, so another Hobart funny, below, would unroll a road in front of itself.

On the following page, look carefully at the picture of a tank apparently crossing a bridge.

HOBART'S FUNNIES (Continued): This isn't a tank crossing a bridge. It is crossing two other specialist tanks which have driven into the anti-tank ditch and extended their folding decks to make a flat road way. It could all be done under fire. And if the Germans were still giving trouble from their pillboxes, a visit from a 'Crocodile' flame-throwing tank (below) would shut them up, or maybe a visit from yet another 'Funny', the Spigot Mortar tank which chucked a charge the size of a dustbin at such fortifications, destroying them.

GRUESOME GATLING: The Gatling gun was famously the first machine-gun, although it wasn't fully automatic, like the slightly later Maxim. You still had to turn a handle, but the rate of fire from one gun had gone up from perhaps three a minute to 200. A large bit of equipment, it replaced field guns rather than rifles, so wasn't that portable. Still, it made a massive impact on ranks of ordinary soldiers – and spear-carrying tribesmen in colonial wars.

What was odd about its introduction just in time for the end of the U.S. Civil War was the way Gatling's salesmen flogged the thing. They turned up at a real battle, on the Union side, and just set to work slaughtering Confederate soldiers. Impressed, the U.S. generals bought the weapons. Dr Gatling claimed his invention would make armies need to be much smaller and thus reduce the slaughter. In fact, it massively increased it, leading to the lethal combination of machine-gun, mud and barbed wire known as the First World War.

Dr Gatling's original patent drawing has survived – unlike those on the receiving end of his lethal ingenuity. With his signature.

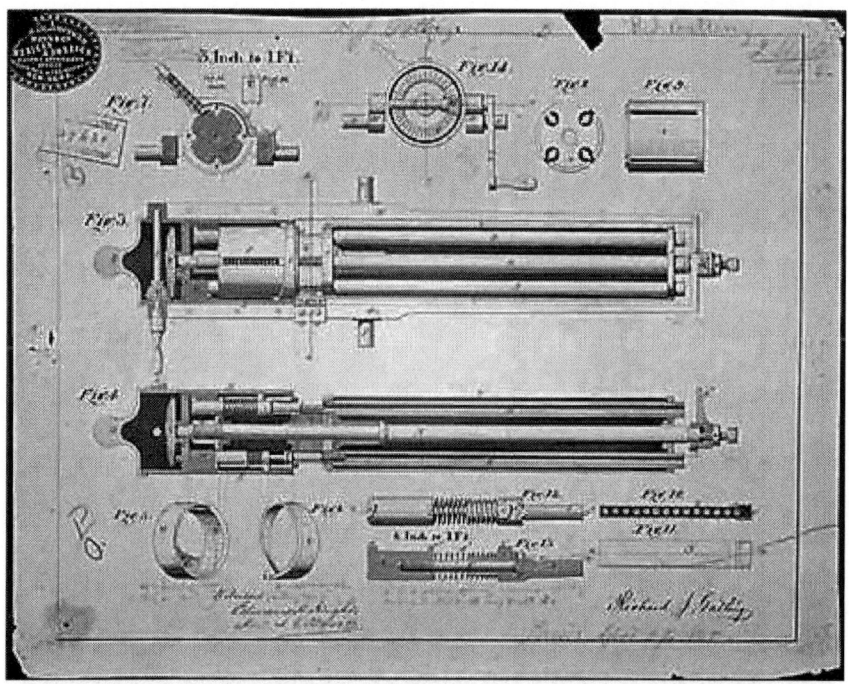

His best shot: Dr Richard Gatling signed this patent application drawing

It wasn't all good news for the side that had the Gatling guns, however. This was the age before smokeless ammunition (which was later devised to stop soldiers giving away their positions on firing). So if one rifle using black powder gave off a puff of smoke, imagine what 200 rounds a minute produced. If the wind was behind them, the gunners would soon be firing into a wall of fog. And if the wind was from one side, the upright position and lack of protection made the four crew easy targets for any snipers not hit by the rage of fire coming out of the Gatling. In fact there were other Gatling guns than the design that became famous. Here's his design for a battery gun:

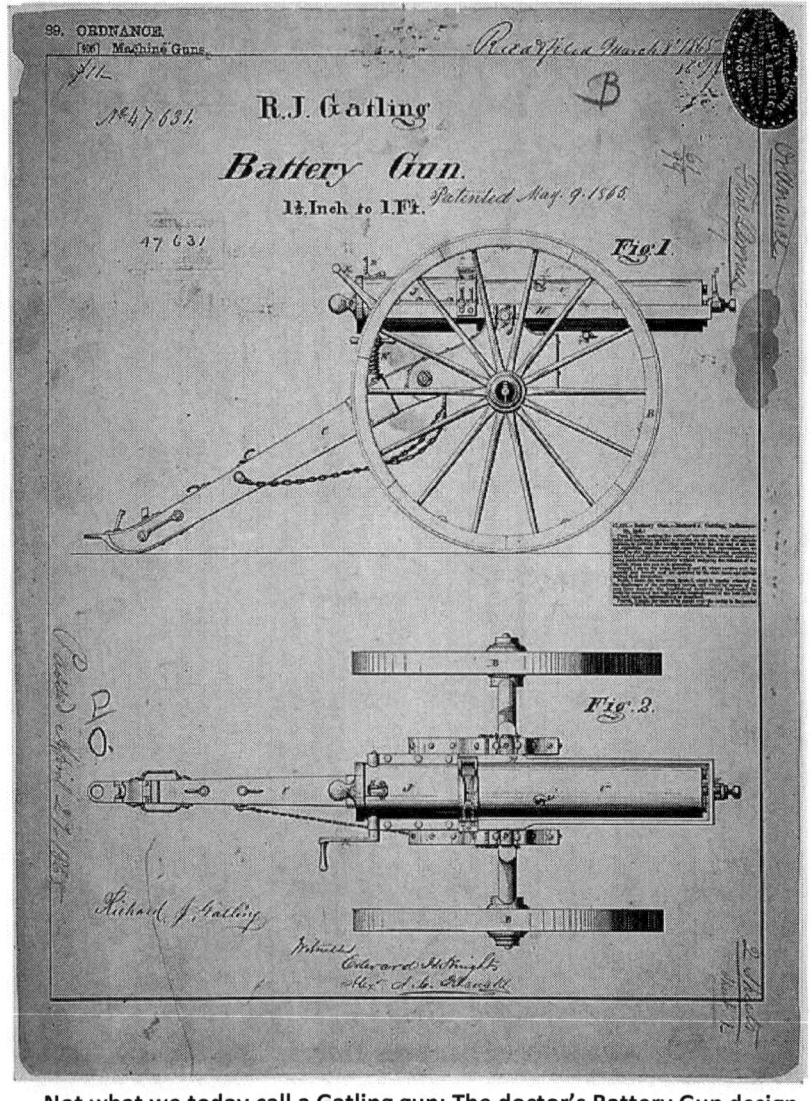

Not what we today call a Gatling gun: The doctor's Battery Gun design

Nevertheless, the Gatling Gun was the huge step away from chivalrous, man-to-man combat (if war ever was really like that) to mechanised impersonal slaughter, where you didn't really see the people you were killing or maiming.

Perhaps that's why, when the First World War got going, people warmed to the idea of aviators facing each other one at a time in their flimsy 'kites' made of wood and canvas. They were hero-worshipped as 'knights of the air' and gallant 'aces' who fought with honour.

That, too, was to change by the time we get to faceless, ruthless, cowardly bombing of civilians from the Spanish Civil War onwards.

Oddly enough, recent years have seen the need for ever increasing firepower bring the return of rotating barrels in modern warfare. The M61 Vulcan, one of which is shown below left, delivers an astonishing 6,000 rounds per minute of explosive ammunition. This was necessitated by the speed of jet aircraft after World War II. They might have only a fraction of a second to try to hit their targets.

But it all started with the Gatling Gun, above, and its strange rotating barrels, which gave a chance for spent cartridges to fall out, the hopper to reload and the barrel to cool a little. It must have been terrifying.

WASP WITH A STING: It could be just the thing in a tedious traffic jam – a scooter with an on-board bazooka ready to fire. The Vespa was the most famous scooter of the post-war years and was built in an Italian factory that had been flattened by Allied bombing because it built aero engines.

The owner, inspired by a paratroopers' lightweight motorbike the Americans used during the war, wanted to produce cheap transport the Italians could afford, and which would cope with war-damaged roads.

He got one functional but ugly design going, then had a stylist emulate those Italian curves later made famous by Sophia Loren, and next listened to the buzzing two-stroke engine and christened it 'Vespa' (wasp) ... and the rest is history, with millions sold.

Roll on half-a-dozen years to the mid-Fifties and the French wanted a cheap and air-droppable mobile anti-tank weapon, and someone came up with the bazooka Vespa TAP 150, named after the Troupes Aéro Portées. They were thrown out of planes in pairs, one carrying the bazooka, and one the spare shells in canisters. They were lashed to a pallet with straw bales either side.

Oddly enough, they worked, and were used in Indo-China and North Africa. They were surely the most dangerous scooters ever devised.

And by dangerous, I should imagine not just to the enemy – fancy being on one carrying all the spare rockets and a full fuel tank while under sniper fire?

WEIRD WAR I, II AND III

BAT EARS: This very odd couple are a junior officer and an NCO from a German Feldartillerie regiment in 1917 using combined acoustic/optical locating apparatus to spot enemy aircraft or guns. Before radar, sound location was taken very seriously – another bit of German equipment under test is shown below left. And Britain between the wars had vast concrete 'sound mirrors' (below right) which can still be seen at sites such as Dungeness in Kent. (See also cover).

Click here for the accessible version

Reply

WORST BRITISH WEAPONS OF WORLD WAR II: It was an era of improvisation and – after the Army's equipment had mostly been left on the beaches at Dunkirk in 1940 – desperation. Some of the bodge-ups or brainwaves were in fact brilliant – such as the Mulberry Harbour, invented by testing out strips of Lilo inflatable bed in a duck pond in Surrey, or the Sten gun, which looks like it's cobbled together from old plumbing – but others looked laughable. Here's a few that, even in the dire days when Britain 'stood alone' (never forget that meant with the loyal Empire and Commonwealth from overseas), invited ridicule from servicemen.

1: STICKY BOMB: This was suicidally stupid type of grenade supposed to be thrown at German tanks, to which it would in theory adhere, and then blow up. It was often a far greater danger to whoever was throwing it than to any potential enemy. The design was just crackers.

The grenade (above) was to be filled with highly unstable nitroglycerine which would be likely to go off anytime with a good knock, and must be kept clean and dry. This was therefore contained in a spherical glass bottle, which was intended to break and deform to the shape such a small amount of explosive needed to be to have any hope of breaking through armour, like a squashed mud ball. Any other shape would be futile.

There are obvious problems already with the concept. Glass is easily broken, the shards highly dangerous to the troops on your own side if it blows up accidentally, but harmless to tanks. Glass is also useless at holding glue. So the bottle was wrapped in a tight sock, which was dunked in glue. Problem solved? Not quite.

The bomb had to be *enormously* sticky to have any hope of clinging to a German panzer. Early test sticky bombs just fell off bits of armour, so some super-sticky glue was required. A civil servant remembered a substance called bird lime, which in those days was spread on the branches of trees and was so super sticky that the poor creatures would be trapped if they landed on it

A tin of it was found, labelled only 'K' and 'Stockport'. A man was sent by express train to that northern town to wander around until he found the manufacturer – which he soon did, a firm called Kay. A suitable glue was rapidly devised.

Now you have something enormously sticky, fragile, explosive, difficult to handle and transport. So it was encased in two hemispherical sticky-resistant cases. These had to be removed by pulling a release pin, and then the bomb thrown at the target where you hoped it would stick until it went off.

Unfortunately there were cases of the bomb getting stuck to the serviceman's uniform or other things. There is one account of a desperate serviceman ripping off his trousers and throwing them attached to the bomb at the target, which it fell off because the trousers got in the way, and blew up. It might have had the effect of incapacitating the troops of both sides with laughter ... although it was probably far more terrifying to have to use the sticky bomb in reality.

Trails of the new device were disappointing. It failed to stick to any surface that was wet or covered with even the thinnest film of dried mud, top brass were told. 'But that is a customary condition of tanks,' Major-General Ismay could not resist pointing out.

So there we have it nearly all of it – the outer shell, the glue, the sock, the glass bottle and the handle all being utterly harmless to

German tanks – and the explosive only any use if squashed to the metal and held there.

About two million were ordered (at a time when the Army had no guns or mortars, it was seen as a morale booster). Oddly enough, courageous Australian troops made them work – by walking up to the German tank and ramming it on, then walking away at an angle. They did that because if walked straight back the handle would be blasted through your back. If you watch the movie Saving Private Ryan closely, you'll see the Tom Hanks officer character getting his men to bodge one up using a GI sock.

And like most apparently crackpot ideas in this book, the thing wasn't entirely without logic. If German tanks and armoured vehicles had invaded Britain, it would have been ideal to drop from an upstairs window onto the roof of the vehicle – where its armour happens to be weakest.

Trouble is, on the open battlefield, German panzers didn't always obligingly drive close to two-storey buildings while keeping themselves perfectly clean...

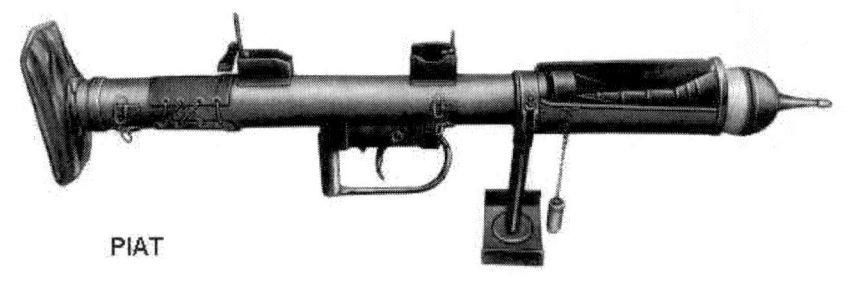

PIAT

2: THE PIAT, an acronym for Projector, Infantry, Anti Tank. Possibly the most-mocked weapon of the war, and some may think, a candidate for worst weapon. This was a shoulder-held rocket launcher (above) that worked with a strong spring which you had to extend and lock with great difficulty, while standing on the shoulder pad and pulling upwards and twisting. It seemed absurd to suggest men would be able to do that and then fire within the puny 100-yard tank-killing range. If they missed, some thought the idea was to stand up again and stretch the spring again and lock it while under fire, but this was a misunderstanding. The action of firing the first round should have re-cocked the weapon, if you had survived that far.

Anti-tank weaponry was absurdly lacking, as recounted in the last item, after Dunkirk. Most of the field guns had been left on the beaches. The Army's other weapon, the Boys anti-tank rifle, was useless. It had never once been documented to stop a German battle tank. There was little metal or time to manufacture whole new field guns, and anything fired from a smaller calibre, such as a rifle, can't contain enough explosive to pierce armour.

Enter the spigot mortar concept. If you launch a rocket or mortar with a hollow tail off a spigot – a metal rod pointing towards the target – you don't have to have a gun barrel (made out of specialist, expensive metals), and the charge at the impact end can be as wide as it needs to be. The parts can be quickly stamped out of cheap metal without careful engineering.

The spigot idea was the baby of Lt Col Latham Valentine Stewart Blacker, an inveterate inventor, adventurer and Indian Army veteran from World War I, although it took others to develop it to the point where it could actually stop a German tank. Another advantage is that the enemy does not see a muzzle flash to give away your position.

So the Piat was born, and did the job until the Bazooka did it much better.

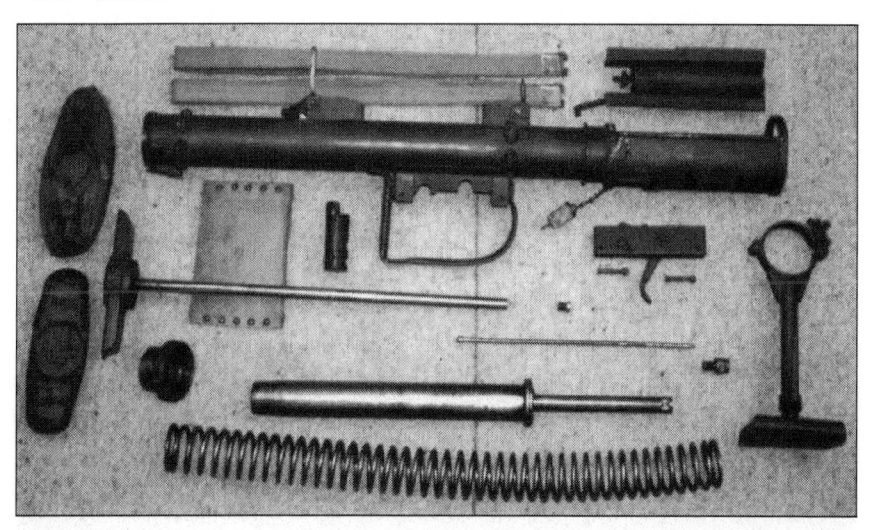

The Piat in bits. That huge spring had to be stretched before each firing

More than 100,000 Piats were built, and used in World War II, the 1948 Arab-Israeli War, the Korean War and possibly the 1971 Indian-Pakistani War. It was extraordinary that troops could be expected to use the Piat under fire – in Burma heroic Indian troops crawled to within 30 yards of Japanese tanks to be sure of disabling them – but any way of stopping enemy tanks was better than none. Asked why they crawled so close, lugging the thing, they said they couldn't be sure of it working from further away.

Having said all that, the Piat did kill German tanks, six servicemen won VCs using them, and when Arab tanks tried to invade in infant Israel in 1948, they were stopped by Piats. Canadians questioned on their return from campaigns voted it their favourite infantry weapon in World War II, so it can't have been that bad, and doesn't deserve the 'worst weapon' tag despite soldiers' cynicism. The rest of us can consider ourselves lucky we never had to use one.

3. THE BLACKER BOMBARD: The above-mentioned Colonel Blacker also produced another stinker of a weapon, the Blacker Bombard. This was a spigot-based anti-tank mortar (that is without a gun barrel), and had an effective range of only 100 yards. As it had to reloaded from the sharp end, you would probably be dead if you didn't kill the tank with the first hit, and you'd also probably be already dead if you let it approach close enough to fire it, without very good concealment. It could either be fired from a huge contraption that unfolded to form a firing platform, or from fixed pillars (above) on which it swivelled. You can still see 350 of these pillars around Britain, the height of a tall stool, twice as wide, with a pin in the middle. This again was fairly ridiculous because the enemy had to obligingly approach whatever was being defended from exactly the right end (e.g. an airfield, which is a big thing). And not notice the contraption and the local version of Captain Mainwaring fussing about it.

The reason the thing got built at all – despite serious misgivings by top brass – was that the demonstration of the prototype was done in West Sussex, in front of Winston Churchill. One of the initial rounds missed the target and hit a tree, blowing pieces off, one of which struck a Free French army observer, not too seriously. Churchill evidently thought this hilarious and stomped off chuckling, saying 'Good show, put them into full production.'

This was a dumb decision because of the weapon's limitations, but it has to be put into the context mentioned above, when 840 of the Army's anti-tank guns had been left in France after Dunkirk; and only a hundred or so were left and the Army was forbidden to waste even one round for those guns in training. The Home Guard, armed in some places with shotguns and pitchforks, were begging for weapons that simply could not be provided. They felt, when a Blacker Bombard arrived, that someone in Whitehall was taking them seriously. Just lucky they never had to use the things in anger.

Oddly enough, Blacker's idea did bear fruit in the long run. In the Battle of the Atlantic, the Royal Navy was desperate to find ways of combating the German U-Boats. One of these was the Sonar detection system – a sort of sound-based underwater radar whereby the ship emitted a ping and a submarine reflected back an echo, giving its location away. Another was the Hedgehog, a development during the battle of the Blacker Bombard but with up to 24 spigot mortars launching projectiles forwards of an attacking ship. These were much smaller than the large depth-charges used beforehand – and they worked only if they hit the target, unlike the enormous bang of the depth charge which went off at a pre-set depth, submarine or no submarine. But one hit was enough to take out a sub.

Firing forwards was important. If a warship approached a German submarine there reached a point where the sonar location was too close to work. The ships had to steam from there and over the enemy to fire its depth-charge, which took some moments to sink to the required depth. German submarine commanders realised this, so they knew that if they greatly altered their course and depth at that moment, they might well evade the attack.

The Hedgehog (above), on the other hand, fired while the sonar was still pinpointing the sub. It had a wider foot print, and if they missed, there was no huge explosion – no explosion at all – to warn German U-boats a warship was on the warpath. It also stopped the sonar 'blindness' that continued several minutes after a depth-charge explosion to aid the U-boat's escape.

Consider the statistics. Depth-charges look impressive with their mountainous plume of spray, but they work only if the depth is set correctly and they are very near the target. The Hedgehog charges work at any depth (and thousands of them must lie at the bottom in the Atlantic mud ready to explode!). One German sub, U-427, survived 678 depth-charges in no doubt harrowing attacks. It was eventually sunk by the British, but only after its surrender at the end of the war. This record was exceptional, of course, but it shows how un-lethal depth-charges could be.

On the whole the record of the Hedgehog was more impressive – one in five Hedgehog attacks resulted in a kill. Only one in 80 depth-charges sunk a submarine (so lucky U-427 had almost used up nine lives!).

Hedgehogs were even adapted to put on the front of landing craft on D-Day. They could clear a certain area of beach of obstacles, mines, barbed wire etc before in the infantry stormed ashore.

Colonel Blacker wasn't such a chump after all.

A Hedgehog is fired forward of the ship. A ring of splashes show where the bombs entered the water but did not explode

A hit! That crippled sub will either surface rapidly to let survivors escape, or just sink - permanently this time

THE GREAT PANJANDRUM: This dramatic but hilariously bad bit of kit (left) – which had a strangely worrying way of attacking its own side when launched – was intended to cope with a serious problem: how to clear a path up the heavily defended French beaches on D-Day without great loss of life. There were minefields in the sand, barbed wire to hold you up and machine-gun nests embedded in 7ft-thick concrete defences to slaughter those attempting to perform this seemingly-impossible task. That part was not at all funny, as the Americans in particular found on on June 6, 1944.

Enter the bonkers Great Panjandrum, a sort of giant double Catherine Wheel which, having been launched at sea, under its own rocket power would roll up the beach, blowing up the mines without itself being destroyed, smashing through the barbed wire, and then with a vast explosion of the large charge in the spindle of the device, blast a giant hole in the defences. Or so it was envisaged…

The prototype was built in East London under great secrecy and was transported stealthily to the test site – which was, ludicrously, a public beach in full view of a busy seaside resort. Just the place if you want something to go embarrassingly wrong. In fact when you consider it was supposed to blast its way up a beach from the sea and kill people at the top of it, having it witnessed by large holiday crowds was a bit batty.

Luckily the prototype was filled with sand in the spindle of the contraption where the large explosive charge was supposed to be. And the number of rockets on the edges of the wheel were limited.

The signal to fire it was given on September 7, 1943, and the Panjandum obediently, and somewhat noisily and explosively, launched itself out of a landing craft, across the shallows and up the beach. There all pretence to obedience ended and everything went awry. Some rockets failed while others kept going, so it veered off and fell over, nowhere near the target area.

Repeated tests failed with the damn thing behaving with all the guided characteristics of an highly inflated balloon allowed to escape your fingers. It shot all over the beach and fell over anywhere.

Rather than do the sensible thing and give up a bad idea, the boffins loaded the Great Panjandrum with more and more rockets, with the results wilder and wilder navigational errors.

Undeterred, they fitted the best possible rockets and invited the Royal Navy top brass for witness their brilliance. What could possibly go wrong? Here is a later BBC account of the event, which was being filmed by an official cinematographer, a certain Mr Klemantaski.

'At first all went well. Panjandrum rolled into the sea and began to head for the shore, the Brass Hats watching through binoculars from the top of a pebble ridge [...] Then a clamp gave: first one, then two more rockets broke free: Panjandrum began to lurch ominously. It hit a line of small craters in the sand and began to turn to starboard, careering towards Klemantaski, who, viewing events through a telescopic lens, misjudged the distance and continued filming. Hearing the approaching roar he looked up from his viewfinder to see Panjandrum, shedding live rockets in all directions, heading straight for him. As he ran for his life, he glimpsed the assembled admirals and generals diving for cover behind the pebble ridge into barbed-wire entanglements. Panjandrum was now heading back to the sea but crashed on to the sand where it disintegrated in violent explosions, rockets tearing across the beach at great speed.'

The Great Panjandrum was then officially abandoned. Oddly enough, someone later claimed it was part of a deliberate misinformation ploy to convince the Germans that the invasion would come in Pas-de-Calais, where the Atlantic Wall defences were indeed stronger. Hence its being demonstrated in quite a public place.

Hmmm. I think the it a case of what I call the MASOOD tendency. That is the habit of historians of belatedly trying to Make Sense Of Official Dunderheads. More likely that dozens of crackpot ideas were tried before the ones that worked actually went into production and then into action.

6 BIZARRE BATTLES

OPERATION ZITRONELLA was one of the most ridiculous raids in World War II, in that it was staggering overkill for such a tiny target, it was months too late to have the desired effect, and it also had the odd result in producing the Germans who held out longest at the end of the war without surrendering.

Admittedly, the setting is a deeply strange, lonely place. The bleak and inhospitable Svalbard islands – Spitsbergen (meaning pointed mountains) being the largest and best-known – are a long way north of Norway, closer to the North Pole than Oslo, and often completely ice-bound. It is the most northerly settlement on Earth.

The weather is punishingly dangerous without the right sort of survival gear, and is a lethal enemy, even without a war going on.

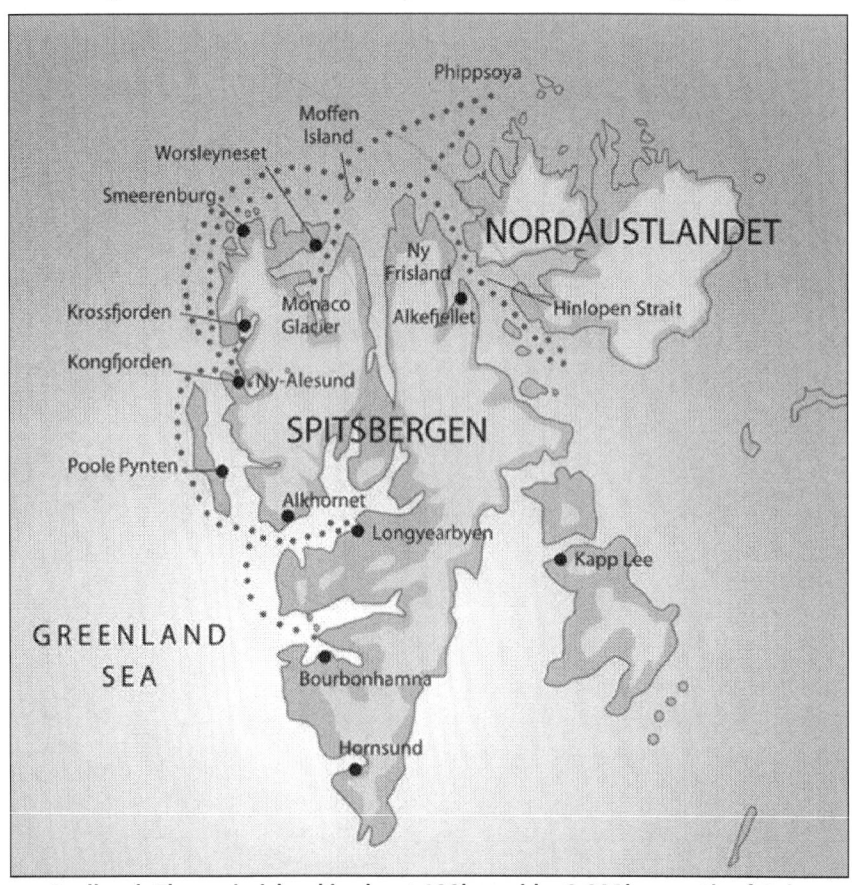

Svalbard: The main island is about 100km wide, 2,000km north of Oslo

The group of islands cover about 200 miles by 200 miles and endure 24-hour darkness during the polar winter, the reverse in the summer.

Before the war, there were two very productive coal mines working on Spitsbergen, one Russian and one Norwegian, and small, rough settlements serving these, with facilities for loading colliers to ship the fuel to their home countries. It could be compared to Britain's Falkland Islands at the other end of the world, and was a base for whaling ships. The capital, Longyearbyen, was not much more than a row of shabby houses along a muddy street.

Worth a massive battle? The capital, Longyearbyen, just before the war

Operation Zitronella was a massive German raid on these islands, but it ignored the fact that the British had already correctly guessed that the Germans, desperate to fuel their war effort, would decide after their invasion of Norway that they could seize the coal mines. An earlier British raid, called *Operation Gauntlet*, in late August and early September 1941, had followed the German invasion of Norway in the summer of the year before.

With the secret agreement of the Norwegian government-in-exile and the Soviet Union, the aim was to seize what coal supplies could be found from under the noses of the Germans and destroy the mines to render them unusable. By this time, the Germans had attacked the Soviet Union, so both the Norwegian and Russian civilians on the islands enthusiastically greeted the British warships.

The Soviet citizens were quietly and quickly evacuated to Archangel, and the Norwegians – who had encouraged colliers to come from the mainland and load supplies with no intention of sending them back again – continued to broadcast weather reports, including fake reports of dense fog, which deterred the Luftwaffe from coming to look. In the end the task force sailed back to Britain, with two captured colliers full of coal, an icebreaker, a tug and two sealers – all valuable for the war effort. A hundred or so islanders joined the Free Norwegian forces based in Britain. Another two hundred French who had escaped from prisoner camps and somehow reached Archangel were successfully ferried to Britain to join Free French forces. Those ships had made a 7,000-mile trip right past German-occupied Norway without loss.

There were no British casualties, apart from a party at the Russian settlement who discovered the vodka store and had to be carried back aboard ship unconscious. The coal mines were wrecked by explosive demolition, and all the remaining coal and other supplies burnt. A German ship was sunk on the way home. *Operation Gauntlet*, well before the German *Operation Zitronella*, had been an all-round success.

It made any German action against the islands utterly superfluous. There was no coal left to seize, no coal mines to work, no locals to round up, no shipping to capture, and the radio stations had been destroyed.

In the intervening period, the Germans had established a weather station elsewhere in the islands, then evacuated it by submarine because the hostile weather and Allied forces in the area made it untenable. The Norwegians had also left a small weather station in a building which was not much more than a hut. The importance of all this weather information is that British and American convoys needed to sneak past Norway to supply the northern Russians ports. Clear weather would enable merciless Luftwaffe or warship attacks with men and supplies going down in the near-freezing seas (more on these convoys in Chapter 10). Fog, rain or storms might allow the Allied ships to get through with their vital supplies of guns, tanks, ammunition and aircraft.

But the place was so vast, empty and inhospitable that both sides could have a small weather station on the islands without knowing the other was there – like two Moon bases.

At this point, some German twit gets grandiose plans. A full-scale – no, massive scale – attack on the Norwegian 'hut' is planned. It was a hut with some military back-up, to be fair – about 150 men.

But one landing ship could have carried enough men to deal with this.

In the event, the Germans sent two huge battleships, plus nine destroyers. The modern battleships *Tirpitz* and *Scharnhorst*, no less. This was the only time the *Tirpitz* was ever used in offensive action, and the only time she used her main guns. She was the biggest ever European battleship, a crew of over 2,000, 823ft long, 12 superheated boilers to give her an impressive turn of speed, eight huge 15-inch guns (one of these shells could destroy half a street, or sink any warship). *Scharnhorst* wasn't quite as big, but still had massive armament, with nine 11-inch guns and about 60 of smaller calibre – more such weapons than any European warship has today.

All of this against a 'hut' and a few men defending it!

They attacked at dawn on September 8, 1943, and most of the Norwegians fled into the hills. At one point the giant German ships just lined up opposite the settlement and let rip. There were a few guns on the Norwegian side but the overwhelming fire power soon silenced them. It was all over by noon.

Overkill: Tirpitz and a line of destroyers entering the fjord in Spitsbergen

Even so, nine Germans were killed, 49 wounded, and three destroyers damaged. It is suspected that at least some of the German casualties were caused by their own bombardment from ships. They had little experience of co-ordinating naval gunfire with ground attack, and it seems some 'friendly fire' fell among their own troops.

Some 11 of the Norwegians were killed, and 74 made prisoners.

The operation was a pointless failure. The Germans blew up facilities that had mostly already been blown up by the British.

The Norwegians established a weather station elsewhere in the islands within a month, with American forces helping supply them.

The small weather station the Luftwaffe had installed under cover of the raid on one of the islands remained until the end of the war, and way beyond.

Quite why *Operation Zitronella* was ordered is not known – but one theory was to impress Hitler and show him the thousands of men, millions of reichsmarks, thousands of tons of fuel and supplies devoted to *Tirpitz* through the war years were worth it. They weren't. She met an ignominious end (see Chapter 10) having taken on nothing more than a weather hut in the entire war. That such major ships were holed up – hiding, in effect – in northern Norway for much of the war showed the importance of the St Nazaire raid in early 1942, when British forces destroyed the one dock big enough to house them in western France, where they could have been well-placed to devastate Atlantic convoys.

Plucky, pugnacious: *HNoMS Stord* pictured in the same year

At least *Scharnhorst* fought a few actions during the war, and went down fighting not so far from here in the dramatic Battle of the North Cape on Boxing Day, 1943, with the loss of over 1,900 men. Her opponents included *HMS Belfast*, the cruiser today preserved in London on the River Thames and, appropriately, *His Norwegian Majesty's Ship Stord* (above) of the exiled Royal Norwegian Navy.

Although relatively small and unarmoured, *HNoMS Stord* fought daringly and helped cripple the huge German ship, British officers of the other warships noted with admiration.

Fought in Arctic winter darkness, and a full gale (which prevented aircraft from being used), it was the last battleship-to-battleship fight between Germany and Britain in the war, and in fact the second to last in all history. The largest British warship involved was the battleship *HMS Duke of York*.

Victory: *HMS Duke of York* **gun crew on their return to Scapa Flow after the battle. The men are wearing anti-flash gear. Picture: Lt F. A. Davies**

Terrible and devastating though that battle was, it that was what navies were intended to do. *Operation Zitronella* was not – with its massive forces, weather station hut, and pointless outcome.

After Germany had surrendered in May 1945, the unit left on Spitsbergen was the last active German military force, holding out until September 1945 simply because they were ignored by the outside world and had no way of leaving. In that month they spotted a passing Norwegian fishing boat, to whom they enthusiastically surrendered. So the whole terrible war in Europe – and this very odd northern sideshow – finally ended at this lonely, godforsaken spot.

Street by street, house by house: Germans attack in the Battle of Stalingrad

THE HOUSE WHERE HISTORY TURNED: You could argue that World War II was turned around at Stalingrad. And in that terrible charnel house of slaughter, there was one particular house where the battle hinged. The huge German military machine of millions of men and thousands of tanks and aircraft ground to a halt right here, and the initiative shifted to the Red Army, who fought from this very doorway to Hitler's bunker in Berlin.

The German attack on Russia, *Operation Barbarossa*, was the biggest invasion in history, and one of the most barbaric in the way it was conducted, and this was the biggest battle and turning point – the highest flood of the seemingly unstoppable Nazi tide before it started ebbing away, if you like.

The Battle of Stalingrad (August 23, 1942-February 2, 1943) was a huge and relentlessly brutal event. Both dictators, Hitler and Stalin, attached huge importance to it, partly for strategic and morale reasons, and partly because the city bore Stalin's name (it is now named Volgograd). More than a million men and 10,000 artillery pieces were employed on each side, plus hundreds of aircraft and tanks. In the midst of the ruthless bombing and house-to-house fighting and sniping was a terrified civilian population, who were deliberately targeted by the Germans.

Hitler had proclaimed that every male, civilian or military, would be murdered; and all woman and children deported and enslaved. Both dictators reached a point of ordering 'not one step back', so the soldiers knew they must face victory or annihilation. A million men would die, or be wounded or captured here.

So it was a fight to the death on the scale of one house at a time, for one city, yet a fight for the whole Soviet Union, and, many historians feel, for the outcome of the war.

If the Germans could seize Stalingrad and the key Volga River that ran through it, then American supplies coming up from the south would cease, and they hoped Russia would collapse, as had so many other countries in the face of the blitzkrieg.

The Russians were pushed back and back towards the Volga, across which supply boats made perilous journeys while being strafed and shelled by the Germans. In the end there was a narrow strip along the west bank, broken in two at times.

One fortified house was a particular obstacle in the ruins of the city. It had been taken once by the Germans, then retaken by the Russians, who decided to hold on there. It became known as Pavlov's House, named after Sergeant Yakov Pavlov, pictured, who commanded the platoon that defended the building so effectively.

Pavlov's House, overlooking 9th January Square, in the centre of the city, was a vital toe-hold keeping the Germans off the bank of the Volga. It had good lines of fire west, north and south. The four-storey block was manned by up to 50 soldiers of the 42nd Guards Regiment. The building was surrounded with land mines and barbed wire, and had machine guns in every window. A key weapon was a PTRS anti-tank rifle. A narrow trench led east, to supply ammunition and food to the defenders.

The PTRS-41 antitank rifle, known as the Simonov after its designer, was used from the roof of the building to ambush German tanks most effectively. The tops of the tanks, the turret roof armour, were thin, and while the tanks' main gun could not be raised high enough to fire back at the rifle, the rifle could fire down on the tanks, and its devastating 14.5 mm armour-piercing bullets, leaving the muzzle at a speed of over a kilometre a second, could rip through up to 4cm of armour.

Lethal weapon: The PTRS-41 antitank rifle could defeat the panzers

The Germans attacked the building several times a day but could never make it past the machine guns and accurate anti-tank rifle fire that came from every level of the building. Soon, as well as mines and barbed wire, there were piles of German bodies and wrecked vehicles blocking access.

The gallant defenders held the building against constant attack from September 27 to November 25, 1942, until they were relieved by a Soviet counter-attack, when friendly troops greeted the exhausted survivors as heroes. Stalin's Order No. 227 of 'not one step back' had been truly carried out.

Soviet defenders: Bitter resistance (elsewhere in Stalingrad)

Ruined: Pavlov's house after the battle ended

As Vasily Chuikov, commanding general of the Soviet forces in Stalingrad, later joked, the Germans lost more men trying to take Pavlov's House than they did in taking Paris. Not without reason.

In the brilliant *Operation Uranus*, on November 19, 1942, the Soviets' massed tanks attacked the thinly held lines north and south of the city – manned by German allies such as the Romanians – and broke though, encircling Stalingrad. Hitler declared the Sixth Army would never leave. Most of them didn't, except as prisoners, and few of them survived. The Germans had attempted to supply the starving, frozen troops by air but lost 488 transport planes in the process. The Axis powers lost 750,000 men and would never fully recover momentum.

As for Pavlov's House, the ruined building was rebuilt after the war and is still an apartment block today. On one wall of the building, there is an attached memorial, made from bricks from the ruins, to commemorate the battle (pictured left).

Pavlov, who was badly wounded in the building, fought on for the rest of the war to Berlin and died in 1981, honoured with the title Hero of the Soviet Union. If ever that had been earned...

WHEN THE USA BOMBED AND SANK BRITISH SHIPS – TWICE – AND GOT CRAVEN SUPPORT FROM LONDON AS A RESULT: If you ever saw the film *Air America*, you might remember it was an apparently far-fetched, light-hearted buddy movie starring Mel Gibson about a fake airline used by the American CIA to intervene in various wars without any evidence of official involvement. 'Yee-haw, let the commie punks have it!' type of stuff.

In fact the basic premise was absolutely accurate – the U.S. *did* create such a spooks' airline as a front for what are now called 'black ops'. And unlike the day recounted in Chapter 7 when America bombed bits of Italy and France, or the day they dropped H-bombs on Spain, this did some real damage – not least to its most loyal ally, Britain.

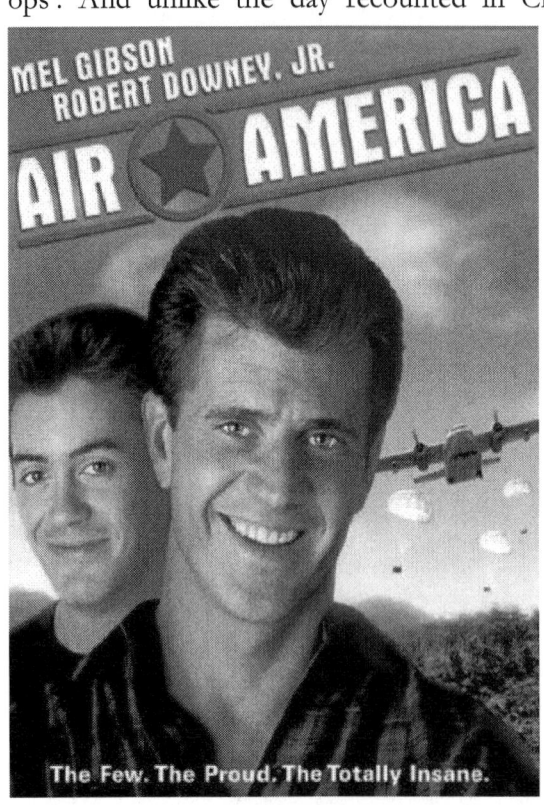

Twice the sham airline sank British ships, and twice it was not only covered up by all parties – who all knew the truth – but also the British poodle gave its U.S. master unwavering support ... as seems to have been the pattern for the post-war decades.

They are both stories too far-fetched to make a credible Hollywood film – but utterly true. They are tales of ruthless Western dishonesty, craven sucking up, downright bullying, bungling incompetence, needless killing and anti-democratic meddling which is hard to defend, even by someone who could see communism had to be resisted during the Cold War. Plus a bit of gung-ho buccaneering thrown in. The stories take in Central America and Indonesia, but start one pleasant day in a picturesque Norwegian port, in mid-1939.

FAKE ATTACK NUMBER ONE: A 2,000-ton cargo ship, SS *Springfjord* was launched in Trondheim, Norway in 1939 for a British company, Springwell Shipping Co Ltd of London.

She was still being fitted out when the Germans invaded in 1940, so the Nazis took her over and renamed her, running her as a freighter during the war. After the surrender of German forces in Norway in 1945, the British military took her over for a while, then handed her back to her owners in 1947 for her original purpose – general sea trading.

Spin the years on to 1954 and the CIA was organising a *coup d'état* in Guatemala, Central America to replace its elected government with a dissident Guatemalan colonel, a certain Carlos Castillo Armas. Why? Well, America's United Fruit Company (UFC) owned nearly half of the land in that poor country, and the elected government was going to nationalise the unused parts to give to the poor. Why was the American company so upset? Yes, they owned the land, but they also wanted the poor kept poor to be a pliant and cheap workforce.

Banana farming was labour intensive, and a poor workforce kept profits up

The Guatemalan government knew the USA was likely to interfere, and had some arms shipped in to defend itself. A Swedish cargo ship MS *Alfhem* had evaded a U.S. sea and air blockade to deliver a cargo of various Czech weapons to Puerto Barrios on the Caribbean coast. The CIA had set up a covert 'Liberation Air Force', disguised as rebels unconnected with the USA in any way, to support the Colonel's rebels, who in fact numbered only a few hundred (and they were being paid to be there). This was earlier than the fully-fledged pretend Air America outfit involved later.

LA HUELGA DE 50,000 TRABAJADORES
HONDUREÑOS EXPLOTADOS POR MAS DE 50 AÑOS POR EL MONOPOLIO DE LA
UNITED FRUIT CO. ES UNA CAUSA JUSTA.

A strike against United Fruit in neighbouring Honduras

As planned, early on the morning of June 27, 1954, the CIA *coup* forced Guatemala's elected President Jacobo Árbenz to flee into exile. At this time *Springfjord* was under charter to the U.S. shipping company Grace Line and was berthed at Puerto San José, Guatemala loading normal cargo, that included coffee and 1,000 bales of cotton.

However, the local CIA chief believed that *Springfjord* was unloading arms, so instead of simply asking the American company which was chartering the ship what was on board, or the British owners, he ordered pilot Ferdinand Schoup to attack the ship.

Schoup, flying a Lockheed Lightning fighter-bomber, black with no markings, attacked *Springfjord* with napalm bombs and set her on fire. *Springfjord* was badly damaged. It was a stupid bomb to use on a ship – you really need high explosive, armour piercing or a torpedo. What napalm does – as we saw later in Vietnam – is coat people and things with sticky burning petroleum jelly, a horrific way to die. And it seems it just hit the structure of the ship, and failed to sink it, but started a fire which resulted in its being written off.

On June 28 the Guatemalan government told the British *chargé d'affaires* in Guatemala City that the aircraft belonged to the insurgents. It didn't.

Suspicions were quickly raised about who was behind the attack and the coup. On July 5, 1954 British Labour MP Philip Noel-Baker suggested that a parliamentary committee should investigate whether the UFC had anything to do with obtaining the aircraft used to attack *Springfjord*.

Attractive artwork may have concealed a ruthless monopoly

In the House of Commons, Labour MPs pursued the suspicion that the USA had caused the coup. Geoffrey Bing MP asked the Conservative government's Minister of State for Foreign Affairs, Selwyn Lloyd, to ask the U.S. government whether it provided weapons to the Guatemalan rebels. Lloyd retorted: **'The hon. and learned Gentleman, in assuming that the United**

States Government are responsible in some way for this, is, I believe, stating something which is wholly divorced from the truth.' He knew what he was saying was untrue, and the Opposition MPs suspected this.

George Wigg MP bluntly asked: **'Will the Minister be good enough to answer Yes, or No, to a simple question? Is it a fact that American aircraft, manned by American pilots, machine-gunned Guatemalan civilians and dropped napalm bombs on Guatemala, and that Her Majesty's Government were well aware of that fact?'** A rattled Selwyn Lloyd insisted: **'That is certainly not the case. Her Majesty's Government have no information of that kind whatsoever.'** *Yes, they did.*

The British Consul at Puerto San José, who knew the truth, told *Springfjord*'s Master, Captain Bradford, to keep quiet about the attack on his ship and took from him a set of photographs of the incident taken by a member of *Springfjord's* crew, and destroyed them.

Was it right to point the finger at UFC's HQ?

In the UK House of Commons on 8 November 1954 the Labour MP Marcus Lipton asked whether Colonel Castillo Armas's military junta had paid any compensation at all for *Springfjord's* destruction. The new Tory Foreign Secretary, Anthony Eden, replied that the junta's foreign minister had said his government was prepared to discuss paying **'a reasonable sum in compensation'**.

A month later no settlement had been reached, so on 8 December 1954 Marcus Lipton asked '...**why, in South America,** this Government appears to be so flabby in protecting British interests? Is he further aware that the Government have become very unpopular with Lloyd's [the ship insurance market]?** A minister replied that the Government was not responsible for preparing the claim, and tried to explain the delay by saying **'legal gentlemen do take a long time over these matters.'**

The haggling lingered until July 1957 when Col. Castillo Armas was assassinated by one of his guards, and General Miguel Ydígoras Fuentes became president of Guatemala.

Thirteen years after the attack, still no compensation had been paid, so in 1967 Marcus Lipton submitted a written question asking the then Labour Government's Foreign Secretary **'what steps he has taken to obtain compensation from the Guatemalan Government'**. On 12 June 1967, the minister, William Rodgers MP, replied to the Commons that in 1963 Guatemala had suspended diplomatic relations with the UK and since then the UK government had been unable to continue to pursue the claim. He, too, should have known it was the USA that bombed the ship.

FAKE ATTACK NUMBER TWO: This outrageous attack on British and other allied countries' shipping involves the shadowy fake airline created by America's CIA – the Civil Air Transport Corp (CAT), in 1959 converted to AIR AMERICA, and immortalised in the rather light-hearted movie of that name.

Air America: It looked like a proper airline, but got tangled up in wars

While, on the face of it, this seemed to be an airline where you would be welcome to book a flight for yourself or cargo hauling – and you could – it was far from light-hearted behind the scenes. You wouldn't be at all welcome at the places where its aircraft turned up unmarked – for that meant illegal attacks and mayhem were about to happen. For several decades after World War II, this outfit ranged around South-East Asia, where the U.S. was not only combating the spread of communism – as in Vietnam and Korea, not with outright success – but also nakedly defending America's own commercial interests, as in the previous item.

CAT was created in 1946 by the legendary flier Claire Chennault (despite the name a man, and quite a man at that!) who had created the Flying Tigers, a fake supposedly all-Chinese air force, to fight Japan before America had officially entered that war. CAT had plenty of WWII surplus aircraft such as the Douglas C-47/Dakota and the Curtiss C-46 Commando, which had been used to supply war-ravaged China. With the end of the world war, CAT easily turned into a support and supply airline for the Chinese Nationalists (above), led by Chiang Kai-Shek, who was fighting a civil war against the Communists under Mao Tse-tung. The Americans wanted the Nationalists to win, of course but, as later in Vietnam, were backing the wrong horse.

By 1950, the Nationalists were beaten out of the Chinese mainland and were forced to withdraw to the island of Taiwan (Formosa). CAT followed them and set up as a pukkah airline, flying scheduled passenger flights, while simultaneously using other aircraft in its fleet to fly covert missions.

Through the Fifties, CAT pilots were involved in secret missions in Korea, China, and Indo-China, and although much of it will never be fully known, we see their plane wrecks near remote trouble spots even today. C-119 Flying Boxcars flew in supplies at the siege of Dien Bien Phu, Vietnam in May 1954. This epic battle was lost by the

French, and led to the disastrous U.S. involvement in that war for nearly 20 years, costing tens of thousands of lives on all sides.

By 1958, with the outcome of the struggles against communism, and Chinese influence, far from clear in Korea, Vietnam and British Malaya, the White House grew alarmed at the threat of Indonesia falling under the reds – as foretold in the 'Domino Theory' of one state collapsing after another.

Indonesian President Sukarno seemed to be letting this nightmare for the Free World come true, and the prospect of the giant South-West Pacific archipelago falling into the Chinese geo-political sphere was worrying the USA. It must have made all the sacrifice of fighting island by island to Japan only 14 years before seem possibly futile. It was a horrific scenario for the U.S. which therefore secretly decided to topple Sukarno.

Only three years before, the U.S. had championed Sukarno in taking over bits of the old Dutch East Indies empire, and had grumbled about the old colonial power interfering with people's free expression to determine their own destiny. Now U.S. interests seemed in danger, that argument was put to one side. It would interfere in an outwardly friendly nation, using force, and topple the freedom-loving hero it had been championing as recently as 1955.

You would think in such a huge rambling country as Indonesia, wider than the United States, with more diverse cultures, languages and religions, it would be easy to find rebellious tribes, towns or islands to take issue with the Javanese elite in power. But the CIA bungled it, big time, by backing the wrong outfit. Again.

The Douglas A-26 Invader: Ones used by the CIA had markings painted over

In 1958, the fake airline CAT supplied a fleet of 20 aircraft from its hidden reserves, which were types of aircraft no respectable civilian airline should have owned (a PBY Catalina, 15 Douglas A-26 Invaders, and four P-51 Mustangs) to a totally unknown insurgent movement PRRI/Permesta in Northern Indonesia, led by a group of Army Officers who revolted against the Central Government in Jakarta. That this group was powerful and committed enough to challenge the Indonesian state was eagerly accepted by the CIA, although in fact this was naive and foolish wishful thinking on their part – as happened repeatedly in this era (think of the similarly bungled Bay of Pigs invasion of Cuba a few years later). They would use this lot to get Sukarno out, the CIA decided. Optimistic reports about the islands all being ready to revolt against the central power were circulated – mostly totally untrue.

What had happened was that a few discontented men had managed to take over an air force base at Mapanget near Manado on the northern tip of the island of Sulawesi (Celebes).

So the U.S. was relying on a flaky rebel group of unknown numbers or quality, applying an unjustifiable policy and donating half an air force, and calling in buccaneering, loose-cannon adventurers to fly the things. Typical were American pilots, William H. Beale Jr. and Allen L. Pope, who had a long semi-mercenary career with CAT. Other pilots and mechanics arrived, not very discreetly, directly from Clark U.S. Air Force base in the nearby Philippines. Fuel, bombs, spares, everything needed was shipped in.

British casualty of CIA war games: The San Flaviano after being bombed

On April 27, Pope in his A-26 Invader attacked the island of Morotai, hours before the island was taken over by a Permesta force, their one big success. That was a bold assault, and worked because of the deep-seated dislike there of the Javanese rulers. It was supposed to kick off a general Eastern Indonesian revolution. It didn't.

But soon, CIA instructions to Pope took his activities into a new direction. Merchant shipping on the islands of Sulawesi and Borneo came under attack by his A-26. Pope – ever enthusiastic, even gung-ho – attacked and sank three ships in one single day, April 28, 1958, which was good combat flying, but with one slight problem: The boats belonged to peaceful, neutral or allied countries – Italy (*SS Aquila*), Greece (*SS Armonia*) and Panama (*SS Flying Lark*). This last Norwegian-built vessel was sunk with the loss of nine crew. The casualties on the other two ships, both British-built, are unknown.

Pope was now going beserk in attacking the City of Palu, shooting up 20 trucks on Ambon Island, bombing an Indonesian air force base, strafing some Indonesian Navy patrol boats, shooting up bridges and army depots, all in a few days. It was becoming not so much a one-man air force as a one-man war.

But the pretend rebel air force had also attacked with spectacular success a ship belonging to America's most loyal ally, the United Kingdom, and this made news around the world. The *San Flaviano* was an oil tanker, much larger than the other victims of the fake air force, and much newer too. Her loss was a major event.

On 28 April *San Flaviano*, built by Cammell Laird in England in 1956, was in Balikpapan Harbour, in the East Kalimantan Province of Borneo, when a Douglas A-26 Invader bomber aircraft, flown by William H. Beale Jr, and painted black and with no markings, bombed and sank her. *San Flaviano* had nearly finished discharging a cargo of crude oil but was at anchor that day.

The CIA aircraft hit *San Flaviano* with one or more 500lb bombs amidships on her starboard side, causing an explosion and fire which spread rapidly along that side of the ship, destroying her starboard lifeboats. The crew launched both port lifeboats within four minutes, successfully evacuating everyone, including a woman passenger. *San Flaviano* sank near the entrance of Balikpapan harbour.

Beale also shot up and sank various other ships that day, including an Indonesian Navy corvette, killing 18 crew. He hit another British tanker, the *MV Daronia*, owned by Royal Dutch Shell, but the bomb bounced off and fell harmlessly nearby. Had the bomb entered the ship, as it had a full load of petrol, the result could have been devastating.

Beale's career as rogue pilot continued until 1962 when, flying a covert mission for Air America, which CAT had become, he was killed in a jungle take-off in Laos.

The San Flaviano: Miraculously, the whole crew was saved

But is some of this conspiracy theory, urban myth stuff? No, some of the crew of *San Flaviano* are still around. Here's the response in 2006 from former Deck Apprentice Bingham Macnamara, to a plea from a crew member's son for evidence about what happened:

I was on watch and making tea for the 1st Mate, in preparation for the return to the dock, when the bomb hit. Kuwait crude is very volatile and the ship was almost empty of oil, but the tanks were full of gas, consequently supressing the oxygen content and likelihood of an explosion. The tank lids were popping because of the rapid expansion of the gas, not because of explosions.

As far as the *Daronia* was concerned, since she was full of petrol, she had a miraculous escape. She was anchored about one-third of a mile upwind of the *San Flaviano* and was built many years before and equipped with unusually high mid-ship pump room ventilators. By the time she was attacked I was already swimming away from the *San Flaviano* and vividly

remember watching the bomb leave the aircraft, hit the port ventilator, bounce to the starboard ventilator and over the side of the ship without exploding.

In its short-term aim of destabilising Indonesia's economy, the CIA-run raid was a success. Royal Dutch Shell suspended its tanker service to Balikpapan and evacuated crews, shore-based wives and families to Singapore.

In June 1958 both the Indonesian and UK governments claimed that the aircraft had been flown by Permesta rebels. In fact the aircraft, the pilot, the bombs and the bullets were all supplied by the U.S., and the CIA pilots had orders to target commercial shipping to drive foreign merchant ships away from Indonesian waters.

For some months previously, UK Prime Minister Harold Macmillan and Foreign Secretary Selwyn Lloyd had supported U.S. policy to aid Permesta. On 6 May 1958, more than a week after the CIA sank *San Flaviano*, Lloyd secretly told U.S. Secretary of State John Foster Dulles that this was still his position. On 18 May, Indonesian forces shot down a different Permesta A-26 and captured its CIA pilot, Allen L. Pope, alive.

The CIA policy then rapidly unravelled, and the U.S. returned to supporting Sukarno, or rather tolerating him. All the governments maintained the fiction that the rebels had got together an air force and sunk some ships. All three were lying.

The bell from the *San Flaviano* was salvaged from the wreck and taken back to London, where it bears a plate (below) listing its history and saying the boat was 'sunk by bomb by Indonesian rebels'. It's still lying. The bell doesn't ring true.

```
S.S. "SAN FLAVIANO" - EAGLE TANKER COMPANY
GENERAL PURPOSE TANKER - 18,219 DEAD WEIGHT TONS
                    BUILT BY
CAMMELL LAIRD & CO. LTD., BIRKENHEAD (SHIP NO. 1242)
        KEEL LAID 1ST NOVEMBER, 1954
    LAUNCHED BY LADY KINDERSLEY 12TH JUNE 1956
         DELIVERED 27TH SEPTEMBER, 1956
                 SUNK BY BOMB
BY INDONESIAN REBELS IN BALIKPAPAN, PAPAN HARBOUR, BORNEO
                 APRIL 28TH 1958
BELL RECOVERED FROM THE WRECK AND RETURNED TO LONDON
```

7 FLYING IN THE FACE OF REASON

FIRST WORLD WAR ODDBODS: Most people 'know' two things about First World War German aviation – that their planes had more wings, with the famed Fokker triplane often recreated in models, films and replicas – and that their ace, the Red Baron, Manfred Albrecht Freiherr von Richthofen, was the first to paint such an aircraft red, to thumb his nose at the enemy.

But this isn't the whole story. There were aircraft with more wings, including the British Pemberton-Billing P.B.31E (pictured below), a quadruplane with a rather astonishing set of armament. The fact that the aircraft company changed its name to Supermarine – as in Spitfire much later – while the first aircraft was being built should suggest it was not a totally amateur project.

Four wings – and lots of guns – didn't make the Pemberton-Billing a success

It was designed for a very specific job – to combat the German Zeppelins which were mercilessly bombing British towns and cities, initially without the defenders being able to shoot them down. This plane was intended to have extreme endurance – as much as 18 hours – and lie in wait for the silver monsters to lumber into British night skies. Nicknamed the Night Hawk, the aircraft had a searchlight in the nose, a one-and-a-half pounder gun on the top level, and two machine guns as well. If it had ever caught up with a Zeppelin, it could have caused havoc with the hydrogen-filled airships. The trouble was that it couldn't catch up with them, in speed or height. It was never adopted in squadron strength.

Oddly, brilliant designer Anton Fokker (right) also went down this road of adding wings to try to improve performance, and built a quintuplane, the V8, which he test-flew himself. It, too, showed no real advantage over the simpler triplane. The picture, below, on first glance seems to show a triplane – until you notice two more wings halfway along the fuselage.

Fokker, by the way, was a Dutchman, not a German. He was credited with the 'interrupter gear' invention, which allowed a forward-firing gun to fire through the spinning propeller of an aircraft without hitting it, thus giving the Germans a massive advantage for a time.

The consequent 'Fokker Scourge' period of German dominance lasted from August 1915 for about six months, until better British and French planes arrived. On the other hand, given the chance to demonstrate his machine by slaying defenceless airmen, Fokker refused – in contrast to the Gatling Gun salesmen (see Chapter 5).

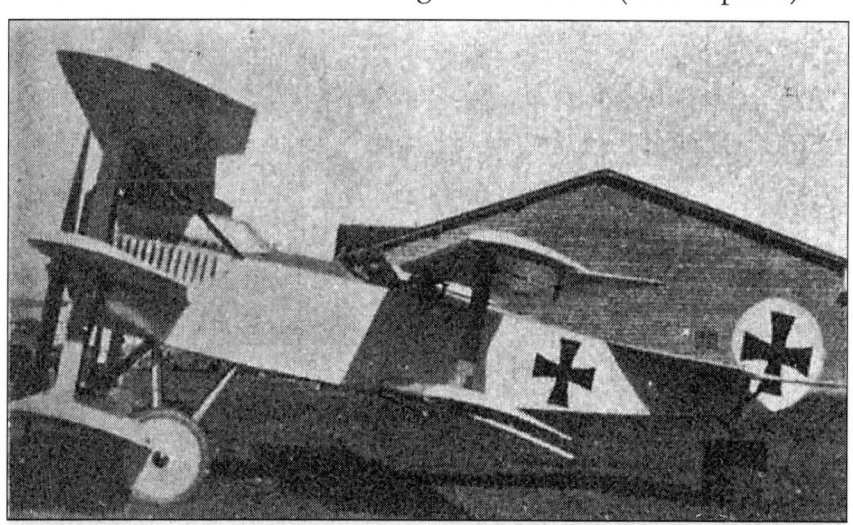

A rare picture of the failed quintuplane. This Fokker wasn't going anywhere

RED BEFORE THE BARON: The first ace in World War I to paint his aircraft red was *not* German, but French. Jean Marie Dominique

Navarre, pictured, who was to become the ace known as **The Sentinel of Verdun**, was born on August 8, 1895 in Jouy-sur-Morin, a commune in the Seine-et-Marne department in north-central France. Navarre was a difficult child who frequently challenged his teachers and often played truant — traits perhaps not rare with ruthless fighter aces, as they are shared with Douglas Bader (see later in this chapter) and, like that Second World War British flier, Navarre was prone to disobeying orders and performing dangerous stunts.

Navarre's short life was, of course, much earlier, right in the infancy of aviation. Fragile 'kites' of wood and canvas limped into the air with not much speed, weaponry, or reliable hope of even getting home again. At the start of the war, you had far more chance of crashing due to your feeble aircraft's limitations than enemy action. This rapidly changed.

Navarre had earned the Civil Pilot's Brevet No. 581 on 22 August 1911. This gained him immediate entry into French military aviation in August 1914, when the war began. In the early days of the conflict, pilots mainly flew reconnaissance missions, and their planes were not armed. Flyers would sometimes wave in a gentlemanly manner at their opponents when meeting in the air. Jean Navarre felt this was war, and they should kill them. At every stage of the war, he tried improvising with different weapons to do this.

Navarre's first victory was on April 1, 1915. Two more wins followed that year, and honours followed — partly for secret missions which we know little of, even now.

Navarre painted his early plane a patriotic red, white, and blue. When he received a new **Nieuport 11** fighter plane, he deliberately painted it red all over to challenge and intimidate the enemy in the skies over **Verdun**, where an exhausting and terrible battle was being waged, well before his German counterpart would copy the idea and gain wider notoriety as the **Red Baron**.

In this new plane Navarre scored one of the first 'doubles' of the war, downing a Fokker E111 and a German two-seater on 26 February 1916, and becoming one of the first flying aces in history.

He was hailed as the first official French ace and praised by the troops on the ground as **The Sentinel of Verdun**. He was feted in the French press – he is pictured below examining a downed and captured German aircraft.

On May 19, 1916 he shot down a German Aviatik over Chattancourt, becoming the first Allied ace with 10 victories. On 17 June, Navarre achieved his twelfth win, but was himself shot down and sustained severe head injuries from which he never fully recovered. Navarre's younger brother was killed in a flying accident at about the same time. Jean Navarre was sent to a sanatorium to convalesce. He would never fly in combat again – although fate, or perhaps recklessness, had something else in store for him.

Navarre became close friends with fellow ace **Charles Nungesser**, as insubordinate and reckless as himself, and equally fond of unorthodox flying stunts… and a raucous Parisian nightlife.

After the end of the war, a victory parade was planned down Paris's Champs Élysées on 14 July 1919. Airmen were ordered to participate on foot rather than flying their aircraft. The headstrong Jean Navarre and Charles Nungesser took this as an insult. At a meeting of aces in a bar, they decided to reply to this affront by choosing one of their number to fly through the **Arc de Triomphe**.

Navarre, as the **first ace**, was considered the ideal choice despite his head injuries. Sadly, while practising for this stunt, Navarre crashed his plane and died at **Villacoublay** airfield on 10 July. He was only 23. Another man performed the stunt.

Menace looming over the heart of London: A Zeppelin at Westminster

DEAD ZEPPELIN AND THE GREATEST HITS: Earlier in the chapter, I mentioned the apparent invulnerability of the German Zeppelins (rigid hydrogen-filled bomb carrying balloons) to British defences, as they could fly too high for the feeble aircraft or anti-aircraft guns to reach them. Oddly enough, I once met in New Zealand an aged relative of mine who recalled as a small boy, running through the blacked-out streets of Norwood, South London, trying to escape the menace of the great silvery balloon in the moonlight seeming to chase him personally!

So how did Britain finally get to grips with this German menace? The answer can be found not so far away, in West Brompton Cemetery in Earl's Court, London.

Here lies a hero, Flight Sub-Lieutenant Reggie Warneford, VC (1891-1915), of the Royal Naval Air Service, pictured left. He, in 1915, was the first airman to bring down one of the much-feared Zeppelins over Ghent, Belgium. It is particularly ironic to find him here in a peaceful corner of West London, as German bombers violently disturbed the dead in Brompton Cemetery in World War II, as the shrapnel marks on monuments near the north gate show. It was even suggested they blew up people previously blown up in World War I. If so, that's Teutonic thoroughness for you. On the other hand, perhaps they wanted to get old Warneford again, just to make sure.

By the way, how long does it take nowadays for a courageous soldier, sailor or airman to be given a medal for bravery in battle? Months? Years?

Consider then this announcement from June 1915:

His Majesty the King has sent the following telegram to Flight Sub-Lieutenant Warneford:

I most heartily congratulate you upon your splendid achievement of yesterday, in which you single-handed destroyed an enemy Zeppelin. I have much pleasure in conferring upon you the Victoria Cross for this gallant act.
GEORGE R.I.

This was from King George V, Rex Imperator (King Emperor) straight to the ordinary airman and the speed of his recognition of Warneford's feat indicates one thing: how desperate the British were to combat the Zeppelin menace.

As stated earlier in this chapter, aircraft with wings were then primitive, made of wood and cloth with puny, unreliable engines, difficult to control and likely to crash at any time. The Zeppelin was a more reliable hydrogen-gas-filled cigar-shaped balloon that enabled the Germans to go high above the reach of British guns and bomb London with impunity. There was little that could be done about these great silver menaces in the sky and even at this early stage there was no German pretence that military targets were being aimed at. Their press published gleeful cartoons of men, women and children being blown to pieces. And postcards were sold of panic-stricken Londoners under the Zeppelins.

A gleeful German postcard, captioned 'Fear in Londoners of the Zeppelins'

So although the number of bombs the Zeppelins were carrying was small, the British were desperate for countermeasures. On May 17, 1915 Flight Sub-Lieutenant Warneford – the RAF had yet to be formed, so he was, in fact, a sailor – was flying a Morane aircraft over Belgium and saw a Zeppelin, L37, returning from bombing Britain. Single-handed, he flew to 6,000 feet and then manually tossed bombs on to the enemy while trying to control the unstable aircraft at the limit of its altitude.

At least one of the bombs exploded, and those who have seen that amazing newsreel film of the German civil airship the *Hindenberg* crashing, will know what happened next – a huge unstoppable conflagration as the hydrogen inside caught fire and escaped from the plunging Zeppelin.

Warneford's plane was caught by the blast, said the *Times* man in a dispatch, and turned upside down so all his remaining petrol fell out of the tank. Warneford calmly landed Biggles fashion on a Belgian road behind German lines, filled up his tank from a spare can, restarted the engine and took off for home.

The Dutch newspapers carried a different account that hints at civilian casualties on the ground, but perhaps would have said explicitly if there were any, and has the action at a lower altitude. On 8 June 1915, *The Tyd* wrote:

Yesterday, at dawn, a Zeppelin appeared near Ghent, pursued by two Allied airmen. The German guns posted on the parade ground and at other points in the town opened a terrible fire on the aeroplanes, which were trying to cut off the Zeppelin's return. The airship was flying over St Amandsberg and attempting to escape the airmen by descending. The Zeppelin had already had a skirmish with its pursuers, as it was listing to the left side. Shots were exchanged with the pursuers, of whom one was daring enough to approach close to the dirigible in an attempt to fly over it. After a sudden bold swoop this airman was seen to drop some explosives on the Zeppelin, which was at once enveloped in flames. The balloon covering was fiercely burning, and, after some minor reports and one big explosion, the dirigible dropped on the convent school of St Amandsberg.

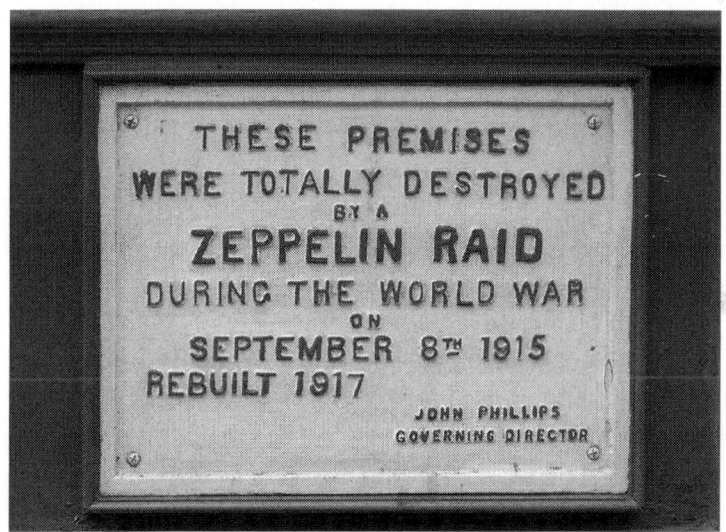

A plaque in Farringdon Road, London, bears witness to the danger

Warneford, an ill-disciplined but brilliant flyer of whom his commander had presciently said during his training 'this youngster will either do big things or kill himself', died in a flying accident recklessly showing off his plane to an American journalist only a month later. He was buried in West Brompton in a ceremony attended by thousands of Londoners.

Not that this stopped the Zeppelin menace overnight. But the aircraft sent up to meet them were improving, and forward-firing machine-guns with incendiary bullets were not good news for the average Zeppelin owner!

In September 1916, the first Zeppelin to be shot down over England fell at Cuffley, Hertfordshire, now just north of the M25, after being attacked by Lt William Leefe Robinson of the Royal Flying Corps. He, too, became an instant hero; he was also awarded the Victoria Cross, a rather good monument was built by newspaper readers at Cuffley and a pub, the Leefe Robinson, was named in his honour, at Harrow Weald, Middlesex (northwest London, above).

One of the few pictures of an Ilya Muromets in flight. This one is fitted with skis and has two men standing on the fuselage, perhaps for balance in tests

RUSSIA'S AMAZINGLY EARLY AIRLINER/BOMBER:

Britain didn't have a four-engined bomber aircraft at the start of World War II, despite films such as *Atonement* annoyingly showing them more than a year before the first one in fact flew. By the end of World War II Britain and the USA has fleets of the things hammering away at Germany, although the Germans never really made a success of their own four-engined bomber designs.

Russia, amazingly, had a perfectly good four-engined bomber, that had also operated as a then sophisticated airliner, right at the start of the war. Not this war, but the *First* World War. Yes, you read that right. In 1914!

This is so astonishing because when this plane first flew, it was only ten years after the Wright brother's faltering first heavier-than-air flight – a feeble hop of a flight shorter than the wingspan of today's jumbo jets.

In Britain there was some military aviation, but the single-engined flimsy 'kites' made of wood, canvas and wire were so unreliable and fragile, they themselves were the crews' biggest enemy. About a quarter of flights ended in a crash, breakdown or a forced landing. Many men died just trying to get the things to fly. All of them had open cockpits.

Yet in 1913 the Russians built the Ilya Muromets aircraft, a four-engined biplane designed by the genius Igor Sikorsky. (The name of the aircraft is that of a revered Russian folk hero/saint, a sort of knight errant who saved several towns from invaders).

It was a revolutionary design, intended for airline service (not a concept Western countries had even got around to) with its spacious enclosed cabin/fuselage incorporating a heated passenger saloon fitted out with comfortable wicker chairs and cushions, plus a toilet and washing facilities – even a private bedroom. The intended customer was the Imperial Russian Air Service, because the Tsar was, of course, still ruling. This was way-ahead thinking for the world's biggest country, where sheer distances were a massive obstacle.

When the Ilya Muromets first flew, it rapidly won the world record for number of passengers carried in one aircraft – 16 – and distance. One flew from St Petersburg to Kiev, a distance of 1,200 km, and back. It was astonishing. The Western powers (or the Central Powers, as the Germans' allies were known) really had nothing like this.

A modern replica of a Sikorsky S-22 Ilya Muromets at Central Air Force Museum Monino, near Moscow. Picture by Alf van Beem

With the outbreak of the First World War in 1914, it was rapidly adapted for a sizable strategic bombing role, the first such aircraft. The Germans were amazed and terrified when they saw it lumbering towards them, and could produce nothing to match it for years.

The military version of the Russian plane was again staggeringly advanced. It incorporated substantial machine-gun defence, including the world's first tail gunner. The four engines were armoured, and this made it hard to shoot down. It tended to bat aside the German Albatross fighters sent up to attack it, and some of these were downed by the powerful propeller wash from the four engines – something they were not prepared for.

Only one Ilya Muromets bomber was brought down by German fighters during the war, in September 1916, and that had clobbered three of the Albatrosses in that fight before succumbing. The Germans gathered up the wreckage and tried to copy the design, but failed utterly.

Of course, the number of aircraft, range and bomb loads was nothing like the Lancasters and Flying Fortresses of World War II. The aircraft managed 400 raids and dropped a total of 65 tons of bombs, and did not change the disastrous course of the war for the Tsarist army.

Even so, it was an astonishing early aviation achievement. As with the first Sputnik after World War II, and the first man in space (Yuri Gagarin in 1961), the Russians showed what they can achieve if they set their minds to it.

The utterly extraordinary Ilya Muromets, with its four wooden propellers, enclosed cabin and tail gunner position (left)

Much feared but in fact vulnerable: A crashed Stuka in North Africa

THE UNDOING OF THE STUKA DIVE-BOMBERS: This infamous German aircraft was hugely feared at the beginning of World War II, and in the Spanish Civil War just before that, because of their screaming sirens and sharp dive angle, giving them a chance to bomb accurately and strafe targets – often including defenceless civilians, such as refugee columns. They were intended to cause terror, which they did – but on one occasion to their own crews.

On August 15, 1939 during a mass-formation dive-bombing demonstration set up at Neuhammer training grounds near Sagan to impress high-ranking commanders of the Luftwaffe, disaster struck. The Stukas dived through a cloud bank and expected to release their bombs and then pull out of the dive.

They were unaware that on that particular day the cloud ceiling was too low and an unexpected ground mist had formed, leaving them with no time left to pull out of the dive.

Thirteen Ju 87s, and 26 crew members were lost when they ploughed into the ground almost simultaneously. An unlucky 13 for the Luftwaffe, and red faces for the commanders.

The aircraft was used initially in the Battle of Britain – and was very effective against, for example, defenceless merchant ships in the Thames Estuary or aircraft on the ground – but proved spectacularly vulnerable to RAF fighters, and was withdrawn after massive losses.

No need to use that bayonet, cobber: An Australian soldier watches as a downed Stuka dive-bomber burns in the Western Desert

'SUPERIOR' GERMAN ENGINEERING: There is a narrative popular after World War II that the German weapons were way better than the Allied ones. Well there's something in that but it certainly wasn't always true. Adolf Galland, commander of German fighter aircraft at Calais during the Battle of Britain, was asked by a furious Hermann Goering what he needed to win the bloody battle, so Hitler could invade Britain in *Operation Sealion*. He replied bluntly: 'A squadron of Spitfires', the nimble little British plane that was outfighting his Me109s over the Channel. Russian aircraft turned out to be a match for the Germans on the Eastern Front too.

Equally, with the heavy bombers, the Germans never produced designs as reliable, powerful or deadly as the British Lancaster or the American Flying Fortress. They could never have mounted the long-range 1,000-bomber raids which Germany suffered towards the end of the war. The Germans had sowed the wind by bombing cities all around them, now they reaped the whirlwind as their cities were, one after the other, reduced to rubble.

Their aircraft just weren't good enough. One such flawed – in fact doomed – German design was the Heinkel He 177 Greif. Its design was intrinsically poor, its engines often caught fire and it took five expensive years to be developed.

German pilots hated the He 177 and nicknamed it the Flying Coffin or *Luftwaffenfeuerzeug* (Luftwaffe's Lighter). Its basic fault was that no one was quite clear whether it was a long-range bomber or a dive bomber, and so it did both rather badly.

Flying coffin: The Luftwaffe's supposed war-winning He 177 was a total flop

It should have had four engines, but Luftwaffe top brass insisted on two, in nacelles. This was meant to streamline the design but it proved under-powered and over-heated, which was never cured. More design changes followed, making it heavier, so a hidden extra pair of engines was installed, increasing weight and over-heating.

What could have been a great plane with high speed and high altitude – better than the Allied aircraft at the start of the war – just floundered. 'Greif' meant Griffin, but in fact it was a turkey.

The He 177 first flew just after the start of the war. It caught fire, and the second broke up in mid-air.

Every time it went back to the drawing board, the changes meant more weight and more drag – going from remote-controlled guns to manned ones, for instance. Heavier fuel tanks. Stronger frames.

It never really came right in time to make a difference in the war, thankfully. At the Battle of Stalingrad, He 177s were tried for casualty evacuation but weren't really suitable as too many aircraft went down.

So 13 aircraft were sent to bomb Russian positions there – and seven crashed in flames – not one of them brought down by enemy fire. Usually the entire crew was lost with each crash. The He 177 was supposed to deliver death. It did – to its own crews. The Flying Coffin had become the Flaming Coffin.

Not what a pilot wants to see: As one He 177 taxis, another burns

GOERING'S FURY: The widely-held notion that German engineering and expertise in World War II was always so superior, like a late 20th-century BMW car compared to a British Morris, is total nonsense – as expressed in the previous item. And it isn't just this author being an attention-seeking contrarian!

Listen to the words of one man who should have really known: Hermann Goering (left), in charge of the Luftwaffe – at a time when it really mattered – on March 18, 1943, the height of the air war – in his address to those who were really responsible – the chiefs of German's most famous aircraft makers, engine builders and research teams. The occasion was a conference – although a cruder term could be used for the event, which amounted to a rage-filled roasting – at Carinhall, near Berlin, that March day in 1943.

Ernst Heinkel was there, as was Willy Messerschmitt, the heads of Junkers, Siemens, Daimler-Benz, the heads of the Luftwaffe, of night fighter operations, of radar research, and what Riechsmarschall Goering had to say is absolutely fascinating for anyone interested in the course of the titanic struggle that was World War II, the one event that shaped all our lives and nations.

These are extracts from the translated transcript of Goering's address, with my headings and my explanations in square brackets:

Goering's general rant:

'Gentlemen, I have called you all together again today to speak about the entire situation on the technical side of the Luftwaffe and to inform you of my views on the subject, and, most important, those of the Fuehrer as well. It would have been very agreeable if I could have commenced my remarks today by acknowledging and thanking you for your efforts. However, I find myself unable to do this and – if I am to continue speaking frankly – quite the reverse. I can only express to you my absolute bitterness about the complete failure which has resulted in practically all fields of aeronautical engineering ... we lag so far behind enemy industry, or rather technology, that it is absolutely childish to attempt to draw a comparison.'

Goering on fighter aircraft:

'The Me 109 [below] has now reached the peak of its performance; no further improvement is possible. The aircraft cannot take a more powerful engine, whereas the British began to improve the Spitfire series [next page] very early with the result that this aircraft is now absolutely and unquestionably superior to the Me 109'.

What a German ace asked for to win the Battle of Britain: A Spitfire squadron

Goering on the 'Amerikabomber' concept:

'In Augsburg I was shown an "America" aircraft which had only to be put into large scale production [the Me 264]. It was claimed that the aircraft would fly from here to the east coast of America and back, or from the Azores to the west coast of America and back and would also carry a large load of bombs ... I was trusting enough to at least go half-way towards believing that something of this kind was possible. Today I know that it is, of course, impossible.'

How Hitler envisaged hitting the USA: The Me 264, never built

Thankfully only artist Kyle Scott's depiction: The Luftwaffe hitting the USA

Goering on the He177 heavy bomber:

'I was promised a heavy bomber [see previous section in this chapter], the He 177, which should have been with the squadrons a year ago. Following a series of calamities, I was told that if there was no need for this aircraft to dive [bomb], it would be the best kite in the world and it could be issued to squadrons immediately. I said at once that there was no need at all for it to dive, as there was no intention of it being used in this way.

However, every time we attempted operation with this type there were catastrophic losses, not brought about by the enemy.

More than a year has since passed and even if the contraption is produced in a reasonably serviceable version in a year's time, it will be obsolete.'

Goering on Allied bombers:

'Fun has been made of the enemy's backwardness and his slow four-engined crates [such as the Lancaster, or Flying Fortress]. Gentlemen, I would be extremely happy if you could reproduce just one of these four-engined "crates" in the immediate future. I would then have at least one aircraft with which something could be achieved. You know that in addition to night attacks [by the RAF] the enemy does not hesitate to carry out daylight operations [USAAF] with these four-engined crates, which have excellent armament and terrific stability, and in spite of our so-called ultra-modern fighters, he gets through everywhere...'

'Do not deceive yourselves, gentlemen. The British will carry out attacks with an ever increasing number of these slow four-engined "crates" or whatever I have heard them called, which some of you hold in such contempt. He will deal with each and every city. It makes no difference to him – he can navigate to Munich or Berlin with the same precision and he can reach Warsaw or Vienna.'

A B-17 Flying Fortress flying high above Germany, taken by Shane Stueckle's great uncle from a dorsal gunner's position of the plane flying below

Goering on technical devices:

'The British and Americans are leaps and bounds ahead of us. If we are lagging, I hoped we would at least manage to keep the gap from widening. I recall just one example ... less than a year before the war they dared to demonstrate to the Fuehrer and myself a recognition device which was to be installed immediately in all aircraft.

When German aircraft were approaching, our flak etc would be able to identify them as such with the aid of this device [which avoids the danger of shooting down your own aircraft and the accompanying waste of ammunition, or letting enemy aircraft through unhindered].

I asked for this device to be put into service quickly and was told it would be fitted to all aircraft immediately. Now, four years later, we still have not one aircraft fitted with a recognition device. The enemy has been using one since the start of the war... It is a disgrace that we should be without a recognition device for our aircraft in the fourth year of the war. This is the greatest scandal...

The enemy navigates with deadly accuracy, far and deep into our land. He drops bombs from above the clouds, in the clouds or below the clouds. He is always producing new radar devices.

All I can say is this: enemy aircraft fly about Germany as they please and only a fraction of them are located, even where there are detection installations [above]. Something or other goes wrong with these installations every five minutes...

They come over in the dirtiest weather and approach the target out of the clouds, fighters and all. However not even our reconnaissance aircraft can get through, as the moment they take off from French bases, they are picked up.'

Goering on the British Mosquito:

'It seems monstrous when I recall that the British – though they are not blessed with aluminium supplies – built a wooden aircraft at the right moment which is almost incredibly superior and unrivalled in speed [The De Havilland Mosquito, dubbed 'the Wooden Wonder']... Today these aircraft stooge back and forth over Germany, sometimes on reconnaissance, but at other times not hesitating to carry out very heavy attacks, without incurring the slightest loss.'

The last thing a German pilot wanted to see, and the last thing many did see – the business end of a Mosquito fighter-bomber

The Wooden Wonder: The De Havilland Mosquito had a speed and range Goering could only dream about

Goering on bombing range:

'In 1940 my aircraft could fly on average at least as far as Glasgow, but this is no longer possible today. When plans for the Ju88 were submitted they drew me the most wonderful pictures showing how this machine would fly back and forth west of Ireland to attack enemy shipping [such as Atlantic convoys bringing vitally needed supplies to Britain from America]. However, this machine has not reached Ireland to this day. You must understand my unbounded anger. What was delivered was absolute rubbish!

Even if the 177 is produced, what am I to do with it? It can hardly get its nose past the hangar doors and [even if it works] cannot even reach Glasgow.'

DID TWO PLANES DOWN EACH OTHER IN A WHITE WILDERNESS? Two aircrews – one British and one German – who fought each other and both crashed in the remote mountains of Norway in April 1940 were commemorated in the 2012 film *Into The White*. The drama came in the fact that the two enemy crews had to decide whether to kill each other or co-operate to survive in the bleak wilderness.

According to the movie, the German Heinkel He 111 bomber and a British Blackburn Skua shot each other down, but the truth is that while the Luftwaffe aircraft was indeed hit, a rather more prosaic problem probably brought the British one down – engine failure.

The episode happened during Hitler's invasion of Norway, *Operation Weserübung*, which came in the 'Phoney War' at the beginning of World War II, before the blitzkrieg Nazi invasion of France. The Germans wanted to seize the country for its ample supplies of iron ore, and the British fought unsuccessfully – in the air, on the sea and on land – to defend Norway from the invasion.

Shot down on a frozen lake: Another Heinkel in the Norway campaign burns

The Heinkel flown by Lieutenant Horst Schopis was shot down by pilot R.T. Partridge and his radio operator R.S. Bostock in their Skua. The Germans' tail gunner Hans Hauck was killed in the attack or the crash, but Schopis, plus Unteroffizier Josef Auchtor and Feldwebel Karl-Heinz Strunk, the remainder of the four-man crew, now faced the snowy wilderness.

Meanwhile Partridge and Bostock had crash-landed on a frozen lake a mile or two away. They were surrounded by forests, mountains and lakes, and there were no roads anywhere near.

Spitting fire: A Blackburn Skua. The boxy cockpit also held a rear-gunner

The Fleet Air Arm men made for an old reindeer hunter's hut they had spotted as they descended. They were ambushed there by the Germans, armed with pistols and knives.

They managed to fool the Germans that they were survivors of a crashed Wellington Bomber (and not the fighter pilots who had just shot their plane down). They offered to let the Germans use the hut while they looked for shelter elsewhere – ending up at the closed, out-of-season Grotli Hotel. The next day the Germans arrived there, and they all shared a meal. The British decided to go for help for both crews, as there was no further food or fuel at the hotel.

At this point a Norwegian ski patrol turned up, and as Feldwebel Strunk reached for his pistol, shot him dead. The other two Germans were taken into custody and ended up spending the rest of the war in a PoW camp in Canada.

Meanwhile the two British crew made it back to England after various adventures in Norway, including commandeering a car during an air raid. A few months later, on June 13, 1940, Partridge was shot down and captured by the Germans at Trondheim in Norway while attacking the battleship *Scharnhorst*. He also spent the rest of the war as a PoW. Bostock was killed in the same raid.

Many years later, in 1977, Partridge contacted Schopis, living in Munich, and they became firm friends. The burnt-out wreck of Partridge's Skua is on display at the Fleet Air Museum in Yeovilton, Somerset. It was burnt out because the crew set fire to it to prevent its use by the enemy; it sank through the ice to the bottom of the lake. Unlikely though it seems, the remains were recovered by a sub-aqua club and returned to England.

So many Skuas were shot down over Norway – eight in that failed attack on the *Scharnhorst* – that Norwegian aviation enthusiasts have gathered enough parts of Skua planes to reassemble one at a museum at Bodo, above the Arctic Circle, and one of the visitors who have examined the aircraft was recorded as Simon Partridge, son of the wartime pilot, who was shown a part of his father's aircraft with a bullet hole in it.

The Skua – which featured a rear gunner as well as forward guns – wasn't a pretty aircraft, and could have been better with a more powerful engine, but perhaps didn't deserve its 'rather useless' reputation (a bit like the Defiant later in this chapter) it garnered when compared to later warplanes which it couldn't possibly match.

Given that it came out well before the war, it did its hybrid jobs of fighter plus dive bomber fairly well.

The Skua achieved one of the first 'kills' on enemy aircraft of World War II when three of them shot down a Dornier flying boat on September 26, 1939 over the North Sea. The design also achieved the first major warship sunk by aerial attack in the war, in fact the first in history, when the German cruiser *Konigsberg* was sunk at Bergen on April 10, 1940.

Meanwhile Schopis's Heinkel is still high on the lonely mountain in that remote part of Norway (not to be confused with the replica wreck made for the film, which has been left by a road in the valley).

The movie made from the saga of the Skua and the Heinkel. Harry Potter star Rupert Grint (right) was one of the actors

THE PLANES THAT FOUGHT FOR THE WRONG SIDE:

If you know the slightest thing about military aviation, and World War II, these next four photographs will seem deeply odd. Disturbing, even. For an explanation, see the following page.

Have you spotted what was wrong in these last four pictures? The unusual photos (above and previous page) show archetypal World War II aircraft in the wrong insignia – that of their enemies. Both sides flew examples of the other side's aircraft which had been captured in various ways. They might have crash landed with repairable damage, been over-run on the ground, or even flown to the wrong base by navigational accident or intentionally to defect.

These were repaired, tested and if in good enough condition, flown. Both sides had a special unit for flying 'traitor' aircraft.

The first picture (previous two pages) shows a B-17 Flying Fortress in Luftwaffe markings. The plane, nicknamed 'Flak Dancer' was shot down on the June 26, 1943 mission to Villacoublay, France, piloted by F/O Delton Wheat. The bomber made a forced landing in Laon, and was later made operational with new propellers by the Luftwaffe, flying with their special enemy planes unit, KG 200. Six of the crew when it crashed evaded capture, two were missing in action and two were made PoWs.

The second picture shows captured German aircraft undergoing maintenance at No. 1426 (Enemy Aircraft Circus) Flight at Collyweston, Northamptonshire.

A Focke Wulf Fw 190A-3, the single-engined aircraft regarded as the best German fighter in World War II, is pictured undergoing an engine service. In the foreground, an airman re-paints the wings of Junkers JU 88S-1, a twin-engined German bomber. The third and fourth pictures show two of the best Allied fighters, a Spitfire and a Lightning, in Luftwaffe livery.

The picture on this page shows a Messerschmitt 110, again in the wrong colours. The way the unit, nicknamed the Rafwaffe, acquired planes varied. Some were crashed and indeed many examples were taken in pieces and tested at Farnborough RAE without being flown again. But the JU-88 in the earlier picture was acquired after the pilot landed at night at RAF Chivenor in North Devon in the belief it was an airfield in France — the crew had made a navigational error after being deceived by a

Meacon. A 'Meacon' is a portmanteau word combining masking and beacon – the German navigational signals were intercepted, masked and then rebroadcast wrongly. Some ran out of fuel and ditched at sea, they were so misled. Fewer to fight, then.

Enemy airmen becoming lost, or in at least one case deliberately defecting were useful – particularly if they brought an aircraft equipped with the latest radio and radar technology. One flown by a defecting crew to RAF Dyce, Scotland on May 9, 1943, was particularly useful as it had the latest night-fighting radar.

So British and American crews who destroyed their aircraft on forced landing (such as the Skua crew earlier in the chapter) were in fact doing the right thing.

THE LEGLESS HERO AND THE WRONG TACTICS: British World War II air ace Douglas Bader is famed for his astounding career in the air force. Less well known is how he got one aspect of the Battle of Britain badly wrong, and the surprising result of that. Nor is the secret advantage of his disability often mentioned.

Having just checked with some under-30s, it was surprising that they had never heard of Bader. But they at least knew of the Battle of Britain, which took place not with ranks of warships on a grey ocean, or vast armies across the plains of Europe, but above the neat rows of Bromley semis with their privet hedges, above the Sidcup bowls green and the Ruislip golf club. It must have seemed very unreal, so let's explore the oddities of Bader's amazing life as a way of taking a fresh look at this crucial few weeks of aerial combat.

That Bader (pictured) achieved 22 aerial victories, four shared victories, six probables, one shared probable and 11 enemy aircraft badly damaged within a couple of years of war was remarkable. What seized the public imagination ever since is that he did it with no legs.

A rebellious, chippy, cocky boy – he'd been sent to various Spartan boarding schools after his First World War hero father died of his wounds, his mother showed little interest and his step-father failed to like him – Bader got into endless trouble but excelled at combative sport. His headmaster tolerated the headstrong, conceited boy. A fellow pupil was Guy Gibson, who went on to lead the 'Dambusters' raid on the German Ruhr in 1943.

Bader eventually joined the RAF in 1928, and soon became known for dangerous, illegal stunts in the air. He had been warned about aerobatics but on 14 December 1931, while visiting Reading Aero Club at Woodley Airfield in Berkshire, he attempted some low-flying aerobatics in a Bulldog Mk. IIA, of 23 Squadron. He had been banned from making any such manoeuvres under 2,000ft and had to keep above 500ft at all times.

His aircraft touched the ground and the plane cartwheeled over. He was rushed to the Royal Berkshire Hospital where his shattered legs were amputated – one below and one above the knee.

He came round and wrote this laconic entry in his log-book:

Crashed slow-rolling near ground. Bad show.

So far, so bad. Here the aviation career of the rebellious but now crippled 21-year-old should have stopped. But his adventures had hardly begun, as it turned out.

Months of convalescence followed, throughout which Bader endured pain so intense he had to take morphine daily. In early 1932, Bader was transferred to a hospital at RAF Uxbridge and fought hard to walk again after he was given a pair of artificial legs. Every step was agony, but soon he was walking, then driving a specially modified car, playing golf, and even dancing. On his way to play golf during the convalescence, he pulled in to visit the Pantiles tea room on the A30 London Road in Bagshot, Surrey. There he caught the eye of waitress Thelma Edwards – and later tried out his dancing on her, and married her the following year.

In June 1932, he took to the air again and proved to the RAF that he could still fly. But by April 1933 pen-pushers at the Air Ministry had decided his situation was 'not covered by King's Regulations' – hardly a surprise that there wasn't a regulation for legless pilots, surely – and that seemed to end his flying hopes a second time. Any sensible chap would surely have hung up his goggles for good. But Bader, who meanwhile joined an oil company, wasn't any sensible chap.

As war approached in 1939, Bader pestered the Ministry for another chance; was turned down; then wheedled his way in using a senior officer friend to vouch for him. He took a test and was soon passed for flying again. He celebrated by turning an Avro Tutor upside down, safely this time. By now the war had started.

In 1940, Bader joined No 19 Squadron at RAF Duxford, and was soon shooting down the odd German aircraft. RAF doctrine at the time was to fly line astern and then attack one by one. Bader – of course – disagreed and thought you needed to attack from altitude, out of the sun, and not fire until the last seconds. In fact, he nearly collided with a Dornier while doing this. But those tactics worked – unlike another tactic which he came to support during the Battle of Britain in the summer of 1940, when Hitler wanted to crush the Royal Air Force so he could launch *Operation Sealion* and invade Britain.

Douglas Bader, tin legs and Hurricane, Duxford 1940. Picture: F/O S.A Devon

The latter tactic was the controversial 'Big Wing' approach. Bader's chief in 12 Group of squadrons (north of the Thames) was Air Vice-Marshal Trafford Leigh-Mallory, who favoured collecting together several squadrons, maybe five or six, and sending the resulting 'Big Wing' against the big German formations coming across from Europe.

Bader was scathing in his criticism of Air Vice-Marshall Keith Park, commanding 11 Group south and east of London, who preferred to husband his resources and commit only small groups little and often. In this debate, Bader was undoubtedly wrong.

Park's airfields in 11 Group, in places such as Biggin Hill or Manston, were far too close to the enemy to get involved in making formations assemble first. Every time 12 Group tried to assemble a 'Big Wing' of perhaps 60 aircraft at Duxford and then attack, they were too late and the Luftwaffe raid had gone.

The controversy raged in a power struggle between the two different approaches – squadron attack or 'Big Wing', sometimes called a Balbo. After the war, air ace Johnnie Johnson summed it up even-handedly:

'Douglas [Bader] was all for the Big Wings to counter the German formations. I think there was room for both tactics – the Big Wings and the small squadrons. It might well have been fatal had Park always tried to get his squadrons into "Balbos", for not only would they have taken longer to get to their height, but 60 or 70 packed climbing fighters could have been seen for miles and would have been sitting ducks for higher 109s.

'Also nothing would have pleased Goering more than for his 109s to pounce on large numbers of RAF fighters. Indeed, [German fighter commanders] Adolf Galland and Werner Moelders complained about the elusiveness of Fighter Command and Park's brilliance was that by refusing to concentrate his force he preserved it throughout the battle.'

And the RAF had the priceless advantage of radar at the start of the Battle of Britain. This meant you could send just enough planes to counter each threat, rather than risk planes – and waste precious fuel and pilots – by patrolling around in big formations like cavalry. Park (a pragmatic New Zealander) would have different units hit and run the enemy formations, with great success.

Park, during the weeks of battle, called on his neighbouring Groups – No 10 to the west and No 12 to the north – to defend No 11's airfields so he could fight the attack, but only No 10's planes got there on time to do a good job. No 12, where big-headed Bader insisted on flying to Duxford, taking off again and personally leading the great group into the air – was always too late. Except on one critical occasion.

In mid-September 1940, the Luftwaffe seriously believed they had bombed and fought the RAF into submission. The airfields in south-east England had been bombed and strafed, and because of Park's careful tactics they rarely saw large numbers of RAF planes. The Luftwaffe were told they were master of the skies now, and to switch to daylight bombing of London. If they had carried on hammering RAF airfields and seeking out air combat for just a few more weeks, they might have won. *Big mistake No 1.*

For one thing, this allowed the RAF to regroup, repair and consolidate its strength. On September 15, the Luftwaffe put up a huge formation of bombers and fighters and headed for London. The pilots were told the RAF was down to its last 50 planes: soon they would be finished like the Poles and the French, leaving the Nazis to bomb mercilessly at will and force Britain to surrender.

A preliminary fighter sweep across the south-east had showed there were few RAF planes around. What the German commanders hadn't realised was that Park knew this was a ruse to get his fighters into the air and get picked off – he wisely husbanded his resources for an expected bomber onslaught.

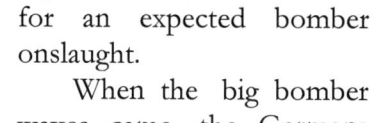

When the big bomber waves came, the Germans were harassed continuously by small attacks and suffered losses (pictured, a Dornier going down) all the way across Kent, with Park deploying for once every single aircraft he had. It was do or die. Churchill, overlooking the plotting table in No 11 Group operations room and seeing the WAAF girls pushing markers around the map, asked Park what reserves he had. Park replied: 'None!' This wasn't quite as desperate as it sounded, as it referred to his own group. There *were* squadrons available in the neighbouring groups that could be called forward.

The German fighters fought badly, because most of them had been ordered to stick to the bomber stream to protect them and only to leave for short fights then return. This put the RAF at an advantage if plunging from altitude. *Big mistake No 2*. And even the winds helped the RAF and hindered the attackers.

And when the Germans got to London, where the fighters were at the limit of their range and had to turn back (having used fuel seeing off 11 Group's fighters), for once Bader's 'Big Wing' turned up bang on time. The Germans were aghast to see 60 more RAF aircraft, all freshly armed and fuelled, storming in to meet them – they'd been told there were hardly any Spitfires and Hurricanes left! The spirit of the RAF pilots astonished the Germans – one Hurricane pilot, angered at having run out of ammunition, rammed his aircraft into a Dornier, baling out at the last second. It worked, and that was one more bomber that didn't get to its target, and one more crew who never flew again.

Bombers were falling all over the place. One went plunging down into the Thames Estuary, a hapless crew member trailing behind because his parachute had caught on the tail wheel.

That day, which changed the course of history, saw the Germans lose 60 aircraft – twice as many as the RAF – with 20 more badly damaged. About 70 of their air crew were killed and as many captured after crashing or parachuting out of doomed aircraft – the RAF having the advantage that it was fighting close to home and any pilots baling out could fight another day, whereas the Germans were rounded up and made PoWs. Equally British aircraft that went down without much damage could be restored to service.

The result was that Hitler realised that *Operation Sealion* wouldn't happen, he wouldn't get a German army across the Channel before the winter storms made the use of invasion barges impossible. And RAF Bomber Command had been destroying the barges in French and German ports in nightly raids as fast the Germans could assemble them.

Hitler turned his back on Britain and his attentions to the invasion of Russia – and it wouldn't have happened without the Few of the RAF, including the surprisingly Many of Bader's Big Wing. *Big Mistake No 3*. Gigantic, as it turned out.

Around the free world, or at any rate the Commonwealth, September 15 is remembered as Battle of Britain Day. If people know one quotation from this astounding era, it's probably Churchill's 'Never in the field of human conflict was so much owed by so many to so few.'

Churchill's ability to weaponise (as we might say nowadays) the English language was probably the most effective in a leader since Elizabeth I's stirring Tilbury Speech, (also facing a Continental invader). Why? Because it conveys powerful, complex matters in what we would today call a sound-bite — a punchy simple headline that said it all, suitable for reproducing on posters (which the Government rapidly did, pictured).

After Dunkirk, Britain had lost some of her Army and most of her weapons, yet Churchill's oratory in the run-up to the Battle of Britain was invaluable in stiffening the backbone of the British, whom the collaborating Vichy French gleefully expected to be beaten at any minute.

Just recall the key phrases 'I have nothing to offer but blood, toil, tears and sweat' or 'We shall fight on the beaches' or 'This was their finest hour'. Interestingly — because it tells you something about the frailty of human memory — you could in later decades meet hundreds of people who were sure they could remember hearing him making these speeches, with his measured pauses and odd speech impediment, almost a lisp. They didn't. Speeches in the House of Commons were not recorded or broadcast at the time. They were remembering the frequent re-broadcast of recordings Churchill made afterwards for record discs.

But the context of the 'Few' speech is worth noting. No one had fought such a vital battle (since Thermopylae) that depended on a few hundred men. Churchill had grown up with battles on land and sea involving tens of thousands of men. This was something new.

Churchill apparently came out of the Operations Room of 11 Group on an earlier day of the battle and said to Major General Hastings 'Pug' Ismay: 'Don't speak to me, I have never been so moved.'

How the Few concept arrived was related by Ismay to publisher Rupert Hart-Davis in 1954. The publisher recalled it like this:

Travelling together in a car, in which Winston rehearsed the speech he was to give in the House of Commons on 20 August 1940 [during] the Battle of Britain. When he came to the famous sentence, 'Never in the history of mankind have so many owed so much to so few', Ismay said 'What about Jesus and his disciples?' 'Good old Pug,' said Winston, who immediately changed the wording to 'Never in the field of human conflict...'

In the public mind, the Few were running out at the moment of victory, reinforced in the histories by Park's comment that there were no reserves. In fact there were reserve planes, and reserve pilots, and aircraft and air crew were being produced faster than the Germans could. If the RAF were the Few, the Luftwaffe were suffering such losses they were the Fewer. But no one cares about them – that was the whole idea. Killing or capturing them.

After the Battle of Britain, Trafford Leigh-Mallory and Bader got the ascendancy in the RAF, and Park was shoved to one side (although he was right and they were wrong about the 'Big Wing'). Bader went on fighting brilliantly in the air, declining desk jobs, and was shot down on August 9, 1941, while attacking German Me 109s over France. Who shot whom down or whether it was a collision was unclear, but as Bader opened his canopy to bail out it became clear that one of his tin legs was trapped under the dashboard. As the wrecked plane screamed down, Bader released his parachute and the terrific jerk pulled him clear, leaving the leg behind.

Famously, the Germans treated Bader rather honourably, the gallant ace Galland (pictured) arranged for the RAF to parachute a spare tin leg to make life tolerable for the prisoner. Galland proposed it, and even Goering rapidly agreed. The RAF slightly spoilt the gentlemanly nature of this unusual arrangement by carrying on to attack targets, including Galland's base, before going home.

Adolf Galland is an interesting character because he stood up to Goering, criticising his tactics such as the close bomber escort. As quoted earlier, when Goering visited a forward base during the Battle of Britain, he asked Galland what on earth he wanted to ensure victory. He bravely retorted bluntly: 'A squadron of Spitfires.'

Goering was speechless with rage but could not dismiss the top-scoring ace. Perhaps Galland and Bader were cut from the same cloth. But it would be a mistake to lionise Galland. He was a great ace – yes, greater than Bader – but he was killing brave young Britons, New Zealanders, Aussies, French and Poles who were fighting for freedom while Galland was supporting the most evil, murderous regime of European history.

Bader, like the troublesome boarding schoolboy he had once been, made an infernal nuisance of himself straight away after being captured. He got out of hospital using knotted sheets (without legs, mind!) before he had even recovered and somehow made it as far as a safe house before being betrayed.

He escaped, or tried to, again and again and was eventually shifted to the 'escape-proof' Colditz Castle – whence he escaped. The Germans even produced a wanted poster of him, saying that although he had no legs, he walked well with a stick. Twenty years later a civilian Belgian prisoner, who worked at a Gestapo office at the time, sent Bader a copy of it. He found it hilarious – he said: 'I walked perfectly well without a stick – never use one!' It was also funny that the Germans were advertising the fact that couldn't keep a man with no legs in their best high-security prison.

Bader saw what he called 'goon baiting' as his duty – by which he meant making himself an infernal nuisance with the guards.

After Colditz was liberated by the Americans, Bader was given the honour of leading a victory flypast of 300 aircraft over London in June 1945. He returned to the Shell oil company, and also became a tireless campaigner for the disabled. He'd met Galland again at the end of the war, when he, Gunther Rall and Hans-Ulrich Rudel arrived at RAF Tangmere, near Chichester, as prisoners-of-war. Bader, according to Rall, personally arranged for Rudel, a fellow amputee, to be fitted with an artificial leg. A debt repaid.

Bader became more famous after the war because of the biography, and much more so because of the film, *Reach For The Sky*, (above), starring the amiable Kenneth More as Bader. Bader was the first to admit that the avuncular More depicted a much nicer personality than Bader really had – he could be foul-mouthed, conceited, nasty, given to making excessive claims (such as about the success of the 'Big Wing') impetuous to the point of reckless – but in war this paid off.

On the personal side, he stayed married to that waitress from Bagshot till she died in 1971, then rapidly married another woman. So surely he had finally given up flying on leaving the RAF? Not quite.

He flew executive aircraft in his Shell job – which he loved – and managed to stay friends with Galland plus Doolittle, leader of the daring raid on Tokyo after Pearl Harbor. Shell gave him the aircraft when he retired and he flew on until 1979, retiring from the skies at the same time as his friend and former foe, Galland.

In 1982, Sir Douglas Bader, as he had then become for his services to the disabled, died on his way home after giving a speech to praise 'Bomber' Harris, the Bomber Command leader during World War II whom the Establishment had found it convenient to distance itself from, as the horror of area bombing in places such as Dresden and Hamburg became apparent.

When Bader died, Galland was on a business trip to California. He made sure he got back to London quickly enough to attend the memorial service held for his friend of 42 years at St Clement Danes, the RAF church in the Strand. Peter Tory wrote in his *London Diary* newspaper column:

Certainly Bader, had he been present, would have instantly recognised the stranger in the dark raincoat. Stomping over to his side, he would have banged him on the back and bellowed: "Bloody good show, glad you could come!"

Bader got a charity, a building, two roads, a school and pub named after him, plus a statue at Goodwood, site of one of his airfields, and a knighthood. The one mistake about the 'Big Wing' theory one can surely forgive. And crashing a plane for no good reason. And, oh yes, another one he crashed by forgetfulness. He damaged a lot more of the enemy's.

And that secret advantage of his disability mentioned at the start of this section? When pilots turn sharply in combat, the G-force is so huge that pilots can black out temporarily. The plane always banks in a way that forces blood away from the brain down into the legs. One way to limit this danger is to wear compression stockings. Or, even better, to have no legs for the blood to go to...

THE WAR DROPS IN FOR TEA: To illustrate how the World War II air battle over London (left) was oddly close to people's normal lives, unlike earlier wars, here's a letter from a witness:

THE year was 1943, and I was 11. It was a lovely summer day in West Norwood, South London. I was in our garden with my mum and dad, watching Spitfires in a dogfight with German aircraft. I can still hear the rat-a-tat-tat of gunfire. A German plane burst into flames and crashed in Norwood Park. Looking up, we noticed something white floating down. A parachutist was on his way down right over our heads. 'Blimey,' said Dad. 'He's coming down in our garden.' There was a huge thump as he hit the ground, just missing our greenhouse. Releasing his huge parachute, he stood up, brushed himself down, smiled and said: 'Guten Morgen.' A handsome young German pilot of about 18 or 20 years old stood facing us.

My dad got a garden fork and told him: 'No funny business or you'll get this.' Pointing to his gun, dad said to hand it over. The pilot understood and gave dad his Luger pistol. Mother came out of the kitchen and asked him if he would like a cup of tea and a biscuit. He smiled and said: 'Danke.' Five Dad's Army-type soldiers then rushed in and took the young airman away. He waved goodbye to us.

*Frank S. Coldrick,
Fakenham, Norfolk.*

Here's the 'King of Lampedusa' - RAF Flight Sgt Sidney Cohen of London, who made a forced landing on Lampedusa and received a guarantee of surrender from the Italians. The Italians wanted the bombardment stopped - and quick - Cohen said. (Photo by radio from London).

Caption from the front page of the Jackson Daily News, Mississippi, June 15, 1943.

NO, WE SURRENDER! Sidney Cohen, a London tailor's cutter, and his crew had decided on being forced to land their Swordfish plane to surrender to the large Italian garrison of 4,300 troops on Lampedusa, but before they could do so, to their amazement, a number of soldiers rushed out waving white flags.

He said later: 'A crowd of Italians came out to meet us and we put our hands up to surrender, but then we saw they were all waving white sheets and shouting: "No, no – we surrender!"' Before long, the Italian troops had declared Flt Sgt Cohen the commander of the island. It made headlines around the world.

The story so cheered up the British Jewish community back home, a musical play *The King Of Lampedusa* was staged in 1943, first at the New Yiddish Theatre in Adler Street and later at the Grand Palais in the Mile End Road. This so infuriated the Nazis that their traitorous radio mouthpiece, Lord Haw-Haw, vowed that the theatre would be bombed to dust. (It wasn't. Haw-Haw was hanged.)

The play was performed around the world and on BBC radio. Flight Sgt Cohen and his aircraft were lost in 1946, sadly – but at least he did get to see the play about his greatest moment on stage while on leave. It would have made a good film really...

An amazing aircraft for its time: The German Ju 287 jet bomber

HITLER'S 'FRANKENPLANE': The above aircraft with its dramatic swept-forward wing looks amazingly advanced for its time – 1944 – with four jet engines (two attached to the fuselage directly – the things under the wing jet engines are booster rockets). That it was under test is shown by the cine camera perched near the tail and the dots all over it which had string attached to show the airflow on film. It flew very well, in fact – surprising, given that it was a Frankenstein plane, cobbled together from spare parts.

The Ju 287 had the nose wheels from the two crashed American B-24 Liberators, the fuselage from the HE 177, main wheels from a Ju 352, and lastly a tail constructed from Ju 388 parts. It was probably the first four-engined jet in the world, and certainly the only one with fixed undercarriage. It flew pretty well but the wings warped badly and it was just too late. The factories were bombed and the prototype destroyed before any production could start.

How desperate the Germans were getting was shown by the fact that their jet and rocket planes were sometimes towed to take-off points by oxen to save fuel. And one late design was a coal-dust powered ramjet, the **Lippisch P13A** (model maker's picture, left). It never flew, but the Americans who captured the design found it was aerodynamically good (in wind tunnel tests) for up to 2.5 times the speed of sound. They didn't try the coal engine, however.

Comin' in on a wing and a prayer

The above song was written about the heroics of getting a damaged B-17 Flying Fortress back to base in World War II, and a fine, folksy song it is too when rendered by such a great guitarist as Ry Cooder. It includes the lines:

Comin' in on a wing and a prayer
Though there's one motor gone
We can still carry on
Comin' in on a wing and a prayer

One B-17 that certainly needed a wing and a prayer and courage and engineering robustness and luck to get home was the aptly-named *All American,* whose survival at all is almost unbelievable. In fact the version of her story widely circulated on the Internet IS unbelievable, because it's total fiction. That story has the plane completing its North Africa bombing run in this state, starting and finishing in England (which is clearly impossible) and the heroic crew holding it together with parachute cords (nonsense, can you imagine the forces involved). You can see Mel Gibson starring in a film directed by himself, looking grimly heroic in lots of close-ups, but that's as accurate as it gets. It's a lovely yarn but should not be presented as the truth.

Somehow the *All American* B-16 continues to fly with its tail nearly sliced off

The truth, backed up by the surviving crew, is amazing enough. On February 1, 1943, bombers of the USAAF 414th Bombardment Squadron set off from Biskra, Algeria, to attack the German-held ports of Tunis and Bizerte in Tunisia. After dropping their bombs and heading for base, the bombers were attacked by German Me109 fighters.

Two fighters attacked the lead B-17 and the *All American* which was flying next to it in formation. The bombers' machine-gun fire destroyed the first fighter, but the second pressed on with its head-on attack. For some reason the second fighter could not complete its duck below the *All American* – the aircraft may have been disabled, the pilot, the German 16-victory ace Erich Paczia, may have been suicidal but most likely he had been hit by the heavy machine-gun bullets and was dead or dying. The Me109 tore through the Flying Fortress's rear fuselage almost completely slicing it off, but not quite. It also tore off the port stabiliser (the little wing on the tail).

How do we know all this? Because the bombardier in the *All American* on that day, Ralph Burbridge, who lived in Des Moines, Iowa, until dying aged 93 in 2013, in later life gave an interview about the most extraordinary survival of an aircraft one can imagine.

Burbridge recalled: 'Long after we had left the target and having sustained more fighter attacks, we saw two more climbing about two miles to our right. They came in to attack us, one of them directly at the nose of the lead ship and one at our plane. I covered one coming at us with the [.30-caliber] front nose gun and Harry (Nuessle, the navigator) covered the other plane with the [.50-caliber] gun on the right side of the nose.

'Between our own fire and fire from the lead ship, we managed to hit the Jerry going after the lead ship. He was last seen going down smoking off in the distance.'

A close-up of the damage: The tail gunner somehow survived

The other fighter kept coming toward them and 'his wings looked as though they were afire from his flaming guns'. When the German pilot was about 300 yards away he began a roll to pull down and away from the *All American* after his attack.

'About halfway through his roll either my fire or fire from the lead ship must have killed the pilot or disabled the plane. He never completed his intended roll and rapid pass under our ship.

'For one horrible instant he was right there – inches in front and above us. He passed over us with a distinctly audible swoosh, followed by a tremendous jar and a "whoomp".'

'That Jerry plane had lopped half of our tail section completely off. The other half and the rudder looked like they would shake loose at any moment,' said Mr Burbridge (left).

'Miraculously, none of the crew was hurt, but somewhere in the shuffle the lead ship was lost.' The ten men aboard his own plane put their parachutes on and got ready to jump in case the rest of the tail started to break off.

When the other crews saw that – amazingly – the *All American* could still fly, they slowed down to her speed and flew in a protective formation around her.

Once beyond German fighter range, the rest of the planes returned to base ahead of them. Now flying alone, 'it seemed like the trip back took 10 years but the base wasn't really that far. Somehow Kenny nursed the damaged plane and got us home later than everyone else.'

Although the *All American* landed back at base safely, its tail wheel wouldn't go down – not surprisingly – and they skidded the last 100 yards. 'I remember our ground crew had given us up so they were really glad to see us,' he said. 'Our crew chief, the head mechanic, had tears in his eyes.'

An ambulance sped down the runway after them to take all the shot-up casualties off. There weren't any.

The picture of the crippled *All American* flying home over the desert was taken by Lieutenant Charles 'Cliff' Cutforth, aboard B-17 *Flying Flint Gun* on that mission. It was fortunate that he did – for otherwise no one would have believed a plane in that state could have made it home.

Ralph Burbridge could so easily have died in the North African desert that day, two weeks before his 23rd birthday. In fact he lived to 92 and died, the last of the *All American's* crew, honoured by his children and grandchildren – and indeed by the 414th Bombardment Squadron which had reformed in 2011, again in the Mediterranean, as a reconnaissance squadron.

When its new commander heard that Burbridge was still alive, and knowing his extraordinary story, commemorated in the 414th association's patch logo, he had a Stars and Stripes hoisted at the base, saluted, and then sent it to the old flyer, framed in a glass case. I bet the old boy really appreciated that...

No, you're not seeing things. The 'beer bomber' Spitfire (left) had a keg of beer under each wing and was used after D-Day to take English beer to the troops in Normandy. At least it would have arrived nice and cool

DEFIANT TO THE END: You'd think, if anyone suggested at the outbreak of World War II, equipping the RAF with a fighter aircraft with no forward-firing guns at all, and no way of tackling a head-on attack, they would be called dolollaly, daft and daffy. The enemy would slaughter them – particularly as soon as they found out what the strange-looking planes were capable of (or incapable of) with their rather odd, powered rear gun turrets.

But this is what the air force did with the Defiant, an odd little plane with a dodgy track record. It is – rightly – not feted along with the Spitfire and Hurricane of the Battle of Britain era. Defiants were indeed shot down too easily. You wouldn't think it would be wise to keep building the aircraft through most of the war, after the crews were downed in large numbers early on, but this happened, with about 1,000 produced, none of them with a gun on the front.

Strange design: The Defiant had lots of guns at the rear, but none at the front

And yet it was not all a disaster. Things were not as one-sided as they seemed. Nor was the design entirely stupid.

In 1935, the RAF had asked manufacturers for a turret-armed defensive fighter to counter the threat of massed formations of unescorted enemy bombers. They wanted it to do 290mph and climb to 15,000ft.

The idea was that turret-armed fighters would approach an enemy bomber from below or from the side and co-ordinate their fire. Fine if there were no enemy fighters flying escort. But, if there were, potentially suicidal.

The Defiant, with the first production model flying just two months before war was declared, had a turret with four Browning machine guns, which could rotate through 360 degrees and even fire slightly downwards on either side. The electrical firing buttons had an interrupter to stop a gunner shooting his own tail or propeller off while chasing an enemy target.

Close-up of a Defiant turret: But you couldn't easily bail out if in trouble

In March 1940, the Defiant finally came into front-line service. The RAF trumpeted their arrival with a disinformation campaign, stating that the Defiant had 21 guns: four in the turret, 14 in the wings and three cannon in the nose. Any German spy might have suspected that the numbers of guns was somewhat exaggerated – but not that it had none at the front at all!

On May 27, the Defiants met three bombers and shot them down. On the next day they tried a novel tactic – when under attack from fighters they would form a tight circle, slowly descending. Attacking aircraft would face more than one turret at a time firing at them. It sort of worked – six enemy planes were shot down for the loss of three Defiants.

On May 29, 1940, the Defiants had their best day in what would soon become the fully-fledged Battle of Britain. 264 Squadron claimed 37 kills. That figure is some answer to those who claim the Defiant was a total failure.

But other squadrons had not heeded 264's advice to form a defensive circle, so when nine Defiants were sent to defend a convoy off Folkestone on July 19, flying simply straight in line, seven were shot down, and the two that survived escaped only because they were rescued by RAF Hurricanes.

The best result for the Defiants was when the Luftwaffe mistook them for the similar-outline Hurricanes. They would 'bounce' them from above and behind in classic ambush tactics – and be surprised to encounter a concentrated wall of fire.

But the Germans learned the Defiants' fatal flaw, and just attacked head-on. The losses mounted, and the crew losses were not helped by the fact that the turret had to be rotated to a certain position to get the hatch open. With an aircraft on fire and falling out of the sky, this was unlikely to work.

Worse, the gunner had to wear strange parachute-included 'Rhino suits' because of the lack of space in the turret. One Defiant air gunner, Frederick Platts, recalled: 'The Rhino suit we had to wear on Defiants was a bear but I couldn't come up with an alternative, even though it killed dozens of us. I forget the details of it but we could not have sat on our chute or even keep it nearby as in other turrets, so you wore – all in one – an inner layer that fitted a little like a wetsuit of today. The chute fitted around this, and then the dinghy and the outer clothing.'

As for getting out of a burning, plummeting plane while wearing that clobber and trying to get the turret to move to the escape position, even if not wounded ... it hardly bears thinking about.

By the end of August, the toll was enormous – about half the Defiants delivered to the RAF had been shot down. You could have seen it coming, frankly. They were being sent to do the wrong job. The faster, more agile Hurricanes and Spitfires were being delivered in enough numbers to fight the Germans, and winning the battle, and the Defiants were switched to night fighting, just in time for the Germans to switch to night bombing of Britain – the start of the Blitz on Britain.

It was difficult to locate the Germans with naked eye alone – plus the odd searchlight contact – and yet the Defiant proved its worth now, shooting down more Luftwaffe bombers than any other type of British fighter. They usually attacked from below and slightly ahead.

By September 1942, a Mk II Defiant with a more powerful engine and radar was produced. But at this point German bombing of Britain eased off as the doomed attack on Russia got under way.

As the war reached its climax, the Defiants were given electronic countermeasures duties, and then were used as target tugs – in fact they were so much in demand for overseas air forces that they continued to be built without turrets for this work. And they were used for experiments for the first Martin-Baker ejector seats. By the end of the war, 1,064 had been built by Boulton-Paul – of a design that seemed to many people crackers from the start, and ridiculed ever since. But they did account for almost as many German aircraft. And had they been used – in say, Scotland – against unescorted bombers, as they were designed for, they would have had an even higher success rate. They were designed as night-fighting bomber destroyers, and at that they were defiantly good.

THE DAY A CIVILIAN AIRLINE HELICOPTER SHOT DOWN AN ATTACKING BIPLANE BOMBER:

That's right, you read that correctly. It really happened just the once – in the late 1960s, when the biplane should have been in a museum, but it was still in combat. And what evidence do we have for this insanely unlikely, urban myth-type event? A photograph? A film clip? No, an *oil painting*. Not any old painting, but one proudly and bizarrely published by America's CIA.

That last organisation's name should suggest that the airline quoted – although outwardly a regular outfit with uniforms, offices, cap badges, tickets, livery and timetabled flights – wasn't quite what it seemed. It was Air America, the spooks' outfit we met in Chapter 6 happily sinking British ships (twice). They called their food drops 'rice runs', and weapons drops 'hard rice'.

The battle of which this odd event was a part officially didn't happen, officially, as the American forces involved weren't even in the military, officially. It couldn't have happened because it was in a country where America wasn't officially fighting, against another army that wasn't officially there either, and two other countries not officially involved also took part.

But the bitter battle was real all right. It would have been commemorated by all sides, had it been official. Indeed, if one of the American services 'wasn't there', how come it suffered its worst ground combat losses of the entire era there?

To unravel the story, you need to know that the event goes by the prosaic name of the Battle of Lima Site 85, and was on the hidden edge of the Vietnam War.

In this war – which America was doomed to lose less than ten years later – more ordnance was dropped by the U.S. than in the entire Second World War, which – you will surely know – involved some pretty appalling bombing campaigns in many countries. One scholarly estimate says the U.S. attempts to destroy North Vietnam's ability to fight used *triple* the bomb totals for that World War. 'The Indochinese bombings amounted to 7,662,000 tons of explosives, compared to 2,150,000 tons in the world conflict,' says one source.

It was a staggering rain of death and destruction – and started with the arrogant claim of the Chief of Staff of the United States Air Force Curtis LeMay that 'we're going to bomb them back into the Stone Age'. How wrong he would turn out to be – militarily, politically and morally.

Keith Woodcock's painting, showing a helicopter shooting down a biplane

THE BATTLE OF LIMA SITE 85 took place on March 10/11 1968 on top of a 5,000ft mountain called Phou Pha Thi in a remote part of

Laos, about 24km from the border with Vietnam, where a full-scale war had been raging for more than a decade between the French and then the U.S. and its ally South Vietnam, and North Vietnam, the Vietcong guerrillas and their Russian/Chinese communist backers.

The late 1960s saw much of that bombing campaign run from a secret radar and radio station on top of this mountain in Laos.

In August 1966, the USAF had installed on Phou Pha Thi (pictured below – can you imagine attacking up that hill?) an autonomous radio transmitter that provided pilots with distance and bearing. In 1967, under the code name Heavy Green, the facility, which had its own generators and living accommodation, was upgraded so it could direct and control attacking jet fighters and bombers to their targets and provide them with precise bomb release points. It began operating in late November 1967.

By late 1967, Lima Site 85's radar directed 55 per cent of all bombing operations – *Operation Rolling Thunder* – against North Vietnam. The biggest bombing campaign in history could therefore continue round the clock, at night and in cloud, without cease. The famous north-south supply line outside Vietnam's borders down through Laos and Cambodia to South Vietnam – the Ho Chi Minh trail – was one of the targets for this sustained bombing.

Because of Laotian political sensibilities, USAF servicemen assigned to work at the installation had to sign paperwork that temporarily released them from military service, and to work in the guise of civilian technicians from Lockheed Martin — the process is called 'sheep-dipping', so they were officially not in the air force. In reality, they operated as members of the USAF Circuit Rider teams from the 1st Mobile Communications Group based at Udorn Royal Thai Air Force Base who rotated to the site every seven days, via the weekly supply flights of the 20th Special Operations Squadron, based at Udorn and operating under the code name *Operation Pony Express,* using Lima Site 85, a 2,300 ft airstrip constructed by the CIA in the valley below.

Two armies who also shouldn't have been there were involved in providing forces to defend the mountain radar station and the airstrip. The Hmong Clandestine Army (the Hmongs are an ethnic minority in the mountains) was alongside the Thai Border Patrol Police forces, both funded by the CIA in this case. The effectiveness of these troops if faced with a determined assault by the communists was in such doubt that all the secret equipment on the mountain top had explosives attached so that if the site was overrun, it could be very quickly destroyed.

This ploy didn't really work out because the group of 'civilian technicians' working on site realised – as they came under probing artillery attacks from the mid-distance – that they were sitting on piles of explosives, so they unbolted them and threw them off the mountain. They were dressed as unarmed civilians and officially provided with no weapons (although some took in personal small arms, this would not have held out against any serious assault).

The local communist guerrilla group, the Pathet Lao, had taken several villages near the mountain, although from time to time were defeated by the Hmong forces. In December 1967 and January 1968, the North Vietnamese army moved closer to the mountain. Clearly the threat was getting serious. The commander of the few Americans running the radar station begged for evacuation or reinforcements, but the former was denied because the base was saving American pilots' lives every night (and more effectively killing communists) and the latter because it was politically impossible to move troops in.

On 12 January, a CIA spotter 'somewhere in Laos' saw something unbelievable in his binoculars – a formation of four aircraft flying towards Lima Site 85. They were ancient Soviet-made biplanes, a 1946 model called the Antonov An-2. We were in the jet and computer era now, but these propeller-driven old crates – not unlike the already obsolete British 'Stringbags' described in Chapter 8 but a quarter of a century later – were lumbering towards the CIA's vital radar and radio station. It was one of the very few outings of the Vietnam People's Air Force during the whole war, and it put the linchpin of the American air war in mortal danger.

Slow, rugged: The Soviet-built Antonov could fly backwards in a strong wind

Two of the planes went into attack. As they flew over Phou Pha Thi, crewmen manually dropped 120 mm mortar shells through hatches and then strafed their targets with 57 mm rockets mounted on the wings. Ground fire shot down one An-2, which crashed into a mountainside. By now U.S. officers at Lima Site 85 managed to contact the nearest friendly air unit – which was an Air America Huey helicopter, unarmed, but faster than the old Soviet biplanes. The pilot, Captain Ted Moore, spotted the remaining An-2, and gave chase.

As he pulled alongside, flight mechanic Glenn Woods, armed with an AK-47 assault rifle (also Soviet-made, and used by the 'airline' for clandestine operations so American weapons could not blamed) slid open the cargo door, opened fire and caused the biplane to crash into a ridge.

This is surely the only time in history an 'unarmed' civilian airline helicopter shot down a combat-mission military biplane. (If, by the way, you recall an image of helicopters lifting panic-stricken people from the roof of the U.S. embassy in Saigon in 1975 as the war was finally lost, yes, that was an Air America Huey chopper too.)

One of the huge Vietnam War-era biplanes is on display in Vientiane today

The North Vietnamese biplane attack had done no damage to the installation – although four Hmongs, two men and two women, had been killed by the raid.

Things got steadily more threatening for the Americans on the mountain and their 1,000 allies around the air strip below. On 18 February, a North Vietnamese artillery spotter team was ambushed near Lima Site 85 by a Hmong patrol, killing an NVA officer. The dead officer, who was a major, carried a notebook which showed their plan to attack Phou Pha Thi with three North Vietnamese battalions and one Pathet Lao battalion. Still the U.S. commanders refused to allow any evacuation or reinforcement, but personnel at Lima Site 85 directed 342 air strikes, some as deafeningly near as 100ft from their own base, to disrupt their opponents' build-up during February 20-29.

But they did not know of another, more secret plan where the NVA would use a platoon from the 41st Special Forces Battalion, led by First Lieutenant Truong Muc – just 33 soldiers, reinforced by a nine-man sapper squad and a communications and code squad. These troops had trained rigorously amidst great secrecy for the mountain assault, and had trekked in from Vietnam carrying over 90lb of supplies per man – food, ammunition, pistols, AK-47 rifles and three rocket-propelled grenade launchers and their heavy rounds. It was some feat, in the rugged terrain and steaming humidity, plus the need to evade relentless American air attacks on anything that moved, by marching by night or under tree canopies.

A graphic of the Air America Huey helicopter

They avoided all contact with locals and with the regular NVA which was preparing its battalion-sized attack. A forward team of the Special Forces had been hidden on the mountain slopes for two months, observing the routines and readiness of the Americans and their allies.

On the evening of March 10, an artillery barrage struck the top of the mountain, so the Americans retreated to shelters – ironically leaving behind the very equipment that could have called in air support to stop the barrage. During the shelling, a few of the NVA special forces climbed the mountain to reconnoitre a route up for the coming assault and to remove landmines and trip wires. The barrage killed no Americans, but it did wipe out their only artillery – a howitzer, manned by Hmong troops – with a direct hit.

Over the following night, the 33 special forces men climbed the mountain and made their successful attack on the radar station at the top. Most of the Americans were killed, and a battle raged around the air strip below. At first light, an evacuation was finally allowed by the U.S. embassy in Laos, but there were few Americans left alive to rescue. While U.S. fighter-bombers bombed and strafed the hill-top site, now held by the North Vietnamese, an Air America helicopter landed on the airstrip and they picked up two CIA officers, one forward air-controller, and five technicians who had hidden during the firefight.

At noon, the Americans turned their attention to destroying the radar equipment, files and bodies left on the hill top and started a series of 96 air strikes on the hilltop, lasting two weeks, which obliterated all remaining facilities.

It is not known how many local forces and NVA were lost in the battle. The Americans lost 14, including one pilot shot down trying to rescue survivors. Oddly, for a battle that 'didn't happen' by forces who 'weren't there', it was the largest single ground combat loss of USAF personnel during the Vietnam War. From a military point of view, the NVA can be credited with a victory in unbelievably tough circumstances and terrain, won against overwhelming air superiority. From an American point of view, the defeat cannot be blamed on the poor intelligence. They knew at every stage what was coming, despite the secrecy about the one unit. The communists were building paved roads from Vietnam towards this point for months, for goodness sake! No, the men on top of Phou Pha Thi were hung out to dry by their own commanders, or rather hung out to die.

In fact the U.S. was losing the war politically in the West as well as on the ground. In the very same month as this very real battle, thousands of demonstrators led by such idealists as Tariq Ali rioted outside the U.S. Embassy in Grosvenor Square, London, chanting: 'Hey, hey, LBJ, how many kids did you kill today?' A young chap called Mick Jagger stood and watched open-mouthed in amazement.

I know because I was there as a naive, perhaps simplistic 15-year-old, and it was terrifying when the dozens of police horses charged, long batons swinging. I climbed a tree and threw my Vietcong flag at them in frustration.

It was amazing, looking back, that a group of us were taken there in a van by a history teacher, and on the way back to boarding school we stopped off to have afternoon tea with my mother – a respectable NHS doctor – who heartily congratulated us on a principled stand while serving cucumber sandwiches, Bourbon biscuits and watching the riot on the TV news!

The young were naive then and espoused many causes which turned out to be doubtful or too idealistic, and I am sure some military types reading this would have disapproved of my bolshie attitude then (now I can see more sides to the argument in most things, and would certainly have a lot more suspicion of what dangerous emotions happen when a mob gets galvanised, and a lot more sympathy for the cops caught in the middle!).

I grew to appreciate our Servicemen much more, but even so, surely the best way to support them when a pointless war is being waged is to stop the fighting? It must have offended grieving families who had lost a 19-year-old son in Vietnam for young people in the West to protest, and ask what it was all for, but stopping the needless war must have saved other American 19-year-olds from joining them in the endless grim bodybags.

A demonstrator is dealt with: The Grosvenor Square anti-Vietnam War riot

On this one, at least, history shows the naïve youngsters were right. Why were children being napalmed for a war that had little point, no moral, military or political purpose? Far from being bombed 'back to the Stone Age' as the Americans had promised, the much-derided 'peasants in black pyjamas' of the Vietcong guerrillas would beat the biggest superpower in the world. While the victory was, to be sure, theirs, the protests in the West had a role too.

As time wore on, Western TV audiences realised the sheer horror of burning children running towards the camera and the war was lost almost as much in Milwaukee and Maidenhead as in the Mekong delta.

We youngsters, of course, at the time knew nothing of the Battle of Lima Site 85 just a few days before, because it hadn't officially taken place, involving forces that officially weren't even there in a country that wasn't involved. No media recorded it.

Shortly afterwards, what remained of one of the downed An-2 biplanes was put on display in front of the That Luang Monument, the golden stupa that is the most important Buddhist shrine in the Laotian capital, Vientiane. This was supposed to be proof of North Vietnamese military activities in the kingdom. Let's look at this logic. The biggest air assault in all history was being conducted the U.S., partly in Laos, killing many innocent villagers. But one failed North Vietnamese air attack (on a U.S. facility, not a Laotian one) by old biplanes was held up as a reason for supporting the U.S. side. What a mountain of wrecked U.S. planes, bomb parts and missile remains could have been put on display!

Civilians being evacuated in Saigon, 1975: It's an Air America chopper again

In a further macabre postscript, after peace returned to the battered region, American investigators tried to trace the remains of MIAs – those missing in action – for proper burial. When they came to this site, they found two sets of remains to return, plus those of the crashed pilot.

But they listened to the NVA veterans who said that during the battle, they could not bury the dead Americans on the solid rock mountain top, so threw four of them off a cliff.

The Americans had them – or younger compatriots – throw dummies off exactly the same spot, and videotaped this from a helicopter (it really was a civilian one this time). The dummies came to rest on a mountain ledge. Investigators abseiled down and found four pairs of military boots, in different sizes, and a few personal effects such as a cigarette lighter. But nature had claimed all the organic remains – there was nothing much to send home to the relatives.

THE DAY THE U.S. ATOM-BOMBED SPAIN: Not every part of American military aviation history in the Mediterranean area has been as glorious as the 'Comin' in on a wing and a prayer' story recounted earlier in this chapter. There was the horrifying day the U.S. Air Force dropped four atomic bombs on Spain by accident. Hydrogen bombs, in fact, otherwise known as H-bombs, each 100 times more powerful than the atom bomb that obliterated Hiroshima.

This now-largely forgotten emergency came over half a century ago, in January 1966. Looking from today, it was closer in history – just over 20 years – to that attack on Hiroshima in August 1945.

The H-bombs did not explode their warheads, otherwise the history of the world would have changed radically. But why were such dangerous weapons dropped over Spain at all? What were they doing there?

The answer is almost incredible to modern minds. As part of *Operation Chrome Dome*, the U.S. was flying fleets of armed nuclear bombers all the time from all directions towards the Soviet Union, their Cold War enemy. It was part of the MAD doctrine – Mutually Assured Destruction. This held that although the Soviets could launch unstoppable intercontinental ballistic missile attacks at any moment on the USA, including destroying its own ICBMs, the fact that flight crews were on attack paths from all over the world all the time meant that the Russians would never risk it. (It does rather assume both sides are led by rational human beings).

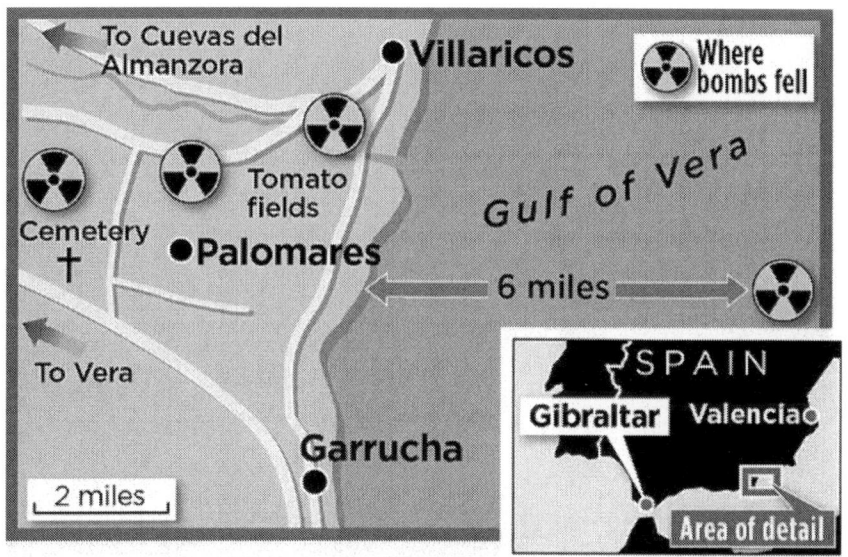

A map showing exactly where the four bombs fell. Courtesy of the Daily Mail

It sounds insanely dangerous – and the chances of a war starting by accident were highlighted in contemporary films like *Dr Strangelove* (a black comedy) and *Failsafe*. But this is how the world worked. In fact, it's not so different today with ICBM-armed submarines patrolling the deep. Like the air crews in the 1960s, they never know whether this patrol will be the one where they fire their appalling weapons, with no homeland worth returning to.

As for back in the Sixties, never mind global warming – no one had thought of that yet, though the pollution caused by fleets of aircraft flying pointlessly around non-stop must have been enormous – but with the danger of nuclear weapons on board, always ready to drop, taken to the edge of 'enemy' airspace sometimes, and with dangerous air-to-air refuelling several times on each trip, global frying was a serious possibility. It was MAD indeed!

On the day in question, January 16, 1966, seven crew took off in a B-52 Stratofortress from Seymour Johnson Air Force base in North Carolina. Because of the enormously long distances to be covered, the B-52 had to be refuelled in the air four times. After turning around over the Adriatic – whence the attack on the southern Soviet

Union would have been launched – the plane headed back to its third refuelling point, where it would link up with a huge KC-135 Stratotanker at 31,000 ft above south-eastern Spain.

Just before 10.30 am on January 17, the planes made their rendezvous as planned. With the two aircraft flying at nearly 500 mph, the refuelling was a difficult task, but the crews were experienced. At the time, the captain, Charles J. Wendorf, 29, was resting and the B-52 was being flown by Major Larry G. Messinger, one of the co-pilots.

The task meant lining up the bomber's receiving receptacle with a fuel boom – buffeted in the powerful slipstream – being trailed by the KC-135. The tanker's boom operator noticed that the B-52 was approaching a little fast.

Cold War warrior: B-52s like this were airborne with H-bombs all the time

'Watch your enclosure,' the operator calmly told the crew of the B-52 as a warning. If the operator thought the situation was perilous, he would have ordered the bomber to break away, but no such order was made. No one seemed to realise how much danger they were in.

'We didn't see anything dangerous about the situation,' Messinger recalled. 'But all of a sudden, all hell seemed to break loose.' The B-52 had overshot and the boom missed the fuel nozzle in the top of the plane and smashed into the bomber with such force that its port wing was buckled.

Air-to-air refuelling isn't easy. A B-52 gets a drink from a KC-135 in later times

Fire quickly spread up the fuel-filled boom and ignited all 30,000 gallons of the tanker's kerosene, causing it to plummet to the ground. Meanwhile, the bomber started to break up, and the crew did their best to get out of the plane using parachutes.

The hydrogen bombs were heading towards the ground at high speed – and if they went off, most of Andalucia and Murcia would be destroyed, killing hundreds of thousands of people.

But as we all know now, the nuclear bombs did not detonate that day. The conventional explosives in two of the bombs did explode, showering some 500 acres around the fishing village of Palomares with three kilograms of highly radioactive plutonium-239.

But the villagers were lucky. Not only did the nuclear bombs not explode themselves (for that to happen the conventional explosives had to operate in a precise sequence) – but even the deadly dust from the fallen bombs blew away from and not towards the villagers. Two of the bombs buried themselves in the land, a third in a river bed, and a fourth out to sea. No one was hurt and no property damaged.

Up in the air, the aircraft crews were not so fortunate. The four crewmen in the KC-135 were burned to death when a huge fireball enveloped their aircraft.

Recovery: Amazed villagers look at the wreckage of the American aircraft

Four of the B-52 crew, including Captain Wendorf, made it out and parachuted to safety. The other three crew members failed to get out in time. Seven men died, but it could have been 70,000.

The American denials of any such incident went on for as long as they could make them credible, aided by the fascist Spanish government of General Franco. A massive clean-up operation on land started – and in fact was resumed in 2016.

The recovery of the intact bomb from the sea was in itself a sorry sequence of further calamities.

Contaminated: The U.S. took thousands of barrels of polluted soil away

Decades later, radioactivity warnings persist locally

The problem was that it was lying 2,500 ft below the surface of the Mediterranean. It took the U.S. Navy nearly three months to find the bomb, and when they finally started to haul it to the surface, the H-bomb was dropped and fell even deeper, a further 500 ft down.

Then, a submarine got tangled up in the bomb's parachute lines and was almost lost. At last, in mid-April, the final nuclear bomb was hauled aboard the recovery vessel, the *USS Petrel*.

Given the potential for greater disaster, the authorities in Washington and Madrid must have heaved a massive sigh of relief.

Recovered: The bomb that went deep into the sea, safe aboard the *USS Petrel*

LIBYA BOMBED A DISCO IN BERLIN, SO THE U.S. BOMBED ... A BIT OF ITALY AND FRANCE (AND ATTACKED CANADA TOO):
In 1986 Libya, then led by arch troublemaker Muammar Gaddafi, was looking for mischief to make – to get at Western allies it blamed for something or other in its default setting of semi-permanent pointless rage.

Gaddafi (pictured on the left with his saner hero, Egyptian president Nasser) was the terrorists' friend worldwide – he was arming and funding the IRA, the Palestinians fighting the Israelis, and Moslem separatists fighting the Philippines. A couple of years after this Gaddafi's agents were to bring down an entire Pan Am civilian airliner over Lockerbie, Scotland, killing 270 innocent people. The year before, his men had struck at Rome and Vienna airport passengers waiting for flights, killing 19. The 'mad dog' Gaddafi label was justified. He wanted nuclear bombs.

Meanwhile in typical sabre-rattling boastfulness, and always attention-seeking, Gaddafi noisily announced a 'Line of Death' to enforce a new 100km territorial limit along Libya's northern coast. The 'Line of Death' would be defended by a whole set of Soviet missile batteries and radar stations.

The USA argued that these

were international waters and took care to send its warships though them regularly, raising Gaddafi to new fury and rhetoric. At 6am on March 24, the Libyans fired at three American warships. They missed. The Americans, however, did not. They destroyed two ships, several missile batteries, several radar stations and killed 35 people.

Gaddafi resorted to lower technology. His agents bombed a disco called *La Belle* in West Berlin which was popular with American servicemen. A bomb went off at 1.45am on April 5. It killed two U.S. Army sergeants, a civilian woman, and injured 229 others, mostly German civilians.

Hit by aircraft: A Libyan corvette burning after the Gulf of Sidra battle

If Gaddafi had hoped to get away with this — and it is doubtful that he would not have boasted about it sooner or later — his congratulatory message to the Libyan Embassy in West Germany put paid to any such chance.

U.S. President Ronald Reagan was furious. With backing from Congress, he ordered retaliatory strikes on Libya. One problem was that not all the Europeans agreed, and would not let American warplanes fly over their airspace.

That meant America had to use its bases in a more reliable ally, Britain. Luckily, the U.S. had been studying how to attack Libya from there. In October the previous year, they attacked Canada instead. Ten F-111Es based at RAF Upper Heyford in Britain flew to Canada. and attacked a fake base in Newfoundland (with the Canadian government's permission, of course) in a secret mission called *Operation Ghost Rider*. It worked – the F-111Es proved their worth over such a distance.

Because of the ban over French, Spanish, and Italian skies, to reach Libya from Britain the planes now had to make a detour of some 1,300 miles. On April 15, 1986, *Operation El Dorado Canyon* (the bombing of Libya) took place. Eighteen F-111 bombers and four EF-111 electronic countermeasure planes left Britain. Their target was Libya's capital, Tripoli.

As they crossed the Mediterranean between Sicily and northern Africa, they saw something odd. There was an enormous dark shape beneath the water... and smoke was coming out of the sea! They must have been a Libyan submarine, possibly preparing to fire. The U.S. knew of no Libyan subs, but guessed the Soviet chums of Gaddafi must have supplied him with some. The F-111Es dropped depth charges on the target and flew on.

Weapon of choice: The F111 swing-wing bomber with afterburners on

At 2am, the first of 60 tons worth of munitions fell – some on Gaddafi's home. The main targets, however, were the Tripoli and Benina airfields, the Bab al-Azizia and Jamahiriyah barracks, the Murat Sidi Bilal Camp, and air defence networks. It was over in 12 minutes. Two American servicemen died as compared to 40 Libyans. The French Embassy – accidentally, of course! – was also hit.

Gaddafi was not hurt, but his two sons were, and his 15-month-old adopted daughter was killed. Typically, he claimed the 'battle' was a victory for Libya over the imperialist U.S. and renamed his country the 'Great Socialist People's Libyan Arab Jamahiriyah.' The last word means something like republic.

And what happened to the deadly smoking submarine bombed by the F111s (one pictured, bending its wings in a tight turn, left)? Libya never had any.

The menacing shape was the submerged Italian island of Ferdinandea – though the British also claimed it, calling it Graham Island. The island with an active volcano rises above sea level, only to disappear again every other century or so. It's clearly marked on charts, so the U.S. pilots taking fright at it was a bit strange.

As for hitting the French Embassy, this was purely coincidental collateral damage. If, as someone quipped, an American diplomat said at the time: 'Well if you'd let our planes fly there direct they might have been a bit more accurate', then that wasn't very diplomatic.

And what happened to Gaddafi, pictured? (We in Fleet Street, by the way, always have a way of remembering how to spell odd names. In this case, how many Ds and Fs? Double Dealing F***er. Once said, never forgotten). He was overthrown by his own people and killed on October 20, 2011, as part of the 'Arab Spring', a flawed process which failed to improve things in Libya.

His political vision of pan-Arab socialism and nationalisation of oil assets were potentially workable, rational choices he was entitled to make. His sponsorship of international terrorism around the world, his encouragement of hatred whenever possible, and his torturing tyranny at home, were certainly not.

8 HOW OBSOLETE 'STRINGBAGS' DOOMED HITLER'S MOST POWERFUL AND MODERN WAR MACHINE

THE Swordfish torpedo bomber, affectionately nicknamed the 'Stringbag' by its crews, was able to defeat Hitler's mightiest, most modern and most lethal battleship *Bismarck* in 1941 not because it was equally good and modern, but because the aircraft was an almost obsolete 1930s design.

A huge biplane (pictured above) with a crew of three but just one engine, the Swordfish was built out of canvas on frames. So bullets and shells that would have crippled other aircraft just whizzed straight through without exploding. The planes would return to their aircraft carriers with dozens of holes, easily patched up. It was also strangely hard for the German gunners to hit the things because they had trained for fast modern aircraft. The Swordfish lumbers along at maybe 50 knots, and in the right head-wind can stop or even go backwards. You might have seen that done at air displays.

The best evidence for this view comes from Scottish hero Lt Commander 'Jock' Moffat, who died aged 97 just before Christmas 2016. He was the last surviving Swordfish pilot of the courageous naval flyers whose attack on the German battleship in May 1941 led to the carrying out of Churchill's order 'Sink the *Bismarck*!'. This now famous command was issued after that battleship had sunk the pride of the Royal Navy, *HMS Hood*, at the Battle of Denmark Strait two days before, in a shocking massive explosion, and the loss of well over 1,000 crew.

The mighty *Bismarck*, seen from another German warship in 1941. Photo by courtesy of the United States Navy History and Heritage Command

On May 26, 1941 the slightly damaged *Bismarck* was about 400 miles west of Brest and heading as fast as she could for the protective umbrella of the Luftwaffe in occupied France and a safe port there. The only men who could stop her in time were the Swordfish crews of 810, 818 and 820 Naval Air Squadrons in the carrier *Ark Royal*, and starting at 7.10pm that evening 15 aircraft were launched into the teeth of a strengthening Atlantic gale.

They found *Bismarck* after an hour and half but hopes of a co-ordinated attack were made impossible by the weather and poor visibility. They very nearly attacked a British ship shadowing the German battleship. Individual aircraft had to launch their own attacks against the now alerted ship's formidable forest of guns, throwing up a wall of flak that looked impenetrable.

With, as their commander later said, 'gallantry and determination which cannot be praised too highly', the obsolete biplanes attacked and dropped 13 torpedoes, two hitting *Bismarck* but not stopping her.

At 9.05pm Moffat dived out of the protecting cloud to begin his attack, and levelled out at 50 feet, almost skimming the surface of the waves, facing a huge storm of bullets and shells, including the battleship's main guns fired into the water to raise waterspouts which could down a torpedo bomber.

A Swordfish being launched into the storm to attack *Bismarck*, as brilliantly recreated by Robert Taylor. The painting is in the Fleet Air Arm Museum

'As we dived through the murk, into a lethal storm of shells and bullets,' Moffat recalled, *'Bismarck's* guns erupted and in the hail of hot bullets and tracer, I couldn't see any of the other Swordfish. I thought the closer we were to the water the better chance we had of surviving so we flew in bouncing off the tops of the waves – and it worked. The great thing about the Swordfish was that the bullets just went straight through. After all, it was only made of canvas. It was like David and Goliath!'

'Nevertheless,' he added, 'the stuff was coming in at such a rate I don't mind admitting that I was petrified. It was coming so thick and fast that I was inclined to duck in my cockpit and, in fact, I think I did so.'

Moffat's crew comprised observer Sub-lieutenant 'Dusty' Miller, and Leading Telegraphist Air Gunner Albert J. Hayman. Miller guided Moffat to his torpedo dropping point, studying the wave pattern so that the torpedo could be dropped in a trough, rather than a crest, and with luck would run deep and true with a fair chance of hitting *Bismarck*.

'Behind me Miller was leaning over the side of the aircraft and calling "Not yet, not yet" and then he said "Let her go!" '

As Moffat (pictured) turned his plane away, gunner Hayman could not resist firing a few a squirts of his puny Lewis machine-gun in the direction of the great armoured battleship. It was as effective using a pea-shooter against an angry elephant.

About the same time a torpedo – probably Moffat's, but in the confusion it could have been another crew's – struck *Bismarck's* stern and the explosion caused shock damage, jamming her rudder, crippling her steering gear, and forcing her to steer wide circles in the heavy seas. The mighty menace was now doomed. Despite all the much-vaunted excellence of German engineering, a design fault had been noted in *Bismarck's* early sea trails. You could not manoeuvre using the propellers alone – as you can with many warships. She just refused to alter course, tests showed, even with props turning opposite ways. This may or may not have helped seal her fate that stormy day.

At 9.15pm the German admiral reported by wireless to his high command that his ship was not manoeuvrable. Now unable to escape the Home Fleet, the German giant was destroyed by pursuing British warships the following morning. And how many warships!

Hitler, who had been at the launch of *Bismarck*, Europe's heaviest ever battleship, complained that the Royal Navy was like the Hydra of mythology. You cut off one head (eg the *Hood*) but others grow. The ships available at short notice in that part of the North Atlantic for the pursuit were two aircraft carriers, six battleships, 13 cruisers, and 21 destroyers (far bigger than today's Royal Navy).

Because the Germans refused to strike their colours – that is surrender by lowering their flag – the British had to keep bombarding the *Bismarck*, gradually disabling her and killing hundreds of men in what must have been a hellish few hours. The assembled fleet fired 2,800 shells at her, hitting *Bismarck* with 400. In the end torpedoes were used – including the only battleship-to-battleship torpedo attack in history (they don't usually get that close) – and even then the Germans claimed they were abandoning ship and had scuttled her with explosive charges themselves. By then the decks were awash and the ship listing badly.

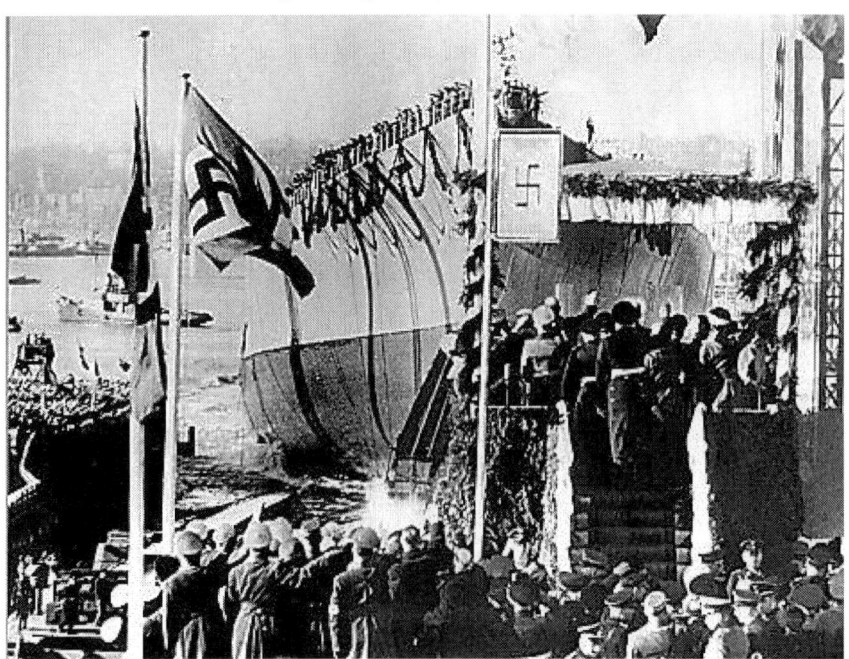

The launch of the *Bismarck* in 1939, attended by Hitler. Note the fascist salutes being given by nearly all. Her superstructure had not yet been fitted

No one can prove which of all these efforts finally sunk the *Bismarck*, but in an unhappy footnote, as British ships lowered nets to enable at least some of the German sailors to scramble up to safety, a

U-boat attack alarm went off and the warships had to steam into action again, leaving some of the surviving crew to drown. Of over 2,200 men, only 114 survived – but even that heavy toll was a more merciful outcome than that of the crew of the *Hood*, where just three survived out of 1,418 – the Royal Navy's worst ever loss of men.

Jock Moffat's story was typical of this heroic generation who lived through a war where they performed astonishing heroic deeds, followed by a peace where life was comparatively humdrum – one minute you are fighting the Japanese with machine-guns, knives and grenades in the jungle and the next you have 40 years of running the Rotary Club and a paint business. Raising children, watching football and paying a mortgage – the perhaps dull stuff of ordinary 1950s and 60s life that their lost comrades never got to live through.

In Moffat's case, it was running the Grandtully Hotel on the River Tay for decades. When he retired from the hotel in 1972, he ran a shop selling Scottish tweeds and tartans and knick-knacks until 1997. He rode with the Lanarkshire and Renfrewshire Hunt, and then with the Fife Foxhounds. When his favourite horse had to be put down, Moffat, then 70, decided to stop riding.

Were his glory days then over? No, not quite. On a visit to the USA, he was taken on a joyride in an aircraft and he rediscovered his love of flying. He joined a flying club back in Scotland, and celebrated his 90th birthday by performing aerial aerobatics.

As for the 'Stringbag', it had lumbered on until the end of World War II, with almost 4,000 being built. The Swordfish outlived many designs supposed to replace her, and was responsible for sinking more enemy ships than any other type of aircraft in the war. A Swordfish sunk some of the first German targets during the war and some of the last – and were even fitted with radar and rockets towards the end – yes, on a biplane! Rockets tended to set canvas wings on fire, so metal undersides were finally fitted.

Moffat was annoyed when his co-written autobiography, *I Sank the Bismarck*, was published in 2009. He thought the title horribly misleading – he had never said such a thing. He said it was uncertain whose torpedo hit the fatal blow, and of course the *Bismarck* would not actually sink until she had absorbed that staggering amount of naval gunfire the next morning. Nevertheless, without an obsolete plane and men like Jock Moffat, the history of the fight to keep supplies flowing from the USA would have been very different.

* * * * *

THE BELL OF THE *HOOD* was recovered from the wreck with the backing of Microsoft founder Paul Allen, and installed in 2016 at the Royal Naval Museum, Portsmouth, with much ceremony – Princess Anne rang 'Eight Bells' on it (meaning noon), albeit quite gently. Many of the families of the 1,415 men who were lost thought this provided a focal point for them, and one of the three who survived had suggested this be done one day. Surprisingly many contacted newspapers to say they or their parents had served in the 'Mighty Hood' – because of course the crew would have changed over time. And one former ship's boy who once rang that bell even took the contrary view it should have remained with the men entombed in the wreck to watch over them, as during their service in the *Hood*.

9 ANIMALS AT WAR

1943: Winkie the RAF carrier pigeon receives the Dickin Medal for helping the rescue of downed aircrew during World War II. Winkie is held – appropriately – by a Wing Commander and is honoured to be receiving the decoration from Maria Dickin, the founder of the medal, known as 'the animal VC'

PIGEON MEMORIAL: There is a splendidly conceived and charming, if somewhat stained, war memorial for pigeons in Worthing, Sussex. It consists of inscribed boulders and a pond on a mound in Beach House Park and is perfectly serious. One stone reads: 'In memory of warrior birds who gave their lives on active service 1939–45 and for the use and pleasure of living birds.'

Hundreds of homing pigeons were dropped to the Resistance in Nazi-occupied Europe and many made it home. Others were with troops on secret missions. Naturally, the Germans tried to shoot down any pigeons they thought might be carrying messages. An astounding 31 of the 53 Dickin medals, the 'animal VCs', went to pigeons, so these brave creatures were not, when it came to war, doves.

THE CAT WITH TWO MEDALS: My all-time favourite of Britain's decorated animal war heroes – even though they include collie dogs that were parachuted into Italy and returned home to their farms after years of fighting the Nazis and still knew their masters, and even though it included stoical war horses of both wars – is a cat.

Able Seacat Simon, wearing one of his medals

A black and white moggie called Simon, hero of the Yangtze Incident of 1949, when a British ship HMS *Amethyst* was trapped up the Yangtze river by Communist forces during the civil war in China. Although Britain had not taken sides and the ship was on an evacuation mission, *Amethyst* was mercilessly shelled for days, causing death and injury, but then boldly escaped down river by night.

Simon, having been smuggled aboard by a rating after being found as a starving stray in Hong Kong, was a cheeky cat, curling up in the captain's cap to sleep. But when one shell hit the captain's cabin he was terribly wounded, and although he was treated and four pieces of shrapnel extracted from him, he was badly burned and not expected to live. He recovered however, and returned to duty (and was promoted to Able Seacat from Ordinary Seacat) and fought off the commie rats, as it were, in the potato store, occasionally bringing one of the dead enemy to a sailor in triumph.

He and the ship's company returned as heroes. Simon's citation when presented with the Amethyst campaign ribbon in Hong Kong on the way home read: 'Be it known that on April 26, 1949, though recovering from wounds, when *HMS Amethyst* was standing off by Rose Bay you did single-handedly and unarmed stalk down and destroy "Mao-Tse Tung" a rat guilty of raiding food supplies which were critically short.'

The Amethyst, and below, some of the crew with Able Seacat Simon

The officer saluted Simon, and the assembled crew gave three cheers. Simon the cat, with predictably stiff upper lip, said nothing...

As the story spread, a sailor had to be detailed to answer the burgeoning fan mail, which Able Seacat Simon declined to read.

Back in Britain, as the crew went ashore to be feted as heroes, Simon stayed aboard on guard, and can be seen briefly in archive

Pathe newsreel of the event. The cat was awarded the Dickin Medal, (and the Blue Cross Medal from another charity) but died before the planned presentation (by the Lord Mayor of London) as a result of complications from his war wounds.

He received obituaries in newspapers and magazines and the British wept when they read one, telling in sentimental Dickensian style of the moment of his death: '...the spirit of Simon slipped quietly away to sea.'

Thousands, including the entire crew of HMS *Amethyst*, attended his funeral. People were in tears as the little coffin came past, draped in a miniature Union Jack. His grave may be seen at the PDSA Ilford Animal Cemetery in East London (a rather fascinating place). It has a proper headstone remembering him, ending with the lines 'carved in granite for all time to read' as a journalist wrote:

THROUGHOUT THE YANGTZE INCIDENT
HIS BEHAVIOUR WAS OF THE HIGHEST ORDER.

He also has a memorial bush at the National Arboretum in Staffordshire. That and two medals and a campaign ribbon. Some cats get the cream. But not many cats get that.

Only in eccentric Britain...

THE REAL WAR HORSE: *War Horse* was a rather good children's novel about a First World War horse by British writer Michael Morpurgo, a truly excellent stage play using puppetry (poster, left) – it doesn't sound like it would work, but it really does – and a rather indifferent film by Steven Spielberg. All fiction, of course, but based on talking to villagers about their real stories, said Mr Morpurgo.

But once, working on a national newspaper, I was

lucky enough to come across the real thing in the form of a letter from an elderly Welshman who could recall the experience. Such moments in journalism are a privilege, I always feel. He wrote to the newspaper:

WHEN World War I began, I was a boy, living on a farm in Monmouthshire. All farms were told by the War Office that horses were needed in France to move heavy guns and wagons at the Front (this referred to an earlier letter to the paper).

I remember how devastated I and my family were to see Army vets on our White Hall Farm selecting from among our mighty ploughing horses.

They took Bowler, my horse — the biggest and best, an enormous Samson of horses, a gentle giant — and another of our eight heavy horses called Elgar.

Bowler and Elgar were given Army numbers, carved on one of their hooves, before being led into a huge closed lorry. My father and mother were distraught and I could not stop crying. Our hearts were broken. We never saw Elgar again: he died on the Somme and the number on his hoof was sent back to the farm.

The war ended when I was 17. One afternoon, as I arrived home from Newport Art School, my mother said casually: 'Stan, go and see what's down in the field.' Imagine my joy — there was Bowler, quietly grazing alongside Leicester, our huge mare. They rubbed their heads and necks together, remembering their past relationship before the war.

I leapt up and down, whooping with excitement. I ran towards Bowler and threw my arms around his enormous neck. He knew me and whinnied with recognition, nuzzling his nose to my face. I was in heaven, and my father, who worshipped horses, was delighted.

We often wondered what story Bowler could have told of his life on the Western Front if he'd had the power of speech.

He lived to be nearly 30 years old. I'll be 102 in December, and I'll never forget the image of that marvellous great horse, grazing and working happily in the fields.

STANLEY C. LEWIS MBE, Oldham, Lancs.

This lovely letter was received in 2007. Sadly, Stanley died in 2009, aged 103. He was a great artist and illustrator of his wife Min's books.

She wrote a weekly children's story for the *South Wales Evening Post* in the 1940s and 50s, which were much loved locally. Later, she wrote a book about Dylan Thomas. Stanley died shortly before his first ever exhibition, which was a great success, but his and her works can easily be found online.

BAT BOMBS: The U.S. military developed a strange programme in World War II to drop bat bombs over Japan. Each bomb would contain thousands of live bats which would be released when it opened close to the ground. The bats would carry tiny incendiary bombs strapped to their legs and, come daybreak, would roost in nooks and crannies of the paper and wood houses of the Japanese cities. It was calculated this could be ten times more effective than just dropping incendiaries at random, and one of the experts predicted: 'Japan can be devastated, with very little loss of life'. (Bat life excepted, of course).

The plan was coming along nicely when one of the canisters burst open at a U.S. air base in New Mexico. The creatures fled to roost in dark places around the base – including fuel tanks and ammunition stores. Boom! This had other serious consequences – the setback delayed the plan long enough for the parallel atomic bomb programme to become the front-runner.

BALLOONATICS: An equally batty Japanese plan, while we are on the subject, was to take advantage of the prevailing jetstream wind across the Pacific by launching balloons with small explosives attached and letting them drift across to America where they would descend and explode, causing mayhem. No need for long-range bomber aircraft, it would seem. And America would be crippled. The problem was that they were most likely to land in the ocean, or merely annoy an Alaskan bear, a Canadian moose or a Mexican mule rather than actually damage the American war machine. They were made of paper pasted together in halls by schoolchildren.

Oddly it worked – a little bit. Some 10,000 were sent off and of these 285 were known to have exploded in the USA. Dreams of starting forest fires were thwarted by heavy rain. The only serious incident was when the family of an Oregon churchman picnicking in the woods found one of the objects. When a child tugged at the strings, all were killed. Tragic – particularly if you think of it as children killing children – but not a war-winning offensive.

An unlikely, lethal ally. Picture: Molly Ebersold, St Augustine Alligator Farm

THE DAY A REGIMENT OF CROCS JOINED THE ALLIES: A bizarre battle where a most effective unit was a regiment of crocodiles took place during World War II, and it is a macabre tale. It was during *Operation Matador*, the British-Indian invasion of Ramree Island, off

Burma, in early 1945. It had been taken by the Japanese in 1942 as they swept across Asia towards India. Now it was urgently needed as an air base to help the attack on Japanese forces in Southern Burma.

The peaceful early morning of January 21, 1945, was shattered when the battleship *HMS Queen Elizabeth's* main guns opened up with 69 rounds of huge 15-inch shells (she was a ship that fought right through the First and Second World Wars). A fleet of smaller warships joined in while beaches were also bombed and strafed by a stream of RAF aircraft, mainly the American-built Mitchells, Thunderbolts and Liberators. Over the several days of action on the island, a staggering 23,000 naval shells of various calibres were fired towards Japanese positions.

The invasion went well (British troops landing there, left) to start with but when cornered, the Japanese army fought stubbornly, surrender not being an option. A unit cornered in Ramree town decided to break out across the island to try to connect with another pocket of Japanese resistance.

This involved crossing a mangrove swamp by night. These are hellish places for humans to try to traverse at the best of times. The mud swallows you whole and drowns you. The tree roots are a dense barrier, needing hacking away, and disease and pests swarm around.

Worst of these is the salt-water crocodile. These, the largest reptiles in the world, grow to 20ft long and over a ton in weight, yet can be surprisingly quick and vicious when hungry. It can beat any challenger, such as sharks, and of course humans. Their sharp, peg-like teeth are designed to seize and tightly grip prey, but not designed to chop up flesh. Small prey are swallowed whole, but larger animals

– including humans – are forcibly dragged into deep water and drowned and crushed. Large prey is torn into manageable pieces by 'death rolling' (the spinning of the crocodile to twist off hunks of flesh) or by sudden jerks of the head. It's horrible to witness.

During the night the British troops were startled to hear blood-curdling screams and rifle shots from the Japanese. Who was attacking them so effectively?

British naturalist Bruce Stanley Wright, who was a soldier in the battle, says the large population of saltwater crocodiles native to the mangrove swamps attacked the Japanese and ate many soldiers. Wright wrote in *Wildlife Sketches Near and Far*:

> **That night [of the 19 February 1945] was the most horrible that any member of the M. L. [motor launch] crews ever experienced. The scattered rifle shots in the pitch black swamp punctured by the screams of wounded men crushed in the jaws of huge reptiles, and the blurred worrying sound of spinning crocodiles made a cacophony of hell that has rarely been duplicated on earth. At dawn the vultures arrived to clean up what the crocodiles had left.... Of about one thousand Japanese soldiers that entered the swamps of Ramree, only about twenty were found alive.**

Since then, the precise numbers given in this account have been subject to some doubt. Certainly a number of Japanese made it back to the mainland in a fleet of small boats (although many of these were sunk by the British). But Wright was there, and was a naturalist too. A massacre by reptile of those Japanese struggling in the mud, perhaps already wounded, certainly took place – and Imperial Japanese Army troops were usefully removed by this most unlikely ally. If you were waiting to combat the Japanese – soldiers of the Wiltshire Regiment are pictured, left, making a meal outside a Ramree temple – then any ally is welcome. Even one that makes a meal of it.

WORLD'S MOST UNLIKLY COLONEL: The Colonel-in-Chief of the elite Norwegian army unit Hans Majestet Kongens Garde – which translates rather obviously to His Majesty the King's Guard – is, rather oddly, a resident of Scotland and never leaves Edinburgh. Even more oddly he – I think it's a he – is a penguin. A king penguin, appropriately, but a perfectly proper penguin all the same, called Nils Olav.

The link between Norway and Scotland goes back a long way – to before Macbeth, when some of the northern isles belonged to Norway – but the involvement of penguins in this odd story started with the presentation of a penguin to Edinburgh Zoo by the Norwegians in 1913, only two years after the Norwegians proved they were superior explorers by reaching the South Pole just before Scott and his ill-fated but heroic British team got there.

That rivalry aside, Edinburgh Zoo gradually became famous for its penguin collection. Roll on to the 1960s, when part of the above-mentioned HMKG attended the Edinburgh Military Tattoo to perform drills, etc, as part of that huge annual celebration of things martial in front of Edinburgh Castle.

During their stay in the Scottish capital, HMKG lieutenant Nils Egelien became fascinated by Edinburgh Zoo's penguin colony. When the Guards returned in 1972, he arranged for the unit to adopt a penguin, which (or who) was named Nils Olav in honour of Lt Nils Egelien, and the King of Norway, Olav V.

Nils Olav started off within the Norwegian army as *visekorporal*, (lance corporal) and each time the HMKG return to Edinburgh he is given a promotion (although I bet he'd prefer a nice raw herring). So in 1982 he became a corporal, and was promoted to sergeant in 1987, gaining stripes on his flipper, as it were. Nils Olav was promoted again in 1993 to the rank of RSM and in August 2005, he was appointed as Colonel-in-Chief. Could his giddy army career and honours go any further?

Colonel Nils Olav inspects his troops. Picture: Marks Owens, MoD

Yes. On August 15, 2008 Colonel in-Chief Nils Olav's proudest moment yet came when he was knighted by command of King Olav V. Colonel Nils Olav was described as the first penguin to receive such an honour in the Norwegian Army. Frankly, we're not surprised. Probably first in the flipping world, Nils Olav!

Anyway, the knighting was conducted with all undue ceremony and seriousness, and if it is an extended joke, no one mentioned that. Or the fact the Nils Olav may have been replaced from time to time – he is clearly going to be eternal.

A parade of the 130 guardsmen at the zoo heard a citation from the King read out, which described Nils as a penguin 'in every way qualified to receive the honour and dignity of knighthood', witnessed by several hundred bemused or amused Scots.

A bronze statue of the Colonel was unveiled at Edinburgh (pictured below), and a similar one at the HMKG base at Huseby, a former farmhouse near Oslo.

Nor is the HMKG some kind of ceremonial only unit. They have a light infantry and urban warfare role as well as guarding the royal palace (this kingdom under its current borders goes back only to 1905, by the way, so the unit isn't that old). In World War II during the German invasion of Norway they fought ferociously in three battles against the overwhelming forces, thus enabling the Royal Family to escape to Britain and lead their countrymen's fight against the Nazis from there.

They fought so ferociously in their black battle dress that they German troops called them *die schwarzen Teufel* or 'the black devils', a nickname the unit retains with some pride.

In August 2016, the Colonel was promoted yet again, to Brigadier, in a ceremony attended by over 50 members of the HMKG. I think they just love doing it – but what next? Field Marshall Nils Olav? I still think he'd prefer a nice herring. He remains Colonel-in-Chief, mind.

Colonel Sir Nils Olav may be little more than a mascot, and one living in the wrong country too. But he is regarded fondly by the troops, is politically neutral – he has a left and a right wing equally – and when they are inspected by him, they must feel they are truly up before the beak.

ANIMALS AT WAR

THE BEAR THAT WENT TO WAR: One of the Free Polish army's most formidable recruits – he stood at 8ft tall, had the strength of three men, could pass ammunition at a prodigious rate and could tear a man apart – was Wojtek the bear (above). But he was officially a proper soldier, with an army number, a rank and paybook. He would swig a beer and scrounge a cigarette like any other soldier, and was hugely popular with his comrades.

His war story started when in early 1942 the newly formed Polish 'Anders Army' left the USSR, heading south for Iran, along with thousands of Polish civilians. These were largely people who had been deported to gulags – slave labour camps – under Stalin's tyrannical version of communism after Poland was ruthlessly split in half by the Germans and the Russians in 1939, causing the start of World War II, from which conflict Russia stood aside to start with. Now, with Hitler's surprise attack on the Soviet Union, the Polish soldiers were suddenly useful again.

The army was led by General Wladyslaw Anders. It, and the Polish squadron of the RAF, are one of the bright sparks in the appalling suffering Poland had to endure in World War II.

On their way to Teheran, one Polish unit stopped for a rest in the railway town of Hamadan, where a young woman among the civilian Polish refugees with them – an eighteen-year-old, Irena Bokiewicz – was very taken with a bear cub that had been found by a young Iranian boy after its parents were shot by hunters.

As a cub: Wojtek the army recruit grew ... and grew

So Lieutenant Anatol Tarnowiecki bought the young bear, who spent the next three months in the Polish refugee camp near Teheran, under the care of Irena, who fed it condensed milk through an old vodka bottle, graduating to fruit and honey.

As the bear grew, it clearly would become too much for her to handle, so it was given to the Polish Army's 2nd Transport Company, which later became the 22nd Artillery Supply Company, and he was dubbed Wojtek by the soldiers. The name is a diminutive of a name meaning 'happy warrior'.

He enjoyed smoking, or eating cigarettes, liked to swig beer with his comrades, and was taught to salute when passing an officer.

The 22nd Company was intended to come under British command, in the Western Europe battle against Hitler. It and the bear moved to Iraq, then Syria, Palestine and Egypt.

The British wouldn't allow a non-soldier onto the ship taking the 22nd to fight in Italy as part of the 8th Army, so Wojtek was officially drafted into the Polish Army as a private in the 22nd Artillery Supply Company.

Bet they didn't get much stolen from their truck! Note emblem on the door

As an enlisted soldier of the company, Wojtek had his own paybook, rank and serial number, and lived with the other men in tents, travelling in a crate on a truck.

The toughest nut for the Allies to crack in the Italian campaign was the Battle of Monte Cassino. There was a hugely costly series of battles to try to take an impregnable German position.

The British, Indians, Canadians, Americans and French had all failed with terrible casualties. In the fourth and final battle, the Poles succeeded – and raised a Polish flag on Monte Cassino, again at huge cost in terms of casualties. The road to Rome was open.

One of those helping the Polish effort was ammunition carrier Wojtek. According to his comrades, he never dropped a single crate. In recognition of the bear's efforts and popularity, the unit adopted the emblem of a bear carrying an artillery shell.

At the end of the war, the Polish soldiers ended up in Scotland. The bear went to live in Edinburgh Zoo. He lived to 21, in 1963.

There are statues or memorials to Wojtek in Edinburgh's Princes Street Gardens, in Krakow, Poland (top), in Grimsby, in Canada, and in London (two separate ones). There were TV appearances on the BBC children's programme *Blue Peter*, there was TV film about him called *Wojtek – The Bear That Went to War* and a music video and a bus named after him too. Not bad for a lost Syrian brown bear.

But he never forgot his friends. In his later years, when he was at Edinburgh Zoo, he would perk up no end when he heard the Polish voices of ex-soldiers who had settled in Scotland coming to visit their old chum .... maybe because they tossed him cigarettes. As there were no lighters in his enclosure, he'd eat them.

Worth a visit: Wojtek's memorial in Edinburgh. The frieze tells his life story

ANIMALS AT WAR

THE RED ARMY'S EXPLODING DOGS: Dog lovers will not enjoy reading this section and maybe should move on. The Soviets in World War II trained dogs carrying explosive backpacks to run under German tanks where – it was hoped – the mines in the canvas pouches would blow up, destroying the tank and, of course, the dog.

Originally, it had been hoped that the dogs could run under whatever was the target, drop the charges by pulling a pin out with its teeth, and then retreat while a timer set the thing off. This proved impossible, so the second more lethal – to the dog – plan was devised.

The concept had been approved by Soviet military chiefs as early as 1924, and in the 1930s various dog training schools were set up, using circus trainers, vets or whoever could be found, and their recruits, mostly what we call German shepherds.

An anti-tank dog in training. Note the stick detonator on its backpack

Dogs were trained by being kept very hungry and their food was placed under tanks. The tanks were initially standing still, then they had their engines running, which was in theory further combined with sporadic gunfire and other battle-related distractions, then the tanks were moving.

Each dog was fitted with a 25lb mine. A safety pin was removed right before an attack, and then a wooden lever extended out of the pouch to about 9 inches high. When the dog dived under the tank, the lever struck the bottom of the tank and detonated the charge. As the underside was the most vulnerable area of the panzers, it was hoped the explosion would cripple or destroy the tanks.

On parade: A Soviet dog training school in 1931

The first Soviet anti-tank dogs arrived at the front line in autumn 1941 and included 30 dogs. There were problems from the start. In order to save fuel and ammunition, most of the dogs had been trained on tanks which stood still and did not fire their guns. In the field, the dogs refused to dive under moving tanks, no matter how hungry they were for the supposed food treats under there. Some dogs ran near the tanks, waiting for them to stop but were shot in the process. Gunfire from the tanks scared away many of the dogs. They would run back to the trenches and often detonated the charge upon jumping in, killing Soviet soldiers. To prevent that, the returning dogs had to be shot, often by their own handlers, who resented having to do this.

So of the first 30, only four exploded near German tanks. Six fled back to the Russian trenches and exploded, killing and injuring their own soldiers. Three dogs were shot by German troops and taken away to be examined. A German propaganda campaign claimed that the cowardly Soviet soldiers refuse to fight and send dogs instead.

Another serious training mistake was revealed later; the Soviets used diesel-fuelled tanks to train the dogs, but the German tanks often had petrol engines. As the dogs rely far more on their sense of smell than other senses, they sought out familiar Red Army tanks instead of strange-smelling Nazi ones, with poor results.

Diabolical device: The stick was supposed to trigger explosives under a tank

The results of using anti-tank dogs remain unclear, given the propaganda on both sides. There are odd incidences where a few tanks were stopped, reportedly, but in a conflict of many thousands of tanks, this would not have made a difference. During the huge battle of Kursk, when German tanks broke through near Tamarovka, Bykovo, it is claimed that 16 dogs knocked out 12 German tanks.

They were certainly hard to hit when running across a battlefield, being low targets. One result of the development was that every German soldier received orders to shoot any dog in combat areas. The U.S. and Japan both tried training dogs for similar missions but gave up.

The morality of it all is, of course, hard to take in modern times. You have to put it in the desperate context of humans being murdered for little reason right, left and centre. Of people being sent to die in suicide missions – even Soviet soldiers running unarmed against the Germans with the hope of picking up a weapon from a felled comrade before they themselves were hit.

One almost unbelievable plan was proposed by William A. Prestre, a Swiss man living in New Mexico, and was taken seriously. He proposed using landing craft filled with thousands of explosive-carrying dogs trained to approach Japanese forces in beach invasions across the Pacific theatre. They would be followed by landing craft carrying soldiers as the Japanese scattered in confusion under the exploding dogs onslaught.

Mr Prestre managed to get Army funding to lease an island in the Mississippi to practise on, but it was never really going to work. For one thing, as the Japanese didn't generally surrender alive, it was hard to get anyone to play their role in training. Some Japanese-American soldiers were called in, and at least trained the dogs to almost lick them to death, but the thing was abandoned as unworkable. These dogs of war never went into action.

Later military forces have used dogs in explosives detection and mine clearance work, at which they are much more successful, and have saved countless lives. Airports use them to check for drugs and explosives. But not to blow themselves up!

A modern Russian mine and explosive detector dog looks rather endearing

THE HEROIC REINDEER BATTALION: In childhood legend, Santa Claus uses reindeer for haulage in very, very difficult circumstances. In World War II they were used for exactly that too, being co-opted in large numbers to help the Soviet campaign against the Germans, and at times against Finland, in North Norway. The Finnish army also used reindeer.

The fighting was so far north – in the Arctic Circle – that conventional military vehicles, such as jeeps, armoured cars, trucks or tanks, were of little use – there were hardly any roads anyway, and the few existing ones were damaged by the retreating Germans, with bridges blown to delay the Russian advance, or roads deliberately blocked with fallen trees and landslides. The winter conditions were so appalling – constant darkness and well below freezing – that no other army has conducted a successful offensive in such circumstances. The main obstacle is logistics. Men and horses die of cold, diesel fuel solidifies, even if you can find a road (or more likely a river) to drive along.

All camouflaged in white: Finnish ski troops with reindeer

But a reindeer can survive the cold and pull up to 110lb on a sledge – making them very effective for transport. When a team of reindeer pull a sledge, they can haul 650lb, allowing the army to move mortars, even artillery in pieces and ammunition through the snow. They could maintain this effort for 20 miles over eight hours.

The first Red Army reindeer transport groups were assembled in 1941 when the Soviets established their Karelian front. The reindeer started with only 1,015 reindeer and around 80 herders, but rapidly grew to 11,015 reindeer, 15 dogs, and 1,477 men divided into five battalions of the 14th Army. The Saami tribes in the Kola Peninsula, who were expert reindeer handlers, were used to recruit from – willingly or not – but there were other groups too.

Unperturbed: Reindeer are oddly able to cope with the din of warfare

To get to the training area before the offensive, most of them had to travel more than 1,200 miles by foot and train. The reindeer, not surprisingly, were not happy at being confined in the trains, becoming sick and hungry. They were forced to stand for three to four days and had no food. When they arrived for training, they were in a weakened state, and so hungry that some escaped to find food and were sometimes shot.

There was also serious friction between the indigenous herders who were frustrated with the Soviet soldiers, many of whom scorned the new units as primitive, and abused them. To the reindeer men, the Soviet soldiers appeared ignorant and lacking the skills of Arctic life, let alone warfare.

The Russians decided to break the reindeer corps up into small groups, ordering them not to communicate with the others. They were told they would be shot if they disobeyed or tried to desert. Luckily a few more enlightened Russian officers took an interest in the Saami people and tried to learn some of their language, earning some respect from them.

During the Petsamo-Kirkenes offensive (that is from a province of Finland to a town in the far north-east tip of Norway), German forces were withdrawing in the face of the advancing Red Army. But they were hampered by Hitler's order that they should leave no equipment whatsoever – difficult in Arctic conditions – and did their best to cause delay by destroying bridges and blocking roads in their wake. The Soviets, in turn, would try to outflank them with amphibious landings, while blocking off certain roads and forcing the Germans in various directions.

Haulage: Finnish troops used the reindeers' strength in pulling supplies

One major advantage for the Russians, however, were the reindeer. They were able to move ammunition and carry essential food, wounded soldiers, and vital equipment. They could even swim to and from vessels that were not able to reach the ice-locked shores. Without their reindeer battalions, the Soviet troops might never have come close to catching up with the retreating German forces.

The reindeer men were proud of the reindeer, and of their role in the offensive. The reindeer were far superior to Russian horses and armoured cars, and were often strangely unperturbed by the sounds of exploding shells. The herders themselves were a great asset, and even as the overall campaign proved largely unsuccessful in capturing many fleeing German soldiers, they proved their worth time and time again by keeping the pressure up.

And why were the Finns at times fighting the Soviets – in effect on the same side as the Germans? This was because Russia had made the mistake of attacking Finland in 1939, after the Molotov–Ribbentrop Pact between Stalin's Soviet Union and Nazi Germany had carved up Eastern Europe into 'spheres of influence' – they had both seized half of Poland, for example. The Soviets waltzed into the Baltic states – Latvia, Estonia and Lithuania, who had to endure half a century of subjugation first by the Soviets, then the Nazis, then the Soviets before regaining their freedom.

The Winter War: Finnish soldiers in camouflage man a heavy machine-gun

But moving into Finland wasn't quite such a pleasant dance. The Red Army, recently purged of all its professional officers by Stalin, who replaced them with political commissars, was relatively poor at fighting against the expert Arctic warfare troops of the Finns, who were of course fighting to defend their homeland.

This had two important effects. First, the world and particularly the Germans, watched the Red Army's humiliation with fascination. Clearly, Hitler thought attacking the Soviet Union a good bet against such useless opposition. So he did, within two years.

Second, Stalin realised his mistake and began reinstating a professional officer class of trained soldiers, just in time to prove Hitler totally wrong about *Operation Barbarossa* being an easy walkover. Hitler's 'good bet' would prove his worst disaster.

When the fighting in the icy north was over, the demobilised reindeer herders refused to put their animals on the trains again. Some reindeer, sledges and equipment were left at the Pasvik River border of Norway and Russia.

They believed that trains would kill their animals, and that boats were dangerous, so they did what they knew best – they set out on foot around the White Sea, arriving in their home territory eight months later. The reindeer they left behind thrived and mixed with the local reindeer populations. As a result, the reindeer of the Pasvik River Valley are still the strongest in Norway. And they – or rather their ancestors – have earned some battle honours too.

ACTING THE GOAT: Wales rugby fans, and that is pretty well all of Wales, love to see the regimental goat mascot in his glorious full regalia – silver-tipped horns, smart regimental badge on the forehead, full uniform with embroidered insignia on his back – leading the military band out at the Cardiff stadium for international matches.

But the Welsh military goats have not always been so well-behaved. It's a story involving scandal – eating a princess's flowers, munching royal fingers, pooing on parade, over-sexed recruits, the Shah of Iran and tranquillised nannies.

It all goes back to the Battle of Bunker Hill, a costly British victory during the American War of Independence. A wild goat walked on to the battlefield and led the Welsh colours forward.

The regiment's goats became royal in the 19th century. A herd of cashmere goats (by the way that means the same as Kashmir in India, where they came from) were given by the Shah of Persia to Queen Victoria on her accession to the throne in 1837. These woolly jumpers had to be put somewhere, so were parked on Llandudno's Great Orme (a picturesque hill behind the North Wales resort) and whether or not they ever made any such garment for the young queen to wear – or a pashmina shawl for the more elderly one – is not recorded. But since 1844, the Crown has presented the Royal Welch Fusiliers – an ancestor regiment of the Royal Welsh – with goats from this herd for mascots.

By the time of the First World War, the regiment's goat mascot was clearly named, and part of a series – Taffy IV of the 2nd Battalion, Welsh Regiment. Taffy (it's a nickname for Welshmen, derived from the River Taff that runs through Cardiff) embarked for the war on 13 August 1914 and took part in the Retreat from Mons, the First Battle of Ypres and the Battles of Festubert and Givenchy, before dying on 20 January 1915. Taffy (pictured) was awarded the 1914 Star, British War Medal and the Victory Medal (posthumously, obviously).

By 2001 the dozen original goats had become 250, given the things old goats get up to, and were wandering into some Llandudnoan (if that's the word) gardens, munching people's prize leeks. A cull was suggested, and although local goat curry fans may have been sharpening their knives, in the end the local council settled for rehoming (about

85 were moved to pastures new) and marksmen firing tranquilliser darts into nannies, who were then fitted with contraceptive implants. Some ended up in zoos such as Whipsnade.

Billy was presented to the regiment by the Queen in 2001, got his Army number 25232301, and his full-time handler carried the title of Goat Major. His job was to lead parades – both in the streets and parade grounds, and on those sporting occasions.

His disgrace and demotion came on 16 June 2006, when he was supposed to lead a parade held to celebrate the Queen's birthday, during Billy's first overseas posting, at the Episkopi base in Cyprus.

Billy (pictured with a young admirer on a different occasion) acted the goat big time. He refused to keep in line despite being ordered to march nicely, he refused to obey. He failed to keep in step, and tried to headbutt a drummer. The goat major – a young fusilier, Dai Davies – was unable to keep him under control. His bowels may not have been totally under control at all times (the goat's bowels, not the goat major's). This was deeply embarrassing for the regiment in front of the invited ambassadors of Spain, the Netherlands and Sweden and the Argentine commander of United Nations' forces on Cyprus. This was not something to be handled with kid gloves.

Billy was charged with 'unacceptable behaviour', 'lack of decorum' and 'disobeying a direct order', and had to appear before his commanding officer, Lieutenant-Colonel Huw James. He said nothing in his defence, and was demoted to fusilier. This meant that other fusiliers in the regiment no longer had to stand to attention when Billy walked past, as they had to when he was a lance corporal.

Various animal rights groups, including a bunch of Canadian goat fanciers, protested to the British Army, arguing that Billy was merely 'acting the goat', and should be reinstated. Three months later, on 20 September at the same parade ground, Billy regained his rank during the Alma Day parade, from the colonel of the Royal Welsh Regiment, Brigadier Roderick Porter.

Captain Simon Clarke said: 'Billy performed exceptionally well, he has had all summer to reflect on his behaviour at the Queen's birthday and clearly earned the rank he deserves.'

As a result of regaining his rank, Billy also regained his membership of the corporals' mess. And if you want a mess ...

Billy is not the first regimental goat to get into trouble, according to some sources. There was, they say, a scandal of certain stud services offered by the regiment's serving goat major to a Wrexham goat breeder – the service being offered by the goat, obviously. The goat major, who had been threatened with the serious charge of *lese majeste* was put on a charge of 'disrespect to an officer' and despite arguing that he did it out of compassion to the goat's needs, reduced in rank.

The Queen with a famously charming old goat (left): Billy on parade in Swansea

Other fusilier goats have tried to snatch a princess's posy of flowers or bitten Prince Philip's hand while being petted. Another royal fusilier goat butted a colonel while he was stooped over fixing his uniform's trouser-strap. The incident – when rank and file didn't entirely manage to keep straight faces – was described as a 'disgraceful act of insubordination'.

Billy retired on 20 May 2009, following eight years of most distinguished service. On the day, Fusiliers lined the route from his pen to the trailer as he left the camp for the last time, in full ceremonial dress that included the silver headdress which was a gift from the Queen. Billy was taken to Whipsnade Zoo

In order to replace Billy, 30 members of 1st Battalion climbed the Great Orme in a dawn assault on 15 June 2009, hoping to catch the feral goats in a docile state by a deft pincer movement. The squad included the commanding officer, the goat major and two vets. An Army spokesman said: 'We are looking for a goat which is calm under pressure and a team player.' Yeah, right, one might say.

It's not clear whether any more nannies were tranquillised on that occasion, although most of the goats evaded the pincer movement attack with little difficulty. But a five-month-old was chosen, and assigned army number 25142301.

The new goat was also to be called William Windsor, Billy for short, with the rank of fusilier while being trained. Promotion later is always possible. He would receive a ration of two cigarettes per day, which he eats and perk him up no end, Army sources said, but would not be permitted his daily pint of Guinness until he is older. As long as he doesn't act the goat too much.

RAVEN NONSENSE: The Ravens in the Tower of London – who legend says will ensure the fall of England if they ever leave – have had similar discipline problems to the Army goats (previous item). They all have names, by the way, and their clipped wings (a painless shortening of feather) means they cannot just fly away.

It was Charles II, according to the stories, who first insisted that the ravens of the Tower should be protected. His astronomer, John Flamsteed, complained that the ravens impeded the business of his observatory in the White Tower and suggested they be evicted to Greenwich, where Charles was considering building a new palace. Having been told that the ravens at the Tower were essential for the survival of his kingdom – and he'd only just got it back after Roundhead republicans seized power and chopped his father's head off – he sent the astronomers to Greenwich instead. So the ravens are responsible for our running the world on Greenwich Mean Time and all maps being based on the Greenwich Meridian.

In more recent times, despite being pampered on a luxury diet, some have misbehaved. Raven George lost his appointment to the Crown, and was retired to Wales for attacking and destroying TV aerials. A special decree was issued about the incident:

On Saturday 13th September 1986, Raven George, enlisted 1975, was posted to the Welsh Mountain Zoo. Conduct unsatisfactory, service therefore no longer required.

In 1981, Grog the raven decided to leave the surroundings of the Tower for those of an East End pub, despite 21 years of faithful service to the Crown, and was dismissed for going AWOL. In 1996, two more ravens were dismissed from the Tower for 'conduct unbecoming Tower residents', whatever that might be. Caw blimey!

A similar legend attaches to the apes of Gibraltar. The British will leave if the apes do, says the story. Well they aren't apes, they are monkeys. And though they were until recently looked after by the Army, now the Gibraltar Ornithological and Natural History Society cares for them. Perhaps to Spanish disappointment, they are thriving, with around 300 at the last count. Just mind your ice-cream!

Old pals having a good old chat: Ravens Jubilee (left) and Munin at the Tower

10 NUTTY OR NAUGHTY NAUTICALS

THE RUSSIAN FLEET IS COMING! In October 2016 the British media were somewhat miffed to see a large Russian battle fleet approach, coming down the North Sea and through the English Channel – though it is an international waterway, after all – to help wage war in Syria.

Not as miffed as when the Russians made exactly the same manoeuvre – getting their Baltic fleet round the world to wage war – in the same week of 1904. Guns were fired, blood was shed, and the spectacular bungling by the Russians nearly ended in war with Britain.

The Russian fleet mistook British trawlers in the Dogger Bank area of the North Sea for Imperial Japanese Navy torpedo boats. They opened fire on them, causing the deaths of three British fishermen. As the firing got going, the Russian ships fired on each other, killing one crew member and a Russian Orthodox chaplain.

One Russian battleship, the *Oryol*, fired 500 shells without hitting anything. On another Russian ship, some crew were ordered to lie on the deck in life jackets because of the impending Japanese torpedoes. Other sailors were ordered to get cutlasses from the armoury and be ready to repel Japanese boarders. After some hours of firing on 48 defenceless fishing boats, all illuminated clearly by the Russian ships' searchlights, and waving swords – which would have been useless – at Japanese ships that were in fact thousands of miles away, the Russians steamed on.

The British were understandably furious. The fishermen had had their nets down and no way of escaping the onslaught. The press raged at the 'Russian pirates'. The Times newspaper, nicknamed 'the Thunderer', ran an editorial saying:

It is almost inconceivable that any men calling themselves seamen, however frightened they might be, could spend twenty minutes bombarding a fleet of fishing boats without discovering the nature of their target.

The Royal Navy, then the largest in the world, ordered 28 battleships to make steam and prepare to go to sea for action. Imagine having 28 capital ships to spare at any time! Britain doesn't have that number of major warships in the entire Navy now.

A cruiser squadron was ordered to tail the Russians down through the Bay of Biscay. The Russians, at last suspecting there might be a teeny-weeny problem, stopped in Spain and put some officers ashore that they said were responsible, to defuse the outrage. An international inquiry was agreed.

Not that they learned their lesson. One of their warships that had become separated now fired over 300 shells 'at three Japanese warships'. These turned out to be a Swedish freighter, a German trawler and a French schooner. Luckily the Russian gunnery was so appalling that nothing was hit. But how do you mistake a sailing vessel for a warship?

The Russian fleet sailed on making trouble. They anchored where they shouldn't have done at Tangiers, Morocco, and when they left pulled up and broke the city's telegraph cable to Europe, cutting them off for a week or so.

The logical, quickest and safest route to the Far East was through the Suez Canal, but the infuriated British (who then owned it) were having none of it and withheld permission to transit the waterway. Progress was slow because the only people who would refuel them (with vast amounts of coal) were the German Navy – the huge British stocks at points all round the world were not made available.

Meanwhile an International Commission of Inquiry met in Paris to examine whether the Russians had been in the wrong at the Dogger Bank Incident. Hull fishermen, wearing bowler hats and Sunday best suits, gave evidence. Astonishingly, the inquiry exonerated the Russians fleet and admiral of any blame. The Russians nevertheless paid voluntary compensation to the fishermen and their families. A monument in Hull (pictured) was soon to be erected and stands today. Its inscription reads:

Erected by public subscription to the memory of George Henry Smith (skipper) and William Richard Legget (third hand), of the steam-trawler CRANE, who lost their lives through the action of the Russian Baltic Fleet in the North Sea, 22 October 1904, and Walter Whelpton, skipper of the trawler MINO, who died through shock, May 1905.

Eventually the Russian Baltic Fleet got to the Sea of Japan, met the Imperial Japanese Navy at the Battle of Tsushima on May 27/28 1905 and the Russians were rapidly sunk, or captured. The besieged city they had been sent to relieve, Port Arthur, had long since been lost.

The Japanese, who were great admirers and indeed allies of Britain's Royal Navy, achieved Nelson's tactic at Trafalgar – crossing the T – twice. This means your ships can fire broadsides with all weapons while the Russians could use only forward turrets. The Russian fleet had suffered such fouling (weed and barnacles growing on their hulls) on their long voyage round the world (they were stuck in a bay in what is now Vietnam for weeks) that they were slow, and their guns were out-ranged by the Japanese. The coal they had managed to scrape together from various sources was poor, slowing them further.

If you think this exaggerates the Japanese emulation of Nelson, consider what order was issued when the two fleets sighted each other and the Z flag was hoisted (they used the international signalling system, and by the way, didn't the Imperial Japanese Navy's red and white ensign, pictured, seem to echo the Royal Navy's flag of the same colours?). This was the order:

The Empire's fate depends on the result of this battle, let every man do his utmost duty.

Sound familiar at all?

The results and lessons of all this were various and more far-reaching than might be at first thought.

1 The Dogger Bank incident showed that costly confusion and mistakes could arise in a North Sea naval engagement – and this certainly soon came true at the Battle of Jutland in World War I.

2 The Russian Romanov dynasty was humiliated and thus began a slow slide to Red Revolution in that world war.

3 The British rapidly understood that the faster Japanese ships with longer-ranged guns could pick off the Russians as ease, and soon therefore started furiously building a deadlier new class of battleship, the Dreadnoughts.

4 It was also the beginning of the end of the idea of white racial superiority – a 19th century racist notion that European nations would always beat Asian ones. This was the start of unravelling this big humiliation, as they might have seen it. The Asian was as good as anyone else, but it would take the West a while to understand that. See next item:

5 The Japanese learned that the adoption of the latest technology and aggressive military action would get them what they wanted. A fact that the world would find out to their cost less than 40 years later. One young Japanese officer wounded by Russian gunfire at the Battle of Tsushima was called Isoroku Yamamoto. Yes, the brilliant commander who would one day lead the Japanese fleet on their surprise attack on Pearl Harbor. Whatever you think of that sneak attack, it changed history.

AFRICAN QUEEN WAR: You may well have heard of *The African Queen*, a great 1951 film starring Humphrey Bogart and Katharine Hepburn. Your author has certainly heard of it – people in South-West London can hear the screeches of the playful green parakeets, which were released from Isleworth studios, where it was shot, at the end of the filming – or rather, their descendants.

As it was an early colour movie, the brightly coloured birds were essential props to make Middlesex seem African.

The unlikely plot is based on a book by *Hornblower* author C.S. Forester and has these two stars reluctantly getting together on a steam launch of that name and attacking a German steamer on a lake way up-river in Africa during

World War I, after many misadventures. The comedy comes in that the starchy, prim British missionary woman Hepburn and the slobby, drunken Yank captain Bogart fight each other more than they do the Germans. But then something wonderful happens…

An unlikely yarn. But not quite as unlikely as the extraordinary real story behind all this.

Lake Tanganyika (below) is staggeringly big – the second largest freshwater lake in the world, holding 18 per cent of the world's fresh water. It's 418 miles long (673km) and up to 45 miles wide (72km), so it resembles a sea when you get there, and is very deep too. Relevantly for this book, it's where the 19th century 'Scramble for Africa' – naked imperialism by European powers – ran out of steam. Or rather ran out of steam and then provided some, as the Germans imported gunboats to control the lake, which was where the British, German, Belgian and Portuguese colonial empires touched.

With three warships, including the substantial *Graf von Goetzen*, the Germans had mastery of the lake, and could deliver troops, weapons and supplies quickly to wherever they wanted (unlike overland travel, which was difficult). Then comes the First World War in Europe. Remote though this all was to the Battle of the Somme raging about the same time, it seemed to matter to someone in London, and certainly to colonial administrators on the spot. The Germans had, after all, sunk a Belgian and a British unarmed lake steamer.

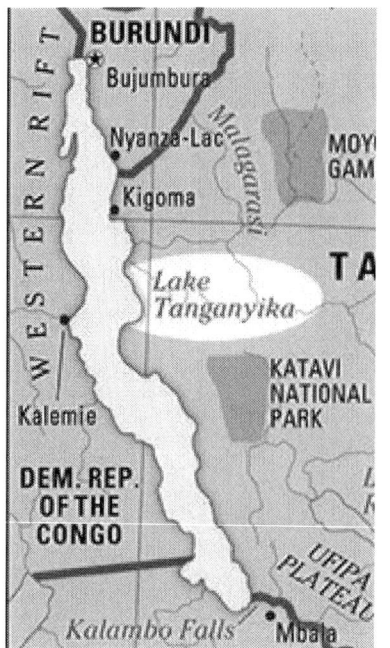

The Admiralty for some reason chose the brilliant but deeply eccentric Geoffrey Spicer-Simson for the job. It was an odd choice, for Spicer-Simson had failed in many of his missions in his naval career. Perhaps the top brass thought they could get rid of him and he'd fail again.

Or perhaps they understood that though Spicer-Simson (pictured next page) was a bit 'East Ham' (that's London slang based on the Underground map, meaning just this side of Barking, or crazy), he had qualities which might just see this amazing mission through.

The monumental task was to take two heavy armed motor launches from the Thames in London to South Africa, then get them somehow overland through jungle and mountains – where there was no road, let alone a waterway or railway – to Lake Tanganyika.

The two 40ft long twin-screw launches, originally ordered from Thornycroft's for the Greek Air Force as rescue launches, were requisitioned by the Admiralty for the job, and fitted with 3lb guns fore and Maxim machine guns aft. The fact that the boats' frames could not endure the recoil of the main gun being fired unless it was aimed straight ahead was rather a limiting factor.

Spicer-Simson wanted to call them *HMS Cat* and *HMS Dog*. His superiors thought this barking mad, so he came up with the even more ludicrous *HMS Mimi* and *HMS Toutou*, which mean the same thing in French slang.

Mimi and *Toutou* were loaded on a ship to Cape Town in mid-June 1915, taken by rail as far as they could, to a rail-head in the Belgian Congo, and then the tough part started. There was no road, so one was built with 150 bridges, many still there today. Two steam traction engines were employed, together with dozens of oxen and hundreds of Africans, to pull the boats and their supplies over the hills, once the road in front of them was built. At times the terrain was so steep that winches had to be erected on hill tops to pull the ships up and let them down the other side. It took a month and half to make the 100 miles to a narrow gauge railway that could get them to a river, which was supposed to ease their journey.

When they got there, the river was too dry. They floated part of the way but had to be carried over the shallows. Eventually the exhausted expedition reached the lake by October, and by December the two launches were ready to launch.

On Boxing Day, Spicer-Simson got his Christmas present – the German ship *Kingani* was sighted, ponderously patrolling the lake. The two launches set off in pursuit and opened fire. With the ship holed below the waterline and the commander killed, the Germans surrendered. The ship was taken ashore, repaired, called *HMS Fifi* (continuing the ridiculous name theme) and joined the British 'fleet'. In fact *Fifi* became Spicer-Simson's flagship.

Spicer-Simson (left, in the skirt) on the day the *Kingani* was captured

The Germans not unnaturally wanted to find out what had happened to their missing ship on a lake without any known enemy threat – it would be absolutely impossible to bring in a vessel except up the railway line they controlled, or so they thought. So they sent another ship, the *Hedwig von Wissman*, to search for it. Eventually, on February 9, the two forces met.

The German ship was twice the size of the *Fifi*, and a formidable opponent, but fled on being fired at. The problem was that *Fifi's* speed was similar, so she could not get close enough to make a hit and sighting was difficult because of the shimmering lake. The motor launch *Mimi* was too lightly armed to make a great impression, but repeatedly closed with the Germans and fired on the *Hedwig*. This made the German ship turn to engage her guns, upon which *Mimi* would zig-zag away, deftly avoiding shellfire. During these periods,

Fifi would close the distance and eventually got a shattering shot in, wounding some of *Hedwig's* crew. Another shot killed everyone in the engine room and crippled the craft.

The boat was sunk and the remaining crew – 12 Europeans and eight Africans – taken into captivity. This action was called the Battle for Lake Tanganyika and earned the commander of *Mimi*, Sub-Lt A. E. Wainwright, a DSC medal. One of history's naval medals earned furthest from salt water, one imagines.

The land campaign went well for the Allies, and the Germans realised they would be cut off, and fled, scuttling the *Graf von Goetzen* – which Spicer-Simson now seemed reluctant to attack – at her moorings. The war ended, Germany lost her African colonies, and Forester's romantic 1935 book based on this story and the 1951 film – which earned Bogart his only Oscar – followed.

As for the steam launch used in the film, *The African Queen,* the old film star (below) puffs around the Florida Keys, where she was shipped in 1968, and is still in service, 70 years after the movie was made.

But back on Lake Tanganyika is something far more remarkable – that German steamer the *Graf von Goetzen* which was scuttled as they retreated. She was refloated, renamed the *MV Liemba,* and still operates as a pleasure steamer. She was in the Imperial German Navy and took part in a war, was sunk and raised, served the British colony of Tanganyika faithfully, and has served the independent Tanzania, and at the age of 100 still steers up and down the same waters. I must go and sail in her one day. What a story!

No guns are now fitted, mind. And here is a sting in the tail. The guns had been taken off by the Germans early in 1916 to use in fighting elsewhere. No wonder they didn't want to engage the British – the heavy guns that kept Spicer-Simson away were wooden dummies!

The *MV Liemba*, retired from warlike service, still steams on Lake Tanganyika

ADMIRAL'S BUNGLE: Sometimes a kid who's showing off in his new car gets it wrong and smashes up his pride and joy. That might have been the situation of the aptly-named Admiral Sir George Tryon, pictured, commanding the British Mediterranean fleet in 1893.

He could have just had them anchor off Tripoli. But no, he had to take the ten enormous warships at high speed in two lines out from the coast in two columns of five, then turn towards each other to form one column, and steer shorewards. Then, after a sharp turn to travel parallel to the shore, the command 'anchor instantly' would have been flown from his signal halyard, and the moment it was hauled down ten midshipmen would have yelled an order, and ten blacksmiths would have hit ten wedges with ten sledgehammers, freeing ten huge anchors to drag ten heavy chains roaring out of their lockers to bring ten battleships or heavy cruisers to a sudden stop, all perfectly in line. Very impressive display of British naval power. Well, so he thought.

Except that the combined turning circle of two of these ships was 1,600 yards, so a safe distance would have been 2,400 yards. Tryon had left only 1,200 yards between the columns. None of the ten huge ship's captains dared query the flag-signalled command from this martinet, who liked to try daring and sudden manoeuvres to keep his men on their toes. Tryon was indeed trying it on and, like a boy racer doing a handbrake turn in front of the girls, was showing off. And some of the senior men thought he had a trick up his sleeve that would prevent disaster.

He didn't; the two lead ships, *Victoria*, carrying Tryon and *Camperdown*, leading the other column, collided. As a witness aboard *HMS Barham* reported to the *Penny Illustrated Paper:*

> "Sir George Tryon, who was on the bridge at the moment of the accident, at once gave directions for the collision mat to be placed over the damaged parts, and signalled for assistance to the rest of the fleet. The order was obeyed with the utmost promptitude, every vessel sending boats to aid in the rescue of the crew.

> "Before they could reach the spot, however, the Victoria, which had been filling rapidly on the side on which she was struck, suddenly turned right over, the steel masts striking the water with tremendous force. The movement continued, until, to the consternation of the rest of the squadron, the great

vessel was seen to be keel uppermost, the twin screws revolving rapidly all the time. As she began to sink, many of the crew were observed to be crawling up the sides of the hull on to the keel.

"To add to the horror of the scene the boiler exploded with two loud reports as the ship went under water.

"The boats of the squadron picked up as many of the men as was possible, but the enormous suction caused by the sinking of the great ironclad drew down with her even the strongest swimmers.

"Admiral Tryon was last seen on the bridge, giving orders with the utmost coolness and courage. It is said that he refused the offer of a life-belt from the coxswain, telling the man to look after his own safety."

The Admiral was right to go down with his ship. Tryon had tried it on one time too many. *Victoria* sank, drowning 358 men, including, fortunately you may think, Tryon, who was blamed entirely for the disaster, disgracefully losing the latest warship named after the reigning monarch – for no good reason, except arrogance.

TODAY'S MOST HATED SHIP IN THE NORTH: Is, according to some sources, this strange Norwegian triangular vessel. Hated by the Russians, that is – she should be loved by us. The *Marjata* is the best spy ship in the world, they say, and keeps an eye on what the Russian Navy is doing, on behalf of the Nato alliance. The unusual hull shape is to give a stable signals and sonar gathering platform. How good is she? Well they say she knew about the explosion and loss of the Russian nuclear submarine *Kursk* in 2000 before the sub hit the bottom.

ANYONE ORDER ICE? An aircraft carrier built of ice was built in World War II, but on a landlocked Canadian lake where it couldn't go anywhere or possibly be of any use.

It was the fault of eccentric London-born Geoffrey Nathaniel Pyke, a slightly mad inventor whose ideas were so off-beam – crackpot even – they were sometimes rather brilliant.

Born in 1894, he came to the notice of the authorities in World War I when he smuggled himself into Germany to try to be a correspondent reporting from hostile territory for the *Daily Chronicle*. He was nearly shot as a spy, but luckily the Germans saw he was just a daft young man with an over-active brain. He escaped and his newspaper made him a hero.

But it was in World War II that his at times crazed creations, always with an underlying brilliance, came to the fore. The start of the war caught him running an opinion poll about the Germans, which he intended to present to Hitler. As a Jew, it was fortunate, to put it mildly, that he got back to Britain before the balloon went up.

He had been inventing things between the wars – not always practical, such as a device for saving coal on railway engines by fitting them with lots of cycle pedals – so he was recruited for top secret work. He was asked to draft stratagems for depriving the Germans of the crucial Romanian oil fields. Problem – how to get the commandos in to blow the things up without the guards stopping them. His ideas included:

- Send in dogs disguised as wolves so the guards would run away.
- Start a few fires and then send in teams of agents dressed as Romanian firemen on fake fire engines. The water they pumped on the blaze would have some delayed incendiary bomblets mixed in with it, so fires would get worse, not better.
- Send in amazingly beautiful whores to distract the guards.
- Send in dogs with brandy flasks around their necks so the guards would be paralysed with drink.

I don't know if the drunken, sex-mesmerised, wolf-chased and half-burned guards would have hated Pyke, thanked him or just shot him. Other ideas of his included marking sabotage equipment in Norway 'Latrines for Officers, Colonels Only' on the basis that rule-bound Germans could never disobey an order and touch the things. Another creative gem was pumping soldiers ashore for invasions inside a pipe. The fluid around the capsules of soldiers in the pipelines could be useful stuff like petrol, he argued.

Pyke wasn't utterly barking, however. One of his inventions – frozen giant ice aircraft carriers half-a-mile long and ice-clad warships – actually made some kind of sense. Project *Habbakuk* was kept secret for many years after the war.

He'd invented Pykrete, a mixture of ice and wood pulp. It was amazingly strong and resistant to melting. He got as far as getting top British commander Lord Mountbatten to show Pykrete to generals at the Allied conference in Quebec during World War II.

Mountbatten got a general to swing an axe at a block of ordinary ice and it shattered instantly. Then he took a swing at a similar-sized block of Pykrete and nearly broke his arms as the axe just bounced off. Mountbatten then fired his pistol at the Pykrete and nearly killed another general with the ricochet. The shot hadn't harmed the Pykrete at all.

Mountbatten even rushed into Churchill's bathroom, dropped a lump of the stuff into his hot bath and said: 'Look, it doesn't melt' which it didn't.

Other neat things about Pykrete were that the ingredients were cheap and plentiful, and the blocks had a strangely self-adhesive quality – put two together at the right temperature and they just welded themselves tightly to each other.

An artist's view of a Pykrete aircraft carrier (top), next to a normal one

Churchill was sufficiently taken with the idea to order a 1,000-ton ice aircraft carrier to be built secretly on Patricia Lake, Alberta, Canada, which, being thousands of miles from the sea, would be the last place the enemy would look for such a ship. As predicted by Pyke, the thing didn't melt in the warm summer of 1943 and was kept running, but only at considerable cost in terms of fuel to run the refrigeration.

So would the unsinkable giant aircraft carriers – floating airfields, nearly – have worked? Had Pyke beaten *Titanic's* iceberg at its own game? The engineers scaled up the energy requirements for the full-sized version and discovered the quantities of fuel needed to power the thing would have been astronomical. The D-Day fleets had already been built, so it was too late by then. The cooling system was turned off and the carrier sank to the bottom of the lake where its remains can still be seen by divers.

Of course, being Pyke, he dressed up a great idea with all sorts of insane notions. His huge unsinkable cork-covered ice ships were to sail into ports and spray everything with supercooled water so the enemy's defences would be frozen solid. Railway tunnels would be blocked with instant ice. Enemy ships would be locked in the stuff. It was science fiction comic stuff, and it didn't help that with his unkempt hair and gabbling speech, Pyke seemed a mad inventor. Nothing more was done about Pykrete ships before the end of the War. Pyke returned to his messy Hampstead flat, dejected; he killed himself in 1948.

It was a tragic end to a genius that could have been put to better use. So many apparently crackpot notions turned out to be good ones in wartime. Pyke's were based on science, but were always just too barmy for the Army ... or the Navy, or anyone.

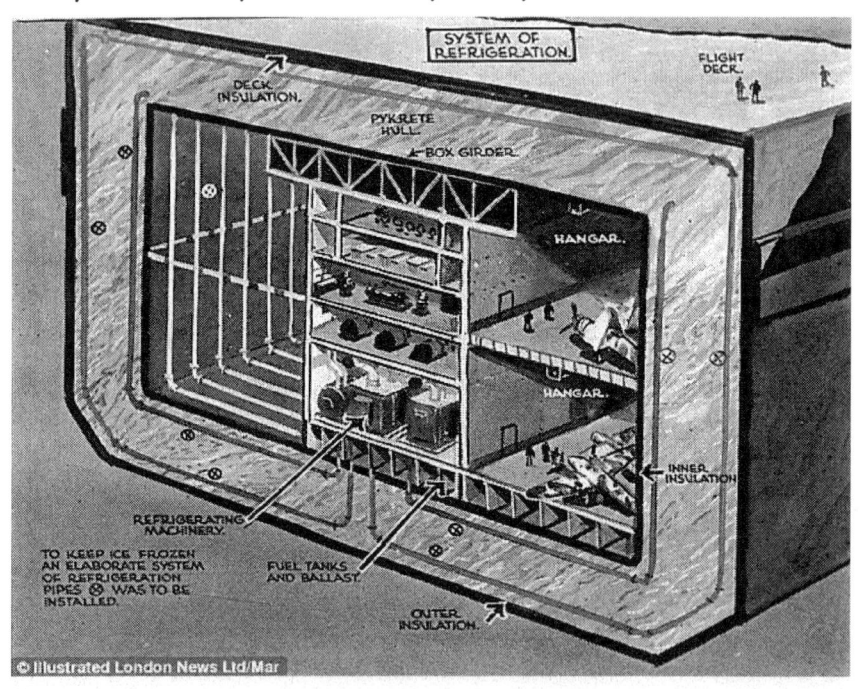

How the Illustrated London News showed the ice-ship design

ACCIDENT TYLER: On February 28, 1844, the U.S. Navy was showing off its new screw frigate, *USS Princeton*, hosting President 'Accident' John Tyler and members of the government (he'd got the nickname by taking over when the President suddenly died). They fired the ship's gun, which exploded, killing the Secretary of State, Thomas Gilmer, and the Secretary of Navy, Abel P. Upshur, and New York state senator David Gardiner. The latter's daughter Julia fainted and fell into the arms of the President. They later married. So 'Accident' Tyler gained two wonderful things by tragic accident.

NAVAL DECEPTION BRANCH: The above ship, the Dutch minesweeper *HNLMS Abraham Crijnssen*, was saved from a terrible fate during the Japanese invasion of Java in World War II by becoming an island. Close-up (left), you can see she's a ship, but further away (right) and from the air, she just seemed part of the jungle. She would navigate by night and then every day she would become an immobile island to avoid being seen by Japanese aircraft that had sunk every other Allied ship in the Java Sea – including *HMS Exeter*, victor of the Battle of the River Plate two years before. The *Abraham Crijnssen* reached Fremantle, Australia, in 1942, joined the Australian Navy for a year, rejoined the Dutch Navy and today can be seen as a museum ship at Den Helder, in the Netherlands.

A radically different approach to camouflage was adopted in the First World War with 'Dazzle' ships. Seen through a periscope in poor weather, it was impossible to see the range of a ship or be certain where the bow was. Both were needed for setting torpedoes to run effectively. Thousands of lives were saved by the ruse.

Dazzle ships: Where IS the bow of this ship? Submarines were out-foxed

Cubist camouflage (previous page) returned in World War II. The *USS Charles S Sperry*, 1944

COAL-POWERED SUBMARINES, SUBMARINE AIRCRAFT CARRIERS, SUBMARINES CARRYING A BATTLESHIP-SIZED GUN: All completely and utterly mad, so all built and tried and all sank. (Yes, they are *supposed* to sink, but they didn't come up again). Actually the enormous coal/steam submarine often ran pretty well if you remembered to put the fire out before submerging. A sailing submarine was once tried in America (on the surface, obviously) but this seems to have been a one-off bit of fun with the mast extended through the conning tower. Here's an aircraft-carrying sub:

The submarine with battleship-sized guns was the deeply strange French vessel *Surcouf* and should perhaps be classed as an underwater cruiser. Launched in 1929 as then by far the biggest submarine ever built, she was as much intended more with an eye to possible conflict with Britain as with Germany (and was named after an anti-British

French privateer). She had a cylindrical hangar for a spotter plane at the stern, so potentially could have been a useful weapon. In practice, as World War II started, she was astonishingly unreliable, and so were her crew, being a mixture of drunks and Vichy (fascist collaborator) sympathisers. Although she fled to a British port rather than be captured by the Germans, relations with the Royal Navy were prickly. The *Surcouf* set off for an ill-fated trip round the world, dogged by frequent repairs and drunkenness, and was lost on her way to the Panama Canal, probably run down by a freighter during a blackout, having achieved little for France except once mistakenly attacking American ships (a failure, luckily).

The extraordinary *Surcouf*, the enormous French submarine that had huge guns (above) and an aircraft hangar (left) but in the end did nothing for the war effort

SUBMARINE THAT ATTACKED A RAILWAY: Subs return home flying Jolly Roger pirate flags they make, showing the ships they have sunk in white outline, or coloured bars. One British sub in the Second World War returning from a patrol off North Africa showed in outline a railway locomotive and a road truck. It transpired that the boat had surfaced in a bay and shelled and destroyed these with its deck gun. The macabre 'Jolly Roger' flags flown on return to base usually showed white bars for enemy ships sunk, daggers for commando raids, etc. This remarkable one (below) from *HMS Ursula* shows two trains destroyed, and oil tanks and a factory – all well on dry land!

RAILWAYMAN WHO ATTACKED A SUBMARINE: At Liverpool Street station in London may be seen a rather moving memorial to Captain Charles Fryatt. In 1915 he was master of an unarmed railway ferry running from Harwich to neutral Holland when a German submarine surfaced and ordered him to stop, or be sunk. The captain ordered 'full ahead both' and turned to ram the submarine, which crash-dived to escape. The Imperial German Navy was thus reduced to an international laughing stock, so in 1916 surrounded the ferry with six destroyers, and captured the master, took him ashore in Belgium and shot him by firing squad.

The captain's grave at Dovercourt near Harwich is blunter than the Liverpool St memorial in its inscription: 'Captain Charles Fryatt, Illegally Executed by the Germans.' (Like shooting nurse Edith Cavell in the same conflict, it was another propaganda disaster for the Germans.) Dozens of shells were later fired at the German trenches with the inscription 'To Capt Fryatt's murderers' on them (above).

DEEPLY UNLIKELY: Would be a submarine having a running battle with cavalry, or a submarine attacking a camel train. Ludicrous, even. But both happened in World War I as British submarines penetrated the Dardanelles and attacked Ottoman land targets.

INVASION OF JAPAN: The need to invade Japan at the close of World War II was famously, or infamously, avoided by the atom bombs that were dropped on Hiroshima and Nagasaki in August 1945. The rights and wrongs of that – whether horrible though it was, it saved more Japanese lives than it cost, plus those of about a million Allied servicemen and PoWs – cannot be settled here.

But there *was* an Allied invasion of the Japanese mainland during the war. On the night of July 22, 1945, eight U.S. servicemen landed on a mainland beach, made a devastating attack, and made their escape. The key elements in this remarkable escapade were a brilliant and exceptional submarine commander, Eugene Fluckley (pictured), his boat *USS Barb* – indeed a thorn in the side of Japan as this sub that caused more losses to their war effort than any other – and his superb crew. The 'barb' in the name, by the way, referred to a fish, not a thorn.

Barb, which Fluckley commanded from 1944-45, sank a total of 17 ships in that time, including three warships. This submarine stranglehold on Japan, preventing her importing fuel, food, raw materials and slave labour, seriously damaged her ability to continue her aggressive war across Asia and the Pacific.

Fluckley had previously commanded the *Barb* on one daring raid right into a very well defended and difficult-to-enter harbour in mainland China, where he sank several Japanese ships and set a new global submarine speed record in escaping under heavy fire and surface pursuit through the difficult channel to the safety of the sea. It was littered with rocks, and mines, so that it could not be done submerged.

He also invented the first ballistic missile submarine by the simple ruse of borrowing a rocket launching rack from the surface Navy, and scrounging 72 rockets to fire from them.

Of course, he couldn't fire them from underwater, as modern submarines can, so the *Barb* (pictured below) had to surface off the Japanese coast, and assemble the rocket launcher on deck to attack land targets. Their launching made his boat highly visible to shore gun batteries, so he had to get the rockets fired, the racks taken down and the boat dived as soon as possible. He also used his deck gun in some of these audacious night attacks.

During these raids, Fluckley noticed heavy troop trains moving up and down the coastal railway. If only he could destroy the track *and* one of these trains.

With his engineering crew, he formulated a plan to land a small boat from the submarine with explosives and blow up the railway. But how to get his men safely back off the beach and still ensure the maximum damage by blowing the charges at the right moment?

Electrician's Mate 3rd Class Billy Hatfield came up with the plan (in fact suggesting he was *first*-class). Take the scuttling explosive charges that are installed to sink the sub in case of capture, and dig them under the track. Then use a switch that would work as the train passed over that point, depressing the rails slightly with its weight. The men – who would probably have been tortured and killed if captured – could be safely gone when it blew up.

It seemed near-suicidal, but plenty of men volunteered to be in the landing party. The *Barb* came in as close as she dared – under 1,000 yards from the beach – and launched eight men in a small boat, with carefully wrapped explosives and electronics. They made it safely ashore, crept through the grassy dunes to the railway and started digging a trench under the track to insert their charges. As they worked, those keeping watch noticed a suspicious tower a few hundred feet away. One of the crew climbed it – and found a sleeping Japanese guard on top.

He silently descended the ladder, and the men carried on digging. An express train came roaring up the coast, causing the men to scatter and hide. But they noted it did make the rails dip over their new ditch. Having inserted the explosives, they next needed to set up the sensitive switch – the most dangerous moment – and despite orders for only one man to stay and risk a premature explosion if he fumbled it, they all stayed with him until it was set up.

They retreated, only to hear just after they launched their little boat into the surf that another train was fast coming. They had to paddle like mad to get away. The locomotive was blown to pieces, and the 11-coach troop train behind telescoped into the wreckage, killing many Japanese soldiers. (No doubt the cacophony woke up the dozing guard in that watch tower.)

All this was witnessed by the entire crew of *Barb*, who had been given permission to come on deck and see the fireworks. They quickly climbed back into the hull, followed by the landing party, and the sub made for open sea, diving as soon as it was deep enough.

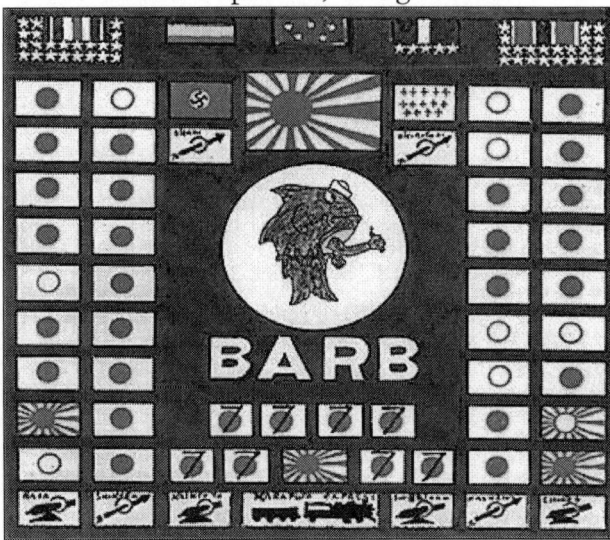

The British sub that had earlier 'sunk' a train on the shores of the Mediterranean, mentioned earlier, was no longer alone in that remarkable feat.

After the war, *Barb* was not retired. She

was decommissioned, then modernised and recommissioned twice. Then in 1954 she joined the Italian Navy and became called the *Enrico Tazzoli*. Not until 1972 was her long career ended in a scrapyard.

When by then Admiral Fluckley heard she had been sold for almost $100,000, to be made into razor-blades or Fiat cars by a one-time enemy, now a firm friend, he said it was a shame – the men of the *Barb* would have bought her and made her into a museum.

But the unique battle flag (previous page) – complete with train, flags for all the ships she had sunk and even symbols for the 14 British and Australian PoWs she rescued from a sinking 'hell ship' which had been torpedoed – is on display at the Submarine Force Library and Museum at Groton, Connecticut. What a career!

BATTLE OF OSLO FJORD: Should you have the good fortune to visit Oslo, go to the waterfront to stroll up and down the trendy Aker Brygge area to see the cool and the rich hanging out in bars, (and then, possibly, go two or three streets inland and eat for half the price!).

If you are interested in history, one of the anchors on display at Aker Brygge tells an astonishing tale of how men in pyjamas, equipped with antique guns, decided to take on the most modern battlefleet the world could throw at them – and won.

At the start of the German invasion of Norway, the attacking forces decided to sail up Oslo fjord and seize the capital in a dawn coup on April 9, 1940.

They were led by the almost brand-new and very advanced heavy cruiser *Blucher*. As they passed the island fortress of Oscarborg, guarding the narrows south of the city, the Germans disdained to take any action against what they thought of as outdated defences manned by a country simply incapable of fighting. The admiral contemptuously ordered the guns on the mighty cruiser, the newest in the German fleet, to be kept fore and aft and not even trained on the old fortress.

The battlecruiser *Blucher*, speeding towards Oslo, seen from the *Emden*

The Germans must have known that three huge 11in guns were there – after all, they supplied the Krupp-made and installed weapons (pictured), but they were 1893 vintage and regarded as useless in modern warfare. The undermanned and largely untrained garrison in the fortress – made of trainees for a different purpose, cooks and retired officers – managed to fire two of them, and both hit the *Blucher*. Good shooting, but it didn't stop the ship, although it started a serious fire which soon spread. What the Germans didn't know was that the Norwegians had installed underwater torpedo launching caves. These (under the command of a retired officer who had been called from his cottage in his pyjamas!) fired and also scored two hits.

The invasion was halted. The fleet withdrew in panic, and the crippled *Blucher* eventually blew up and sank with the loss of 830 crew and invasion troops. To put a cap on a very bad day for the German Navy, one of the retreating ships was sunk by a British submarine.

Going... the *Blucher*, now seriously on fire, drops anchor

Going... A severe list causes the order to abandon ship to be given

NUTTY, NAUGHTY NAUTICALS

Gone: Despondent Germans row away from the sinking *Blucher*

The delay this caused to the German plans to subdue this country and its tiny population rapidly with overwhelming forces allowed the Norwegian Royal Family and government to escape and direct the free forces from exile. Even the country's gold reserves made it across the North Sea to help the struggle for freedom.

Nor is this ancient history – some of the older people you see in Oslo would have heard these events within earshot of this city. Some very elderly may have fired the guns.

It's a lot to think about as you pose for photos next to an apparently harmless anchor, salvaged from the wreck, on Oslo's trendiest waterfront.

A MAN PUGNACIOUS, AUDACIOUS, A BARONET, A MARTINET: Sir Robert Arbuthnot (left) was a Royal Navy commander of such pugnacious stupidity that he boxed everyone he could, was an insane rule-follower (requiring men to follow with strict discipline rules he created by the hundred – in fact he was a baronet who became a martinet) and twice caused sea battles with the Germans in World War I to go badly wrong because of these two faults. On one occasion, he let a German fleet that had just bombarded civilians in British coastal towns escape unscathed because of stupid rule-following. On another, he threw away his ship, and the lives of his crew (about 900, including his own) by his impetuous and very unwise charge against the enemy.

His personality meant he would have been unbearable in command of a pedalo on a park lake, but the Navy gave him command of a major warship – in fact eventually a whole squadron of them. His attitude – in an already highly disciplined Navy – was described as 'the highest authoritarian standard of discipline, mercilessly enforced'.

He was a boxer from his school days, and as an adult, after dinner parties Arbuthnot would bring out boxing gloves and spar with his guests. He was generally hated by his crews for his obsessive, disciplinarian rule following and interference in everything they did. Not content with hundreds of rules in the *King's Regulations*, he wrote *A Battleship Commander's Order Book*, containing some 300 pages of detailed standing orders for his crew. This made him hated. On one occasion when two sailors were angry about a punishment he had inflicted, he gave them boxing gloves and proceeded to take them on and knock the pair to the floor. Another time, when three of his men jumped him when he was ashore, he took on all three and put two of them in hospital. He kept a racing motorcycle in his cabin which he would race ashore when he could at dangerous events such as the Isle of Man TT. Unluckily for his crew, he always survived ...

He'd come to public attention as somewhat unwise in 1910. While commanding officer of the battleship *Lord Nelson*, Arbuthnot made a speech about the German menace and the need to take urgent measures to combat it. Even worse – given the standing orders to avoid any political involvement by senior officers – a General Election was under way and he warned that the German Kaiser was planning to invade Britain and 'to prevent that, the first thing to do was to keep the Liberals out of power'.

This caused outrage at the German Embassy and deep embarrassment in the British Admiralty. The German government made a formal protest and the Navy demanded an explanation from Arbuthnot. He refused to recant his remarks or apologise, and was quickly relieved of his command and placed on half-pay.

When war came – and having been proved essentially right about that, if deeply unwise – Arbuthnot was sent to sea again. He was second-in-command of the Second Battle Squadron, flying his flag from the *Orion*.

Children gaze at the damage caused by German shelling of Scarborough

Arbuthnot's slavish rule-following soon proved harmful, particularly during the German raid on Scarborough (they shelled the town on December 16, 1914) when he allowed a group of German light cruisers and destroyers to escape because he had not received official orders from his superior, Vice-Admiral Sir George Warrender, commanding the Second Battle Squadron, to open fire.

It was bonkers. The enemy had been mercilessly bombarding defenceless civilians. Now the *Orion* had her 13.5 inch guns trained on their ships. This is what they were equipped and trained for. After years of arduous gunnery practice, this was their chance and their duty. Yet nothing happened.

Orion's captain, Frederic Charles Dreyer, repeatedly requested permission to fire, but Arbuthnot refused to allow this before receiving Warrender's explicit order (via flag hoist) to do so. By the time Warrender (attending to other aspects of the battle) realised the cause of Arbuthnot's inexplicable reluctance to fire, and had the order hoisted, the German ships had escaped.

Rather surprisingly, given this failure, Arbuthnot was appointed commander of the First Cruiser Squadron in January 1915, with the old cruiser *HMS Defence* as his flagship. His superior officer, Admiral John Jellicoe, commanding the whole Grand Fleet, noted: 'Arbuthnot is one of the finest fellows in the world, but somehow can't run a squadron. His ideals are too high and he can't leave people alone.' Yet he let him carry on, fatefully.

Defence was sunk at the Battle of Jutland on May 31 1916, in circumstances described by Admiral of the Fleet Lord Fisher as 'a glorious but not a justifiable death'.

The British 3rd Battlecruiser Squadron had exchanged fire with light cruisers of the German 2nd Scouting Group, damaging several as they steamed away north early in the battle.

Arbuthnot had seen the engagement and impetuously decided without orders to engage the German cruisers at close range before they could escape, even though his ships were of the wrong type for the job and would disrupt other British warships taking part.

Arbuthnot turned his squadron in pursuit, cutting directly across the path of the 1st Battlecruiser Squadron, which could have made a difference without this sudden intervention. *Defence*, followed by *Warrior*, cut directly in front of *HMS Lion*, missing a collision by about 500ft. *Lion* and the other battlecruisers were firing at the Germans at the time, and had to desist as they made emergency turns. This put Arbuthnot into the deadly killing zone of falling shells, an area which the other ships had been careful to keep clear of. Arbuthnot's ships blocked the return fire from the British ships, by laying down an effective smokescreen to protect them, and also stopped them pursuing the Germans.

Both the British and German officers watching all this reported it with an air of disbelief, not unlike those watching the Light Brigade charge straight at the mouths of the Russian guns in the Crimean War.

A lieutenant watching aghast from HMS *Malaya* later noted 'When I first saw them, I [knew] they were doomed.' Walter Cowan, the captain of the battlecruiser HMS *Princess Royal*, was equally shocked. He saw the old cruisers approaching the German fleet and commented he would 'bet anything' it was Arbuthnot. No one else would be that recklessly impetuous.

The manoeuvre had three results: it stopped the fire from much better-armed British ships, stopped them pursuing the Germans, and it made Arbuthnot's poorly armoured ships an easy target for German Admiral Franz von Hipper's modern battlecruiser squadron.

HMS Defence: Recklessly sacrificed by Arbuthnot at the Battle of Jutland

Within minutes, *Defence* was destroyed with all 903 crew in a massive explosion after taking hits from SMS *Lützow* at close range. Captain Gunther Paschen of *Lützow* recorded, 'From left to right there appears in the field of the periscope a ship, improbably large and close. At the first glance I recognise an old English armoured cruiser and give the necessary orders...Range 76 hm...Five salvoes rapidly follow, of which three straddle: then there was repeated the now familiar sight of a ship blowing up.'

Warrior fought on, but was crippled by 15 shell hits. She was luckily saved from immediate destruction by the super-dreadnought *Warspite*, forced to circle around *Warrior* because of a stuck rudder, drawing the enemy fire. *Warspite*'s superior armour allowed her to withstand the attack and return to port under her own power, but *Warrior* limped away and sank the next day while under tow. During the battle, British Vice-Admiral Sir David Beatty famously remarked as vessels blew up: 'There seems to be something wrong with our bloody ships today!'

Black Prince was blown up with the loss of all hands that night after blundering into the main German battle line in the dark at about midnight – she had been out of contact with the British fleet for hours. It is believed *Black Prince* may have thought the German ships in the dark were her own fleet, and tried to join the line. She was quickly fixed by searchlights and bombarded by the whole line and quickly destroyed before, realising her terrible mistake, she could flee. This left *Duke of Edinburgh* as the only vessel of the four in the ill-fated First Cruiser Squadron to survive the Battle of Jutland.

One curious consequence of the Arbuthnot fiasco was to help ensure the destruction of the German battleship *Bismarck* in World War II. At Jutland, a destroyer *HMS Onslow* was making a torpedo attack on the German fleet. It failed, and the thinly armoured destroyer would probably have been doomed – there were a lot of them in each squadron because they were, frankly, expendable.

Then Arbuthnot's cruisers blundered in and drew all the German fire. *Onslow* escaped, with her commander John Tovey, who went on to be the Commander-in-Chief of the Home Fleet who co-ordinated the brilliant pursuit and destruction of the *Bismarck* in 1941.

The two halves of HMS Invincible, blown up in the Battle of Jutland

Arctic convoys: If the Luftwaffe or U-boats don't sink you, the ice might

RETURN OF THE GHOST SHIPS: On July 24, 1942, three weeks after the disaster of Convoy PQ17, when the Germans sank ship after ship in that doomed voyage headed round Norway to aid Russia in World War II, a startled Soviet lookout at Archangel shouted a warning. Out of the mist and murk were coming a line of ghostly white ships, resurrected — it seemed — from the icy grip of Davy Jones's locker.

The Russians peered in disbelief. If these spooky vessels, presumed all sunk in the disastrous massacre, were real, how had they escaped one of the most ruthless turkey shoots of the war? And where had they been while two warring navies and air forces searched desperately to sink them or save the crews, combing the seas between Norway, Scotland, and the Arctic ice? Large cargo ships can't be made to just disappear!

The key figure who achieved this miracle was a dapper British chap called Leo Gradwell (pictured). He wasn't a career naval officer but a barrister who was also a keen amateur yachtsman. He had ended up in charge of what wasn't a proper warship, but a trawler hurriedly adapted, like himself, for war duty. Leo Gradwell was born in Chester in 1899 and was educated at

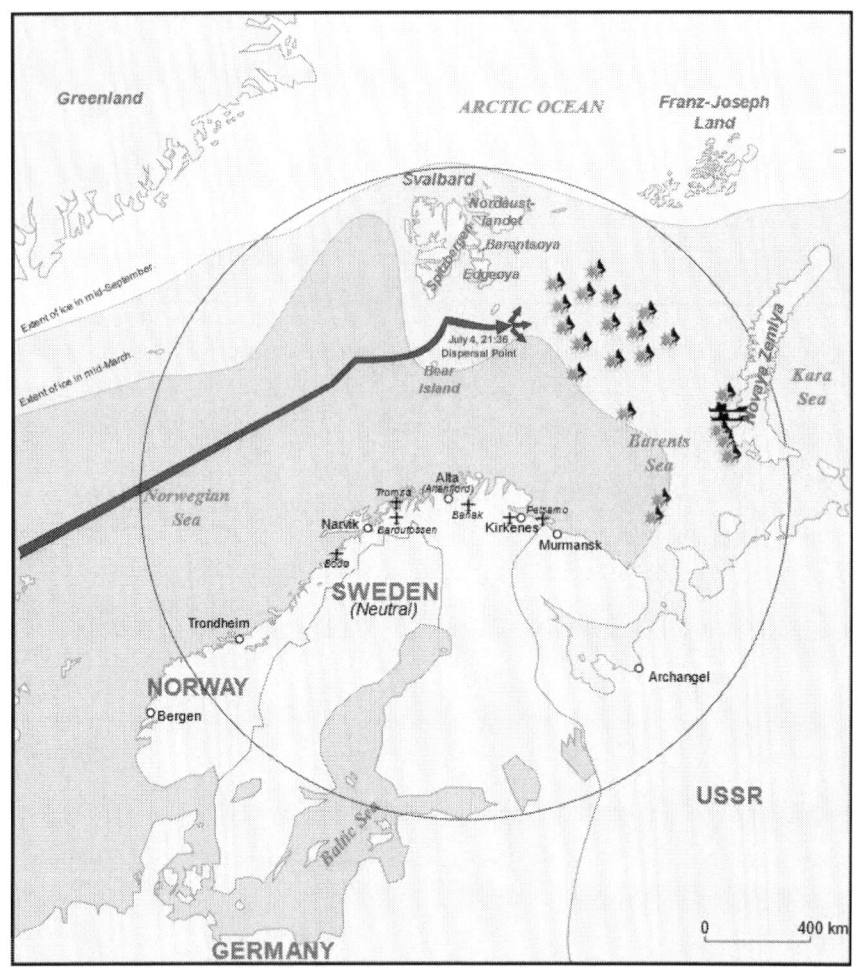

Doomed: Track of convoy PQ17. The sinkings are shown to the right

Plucky: the converted trawler *HMS Ayrshire*, Gradwell's command

Stonyhurst College, the Roman Catholic public school in Lancashire. He read classics at Balliol College, Oxford.

Gradwell was called to the bar in 1925 and worked at chambers in Liverpool. He spent his days off sailing in the Irish Sea. When World War II started, Gradwell was commissioned into the Royal Naval Volunteer Reserve as a lieutenant and given command of the trawler renamed *HMS Ayrshire*, adapted for anti-submarine work. In July 1942, the tiny *Ayrshire* joined the 36-ship Anglo-American Arctic Convoy PQ17 heading for Russia, to aid the Red Army in its titanic struggle on Hitler's Eastern Front.

This meant running the gauntlet of rounding the North Cape in Nazi-occupied Norway. The Germans had submarines, the Luftwaffe, torpedo boats, and a battleship available to stop them. And not just any battleship – the mighty *Tirpitz*, the heaviest European battleship ever built.

On July 4, First Sea Lord Sir Dudley Pound, alarmed by reports that the *Tirpitz* was on her way to engage the convoy, gave the order – controversial for decades afterwards – for the convoy to scatter. Had an attack by *Tirpitz* taken place, it would have indeed been disastrous for the convoy – not only for the slow, old merchant ships ferrying vitally-needed war supplies to the Soviets, but also for the destroyer and cruiser escorts, which would have had little to stop the salvos from the *Tirpitz's* eight 15-inch guns. A hit from just one of these huge shells tearing through the air at supersonic speeds would sink most ships.

Massive threat: The *Tirpitz*, biggest battleship ever built in Europe (artwork)

But the order to scatter was a disastrous mistake. *Tirpitz* was not on the horizon, nor was there any surface threat. Twenty-four of the scattered ships, deprived of anti-aircraft cover and anti-submarine vessels such as Gradwell's trawler, were easily picked off by German U-boats and aircraft. Some 153 sailors died, thrown into the icy water where survival was minutes, not hours, and some horribly wounded.

As the convoy scattered, lone ships making all speed they could for the safety of Scottish waters or plugging desperately on for Russia, Gradwell hit on the brilliant idea of heading not for any known port but to the last place the Germans would expect them to go — north, deeper into the Arctic Circle.

Like a sheepdog, Gradwell rounded up the American ships *Troubador*, *Ironclad* and *Silver Sword* and led them towards the ice pack, the last place any sane Merchant Navy officer would have steered towards. None of the ships had a chart of these waters, so Gradwell navigated using a sextant and a Times Atlas.

Through the mist: Gradwell led the ships north. (Picture of a similar vessel)

Troubador, crucially as it turned out, carried a cargo of coal and drums of white paint. Locked in the ice pack, these ships stopped engines and Gradwell ordered them to paint themselves white to fool German reconnaissance aircraft. If they had their port side to the ice, he'd get the starboard side painted white. No patrolling Luftwaffe aircraft would think of crossing to the ice-cap — no ships could possibly be there. Only the view from the south mattered. White sheets were spread over the decks and the deck cargo Sherman tanks were started up, moved to face possible threats and he had their guns loaded. Each ship thus became a multi-turret warship. The tanks were painted white too, at least to the south.

On a trawler, men load a 12-pounder gun. Picture: Lt F.A. Hudson

The boilers extinguished, the ships' funnels made no smoke while the men shivered. This gamble with the crews, ships and cargos was a risk, but it saved them all. Eventually after keeping quiet for a couple of weeks, they relit their boilers, cast off from the ice, and reached Archangel safely on July 24, weeks after they were thought to have been lost. What the Russians made of their white painted tanks isn't known – perhaps they thought they had been sent with winter camouflage – but they were desperately needed.

Gradwell rightly received the Distinguished Service Cross for his actions (completely against the orders to scatter the convoy, one must note), on September 15, 1942.

Tirpitz, like much of Hitler's surface fleet, turned out to be rather useless and never did fight a naval battle. Having entered service as recently as 1941, she spent years hiding in a Norwegian fjord; was damaged by courageous mini-submarine attack; damaged by bombing; and then finally hit by RAF Lancasters dropping massive 12,000lb Tallboy bombs (pictured) and sunk in November 1943.

About 1,000 men died as she turned over. She had been a constant threat to Allied shipping, but never more than a threat. Yet that was enough to sink most of convoy PQ17.

After the war Gradwell became a stipendiary magistrate at Marlborough Street Magistrates' Court, London, in 1951. As with so many unlikely war heroes, it was back to a humdrum civilian life – in his case dealing with the capital's minor crimes and misdemeanours on a day-to-day basis, and his legal career endured almost to his death in 1969, aged 70.

But there were moments of drama, such as handling the committal hearing of Stephen Ward during the 1963 Profumo Affair, or as a judge, presiding over the private obscenity prosecution brought by Sir Cyril Black, Conservative MP for Wimbledon, against the publishers of the book *Last Exit To Brooklyn*. That action succeeded, but was overturned on appeal.

Dramatic stuff, but not nearly as dramatic as defying the terrifying, ruthless onslaught of the U-boats, the screaming Stukas of the Luftwaffe and the warships of the Kriegsmarine by hiding ships in the frozen north. A David of a trawler versus a Goliath of a monstrous warship. A glimmer of heroic, resourceful success amid one of the war's darkest disasters.

THE CIRCULAR WARSHIPS: Even the most non-technical landlubber can see that ships are pointy for a reason. They obviously need to be as thin and sharp as possible to cut through the sea and maintain a straight course while being buffeted by wind and waves.

So it was rather surprising that the Russian Tsar — or rather his admirals — ordered a series of clumsy circular warships in the late 19th century.

The need for more river monitors — which are heavily armed but shallow draft warships — arose a few years after Russia repudiated the Treaty of Paris (ending the Crimean War, in 1856) under which the Black Sea had been neutralised and the Danube opened to shipping for all nations. In 1870, Russia began to rebuild its Black Sea fleet.

The Russian navy demanded a new fleet of monitors to guard the Kerch Straits — which gives access to the Sea of Azov at the north of the Black Sea — and the mouth of the Dniepr River. A year or so before, a Scottish shipbuilder John Elder had called for new designs to widen a battleship's beam to reduce the area that needed to be protected and allow it to carry thicker armour and heavier guns. Russia's Rear Admiral Andrei Alexandrovich Popov took that idea to an absurd extreme and proposed a fleet of ten circular ironclads.

In 1874, Popov had the first one, the circular *Novgorod* (above) built and launched. It weighed 2,490 tons, had a diameter of 101ft and had two 12in guns which could be retracted into an armoured turret. The ship had six engines, each powering one propeller. It didn't sound very sea-worthy, and indeed wasn't at all easy to handle.

Popov was not put off. A larger monitor, the *Vitse-admiral Popov*, was launched in 1877. This 3,550-ton ship had a diameter of 120ft. It was armed with two 12in guns and four 3.4in guns. The two ships cost 11 million roubles but almost as much had to be spent modifying the dockyards to accommodate the strange shapes. In practice, they were appalling vessels to try to control. On the Dniepr, they couldn't even go against the current. Firing even one gun once caused them to spin out of control. Even contra-rotating some of six propellers was not enough to keep the ships on a straight course.

In rough weather they were prone to severe rolling and their guns couldn't be aimed or loaded in such weather. Despite this, both warships were used in the Russo-Turkish War of 1877-78 and the *Novgorod* and the larger *Popov* continued to serve in Russia's naval forces on the heavily militarised Danube until 1903. They were scrapped in 1912. But they were always hard to steer in a straight course, because they weren't – well, it's hard to avoid — ship shape.

VETERAN OF ALL VETERANS: Not so far away from the waters where the last item's extraordinary circular river monitors (small but heavily armed warships with shallow draught) sailed, or tried to sail, lies even today another monitor, a vessel with an utterly amazing life story.

The *SMS Bodrog* fired the first shots of World War I. She has fought for five nations, including for and against Hitler. She fought for imperialism, for capitalism, for fascism, for communism and for royalty. She has fought against Serbia, Russia, Britain, Romania, Germany and Yugoslav partisans.

She was attacked by Stuka dive-bombers, she was sunk twice – and amazingly she still works for a living on the Danube, as a gravel barge.

The *Bodrog* was launched in 1904, and named after a river, like all the monitors of the Austro-Hungarian Empire.

As we all know, as a result of the assassination of Archduke Franz Ferdinand in Sarajevo on June 28, 1914, the empire of Austria-Hungary declared war on Serbia on July 28. On that very night *Bodrog* and two other monitors fired the first shots of the world war against Serb fortifications on the Zemun–Belgrade railway bridge over the Sava river.

After a vigorous war of campaigns and fronts moving up and down the Danube and tributary rivers, at the close of that war *Bodrog* was the last Austro-Hungarian monitor to withdraw towards Budapest and was the only one that failed to reach the city. On October 31, 1918, *Bodrog* struck a sand bank while navigating through heavy fog near Vinča. She was captured by the Serbian Army and briefly flew Serbia's flag.

SMS Bodrog, with two turrets visible, on the Danube in 1914

From the end of the war *Bodrog* was crewed and operated by the new Kingdom of Serbs, Croats and Slovenes and renamed *Sava* (another river). She was based at Dubovac, and was responsible for the Romanian border on the Danube, having a whole inter-war career on the rivers.

On April 6, 1941 Nazi Germany invaded Yugoslavia, and on the first day *Sava* and a fellow monitor fought off attacks by Luftwaffe aircraft on their base. The two monitors laid mines in the Danube near the Romanian border for three days, but were then forced to withdraw towards Belgrade, coming under repeated attacks by German Stuka dive bombers (pictured next page), fighting these off with heavy anti-aircraft fire and evasive helming.

Sava and two fellow monitors were undamaged, and anchored at the confluence of the Danube and Sava near Belgrade. There was no escaping the German onslaught, however, as high water levels in the rivers and low bridges gave insufficient clearance for the monitors to navigate freely, and they were trapped.

The three captains met, and decided to scuttle their vessels to stop them being used by the Germans. Due to that high water level, when the tugboat evacuating the crews scraped under a railway bridge, demolition charges fixed to sabotage it in face of the German advance went off and the bridge fell onto the tugboat, killing 95 of the 110 men aboard. Another group fought their way overland to the Adriatic sea at Kotor.

Sava was raised and repaired, joining the navy of the German puppet state called the Independent State of Croatia. She served in that navy until in 1944 it became obvious to her crew that the Germans were losing the war and their loyalties lay increasingly elsewhere.

Her crew scuttled her on the night of September 8, 1944 and defected to Tito's anti-fascist partisans.

Sava was again raised and refurbished after World War II, given new guns, and served in the Yugoslav Navy until 1962. Afterwards, she was sold to a state-owned river transport company, which was privatised after Yugoslavia broke up.

The last I heard, *Sava*, formerly the *Bodrog*, was serving as a gravel barge, an extraordinary ship that is still earning a crust (but has never seen the sea).

There are older warships in preservation, but surely none still working and still afloat that have fought for, and against, so many countries, kingdoms and empires, repeatedly on the bow wave of history, but never on the sea.

Q-SHIPS: Were famously those decoy ships, apparently unarmed, in the First World War that helped combat the German submarine menace. When a U-boat surfaced to threaten the merchant ships with its deck gun – cheaper and easier than using the few torpedoes they could carry – the British sailors would have to abandon ship or be killed. Except on the Q-ships, where flaps on deck houses were lowered to reveal powerful guns ready to fire and battle colours were run up, causing a few German subs to be lost with all hands (or all Hans, as an ex-WWII convoy destroyer officer put it to me once!).

But when in WWI the Germans started picking off the sail-powered fishing fleet, unarmed, unable to move with their nets down, a fishing smack, similar to that in the picture above, was recruited. *HM Armed Smack Inverlyon* was fishing when German sub UB-4 surfaced nearby and the captain started yelling orders at the fishermen. *Inverlyon* ran up the White Ensign, uncovered her gun and scored a hit on the conning tower, while other crew members used small arms fire to keep the Germans off the decks. More hits followed and the sub went down, permanently. A rare case of a sailing vessel defeating a modern warship.

BATTLESHIP AHOY! In August 2017, large crowds gathered to admire the skill with which the Royal Navy navigated its biggest-yet ship, the new aircraft carrier *Queen Elizabeth*, through the narrow entrance to Portsmouth Harbour.

Just as they did at the same spot in the same month of 1960, with somewhat less pride as a result, when the Navy's last battleship *HMS Vanguard* very publicly hit the east side of the harbour mouth. She had been decommissioned and was being towed to the breakers, initially by the harbour tugs – which just weren't strong enough for the 42,000-ton giant – and suddenly veered towards the Still & West pub. This, like the entire waterfront, was crowded with sight-seers and holiday-makers keen to see the last battleship leave Portsmouth (not expecting the close-up view they were about to get!).

When it was clear she was heading for the pub and wouldn't be told otherwise, the pilot, Mr R.D. Ottley, had the quick wits to order the starboard anchor to be dropped in the hope of catching the old ferry chains which lay on the harbour bed. This worked and slowed the ship and turned her a little to starboard, so she just nudged up the pub and stopped short by a few yards – but it would have been very different had the pilot not acted as quickly as he did.

We then had a massive battleship embarrassingly aground at the bow and, about 40 minutes later, the tide would turn, and then soon ebb fast, pulling the stern round across the harbour mouth and then breaking her back and sinking her at low water.

Skill: The giant *HMS Queen Elizabeth* eases into Portsmouth Harbour in 2017

Embarrassment: The *Vanguard* nudges up to the Still & West pub in 1960

This would have achieved exactly what Hitler had wanted to do 20 years before by sinking a blockship across the entrance to this vital naval port, trapping all the warships inside. All highly embarrassing and on the Queen Mother's birthday too – August 4.

The sea-going tugs waiting outside to take over the tow came to assist and after a lot of thrashing the water pulled the reluctant *Vanguard* away from the Still & West's saloon bar (where I suspect a few doubles had been swiftly downed as the battleship stopped yards away) and out to sea. Some old salts on the day ventured that she didn't want to leave the Navy, and was resisting like a horse digging its hooves in when being taken to the knacker's yard.

She had been completed in 1946 too late for the Second World War – the last battleship ever built in a world where they were already obsolete. She did ferry the King around the Empire before the Royal Yacht *Britannia* was built, but fought no wars and had a short life – in contrast to the previous *Queen Elizabeth*, a battleship featured in the Animals At War chapter which, like some unlucky servicemen, had to fight through both world wars, and survived too. But as for the new carrier of that name, how many watching her negotiate the harbour entrance remembered what a massive mishap once happened here?

THE DAY TWO LUXURY OCEAN LINERS FOUGHT A DUEL TO THE DEATH ON THE HIGH SEAS: Even odder, one was disguised as the other. *RMS Carmania*, (below) when launched by John Brown's shipyard in 1905, was at 19,500 tons Cunard's largest liner (along with her sister ship, *Caronia* – they were dubbed 'the Pretty Sisters' by sailors and public). In fact *Carmania* was slightly faster, as she had the novel steam turbines while *Caronia* had piston engines – they were to decide the future of steam propulsion.

Carmania rather jammed in the steerage passengers although the upper class areas, as it were, were pleasant enough. The accommodation totals of 300 first, 350 second, 1,000 third class and

1,000 steerage hints at a somewhat pre-*Titanic* way of packing 'em in. Getting poor emigrants to America might have been part of her intended role.

Carmania plied the North Atlantic run from Liverpool to New York for nearly 10 years, carrying H.G. Wells on his first visit there.

Almost equal in size was a German liner, *SMS Cap Trafalgar*, but launched in 1913, she was more modern and was, frankly, considerably more luxurious.

The *Cap Trafalgar*: Elegant, luxurious – the best Germany could offer

Built for the Hamburg-South America trade, she had on her upper decks a swimming pool and a Garden Cafe in a sort of conservatory. The elegant 1st class areas were decorated with gold filigree and elegant ironwork, and her staterooms were luxurious – she offered the best that Germany could provide.

When these two liners finally met, on September 14, 1914, things were very different. In July, the First World War had broken out and was now raging in Europe. As had been planned from the beginning, *Cap Trafalgar* was to adopt a role in the Imperial German Navy. She was ordered to coal up in South America and then make for a secret rendezvous at the uninhabited Brazilian island of Trinidade, 500 miles east of the mainland.

There she would meet German small gunboat *SMS Eber*, which had brought naval officers, ammunition and weapons to convert *Cap Trafalgar* to an armed cruiser. She was armed with two 4.1 inch guns and six pom-pom guns, manned by an experienced Naval crew and ordered to ruthlessly sink unarmed British merchant ships.

Interestingly, given what was about to happen, her dummy third funnel was removed, so her victims could think she was the British liner *Carmania* - until it was too late to escape. What better disguise than as one of the well-known 'Pretty Sisters'?

She went on the hunt for British shipping in late August 1913, and finding none, returned to the secret base at Trinidade on September 1913 to refuel from German supplies.

Who should turn up the next day, having spotted *Cap Trafalgar's* giveaway smoke while she was in harbour, than *Carmania*, the very source of her disguise? *Carmania* had also just been fitted out as an armed cruiser, equipped with eight 4.7in guns, and sent down from Liverpool via Bermuda to hunt for just such German raiders, and flush them out from hidden bases.

One can imagine the consternation as both ships went to battle stations, but they could not fight in the narrow harbour. Both captains were desperate for a victory and believed they could and should sink the other ship, so *Cap Trafalgar* sailed out to where there was sea room to fight.

Undergoing disguise: *Cap Trafalgar* **at Trinidade with** *SMS Eber* **alongside**

It went badly for the British to start with. They opened fire too soon, missing, and then the Germans' skilled gunnery hit home – with two hours of relentless duelling resulting in an estimated 79 hits on the British ship. *Carmania's* bridge was totally destroyed, killing several officers, and she was holed in many places including some below the waterline, for which furious pumping was needed to keep the ship stable. She was on fire, and as the ships closed it was a question of old-fashioned broadsides at each other, hammering away as fast as the ammunition could be manually carried to guns. Sailors manned the rails and used machine guns and rifles to rake the enemy. It was a fight to the death.

Then one decisive British hit sliced through many bulkheads below the waterline and exploded. This doomed *Cap Trafalgar*, which turned away, listing. The unarmed colliers in the harbour came out and rescued most of the crew – 279 men – who were interned in South America later. The German ship sank with up to 50 men killed.

Carmania was in a terrible state too, holed below the waterline, much of her equipment wrecked, nine men killed, many injured, listing somewhat. It seemed that out in the open Atlantic, she would sink too, but the engines still worked. The fires and leaks were got under control and she was met after a couple of days by Royal Navy ships that got her into a port in South America.

Amazingly, she survived and had a long career, patrolling the coasts of Spain and Gibraltar, as a troop ship taking men to and from Gallipoli, then taking Canadians home from the war, then refitted as a liner and running for more than ten years more. *Carmania* was scrapped in 1923 – a remarkable ocean liner that had fought a heroic, furious battle against her own ghost ... and won.

The painting *Sinking Cap Trafalgar* by Charles Dixon (1872-1934), National Maritime Museum, Greenwich. The German ship is in the distance, left

HMS Venturer, on her way to make submarine history off Norway

THE ONLY SUB THAT SANK ANOTHER SUB – WHILE BOTH WERE UNDERWATER: It's hard to hit a moving ship with a torpedo from a submerged submarine. You are firing at where you think the target will be in three or four minutes. You might get the calculations wrong, and if the ship knows there is a submarine danger, it might zig-zag in that time. Or speed up or slow down. It's free to move in two dimensions – towards and away, left to right.

But a submarine chasing a submarine faces another dimension – up and down. The hunted sub will, if aware of the hunter, dive and rise as well as zig-zag.

This was the situation faced by 25-year-old Lt Jimmy Launders, commanding British submarine *HMS Venturer* on February 9, 1945. He had orders to find and destroy a much larger German submarine, *U-864*, which was on a top secret long-range mission to aid its ally Japan with high-technology weapon materials.

The British knew about the mission because of their Ultra intelligence being gained by decrypting German messages sent by the now-famous Enigma machines – the code system that the Germans were utterly confident could never be broken but which, by this stage of the war, was being routinely decoded by the maths geniuses at Bletchley Park.

Lt Launders was a maths genius too. He'd need to be.

The German submarine was on her maiden voyage, and on a vital mission to help keep Germany's ally, Japan, in the war – Operation Caesar. She was carrying 65 tonnes of mercury, an essential element for weapons manufacture that the besieged Japan had run out of. After Italy's surrender, Japan had no source of this metal, essential for making primers and detonators.

German submarine *U-864*, sent on a very long-range mission to aid Japan

She was also carrying aero engine parts and guidance systems that could have allowed Japan to produce jet engines and V2 long-range missiles. Given that Japan was now reaching the desperate straits of using kamikaze suicide bombers, such technology transfer might have had a huge impact on the course of the war. It seems most unlikely, but suppose the atom bombers in August that year had faced jet-engined interceptors? Or V2 attacks on their bases?

But of course no one in the Royal Navy in February 1945 knew the war would end like that, or that soon.

Also on board the *U-864* were some top Japanese scientists who were to help take the technology into war production.

The German mission, *Operation Caesar*, went badly from the start.

On December 5, 1944, *U-864* left her base at Kiel and headed north. Yet even while leaving the Kiel Canal to access the North Sea, the sub hit the bottom hard and damaged her hull. Her commander, **Korvettenkapitän** Ralf-Reimar Wolfram, knew returning to Kiel - being frequently bombed by the British - would be dangerous and look like failure. He made instead for the German submarine base in Bergen, Norway. There repairs were further delayed by British bomber attacks.

On February 6, 1945, *U-864* set sail for Japan again - but didn't get far. One of the diesel engines was misfiring badly. These could be run while submerged at periscope depth, thanks to the ingenious snorkel breathing system and would be vital if the sub was to make it all the way to Japan. She signalled Bergen that she was coming back for more repairs - a signal picked up in Bletchley Park.

HMS Venturer, a submarine launched in Barrow-in-Furness in 1943, and one that led a new V-class of boats, was diverted to the area. Near the island of Fedje, she detected the noisy engine of *U-864*, which was cruising at periscope depth. They pursued the Germans, waiting for them to surface, possibly when she met their scheduled escort ship to take her into to Bergen through the rocky islands.

This was indeed possible. *Venturer* had surprised and sunk *U-771* on the surface three months before, off the Lofoten Islands, northern Norway. The British felt sure *U-864* would surface very soon for air, because they mistook its engine-breathing snorkel for a normal periscope. *Venturer* did not use the ASDIC system to track the Germans because they knew the 'pings' would give away not just their presence but also their position.

But the Germans soon realised they were being hunted by another sub, and started sailing fully submerged under quieter electric power - almost silently. In this deadly cat-and-mouse game, the British realised from *U-864's* zig-zags that the Germans knew they were there. The British could neither see nor echo-detect the *U-864*; just listen, yet somehow they hung her for three hours, until *Venturer's* batteries were running low.

Lt Launders (pictured) sat at a chart table computing the first ever underwater to underwater torpedo attack, which need to be in three dimensions. He had four torpedo tubes, and needed to fire them in a pattern that would intercept where *U-864* would be four minutes after firing, if she took evasive action. Different depths, different angles. Speeds, timings, bearings and depths needed to be calculated using - of course - just pencil and paper.

Then he ordered a slight change of course and ordered 'Fire One!' Then he ordered another change of course and precisely 17.4 seconds later 'Fire Two!' This was repeated for the last two tubes and the British waited silently, diving in case of counter-attack.

On the German sub the crewmen listening at the hydrophones would have heard the torpedoes whirring through the depths towards them. They would have called 'Achtung! Torpedo!' to the commander, who would have ordered a radical change of course and depth. This seemed to work fine, as one torpedo hissed past. Then 17 seconds later, the second. Then the third. It looked like they were going to escape this attack, and leave their pursuer with empty torpedo tubes.

But Launders had predicted the way the Germans would turn after the first three attacks. The fourth torpedo hit *U-864* amidships, blowing her in half. The sub and its deadly cargo went straight to the the bottom. None of the 73 crew survived.

Lt Launders, already a decorated and popular submarine commander, was awarded a bar for his Distinguished Service Order (that is, a second one). He met King George VI who praised him as a fearless, bold commander. After the war, the now famous *Venturer* was taken on by the Norwegian Navy and served two more decades as *HNoMS Utstein*.

The fate of the German submarine and crew was, of course, very different. In 2003, the two halves of the submarine were discovered. Divers found that mercury was leaking into the surrounding seabed from the rusting containers and fishing was banned near the wreck site – the metal travels up the food chain and poisons humans who consume the fish.

The Norwegian government and experts debated what to do. A salvage lift was considered - but you would be lifting two halves of a wreck containing deteriorating containers of deadly poisons and unexploded torpedoes that might go off, greatly increasing the environmental disaster. It was also a war grave, containing the remains of 71 Germans and two Japanese.

Another solution was what was called an 'Underwater Chernobyl'. You entomb the wreck in a concrete sarcophagus for all time. Difficult to do at depth without disturbing the wreck.

In the end, a solution was found. A layer of deep and impermeable sand was put on top of the wreck and that was covered with thousands of tons of rock armour to hold it in place against tidal erosion. The site will be monitored for ever.

But fishing is still banned in the area, a long-term consequence of one of history's strangest naval battles, still said to be the only recorded instance of one submarine sinking another intentionally while submerged.

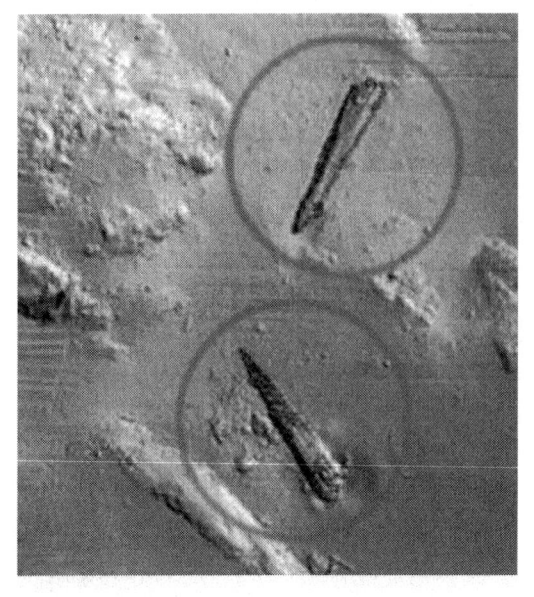

Found! The two halves of German submarine *U-864*, complete with highly dangerous cargo, lying on the sea bed

11 BARMY ARMY: ECCENTRIC SOLDIERS

TRAGIC HERO OR RECKLESS FOOL? The last Allied soldier killed in World War I was Henry Gunther, an American (pictued). Charging a German road block manned with machine-guns, he was shot at 10.59am, a mere 60 seconds before the guns fell silent at 11 on 11/11. He was aged 23.

It sounds heroic, and it was certainly brave. It was ironic, for sure, as Gunther – as the name suggests – was born of German stock and grew up in a largely German community in East Baltimore, Maryland, attending a Roman Catholic church and working in the Baltimore National Bank.

At the time of his death, he was angry at having been demoted from Sergeant. This came about because he'd written to a friend back home, telling him that life was horrible on the Front, and to do anything he could to avoid being drafted. The Army Censor read the letter – as the men surely knew they did – and Gunther lost his stripes.

So there he is charging the enemy, against the orders of his sergeant, with one minute to go. The Germans knew the war was about to end and didn't want any more killing – they shouted at him and waved him back. But Gunther kept on coming, firing as he ran, fixed bayonet ready to kill. They had to shoot him.

Which leaves the question about this individual – why?

Perhaps he was simply a committed hero, fighting for the cause until the last moment – and this is how it was presented at the time. Given his letter home, this really doesn't wash.

He could have wanted to prove himself one last time. A local newspaper in the USA recorded how a comrade said: 'Gunther brooded a great deal over his recent reduction in rank, and became obsessed with a determination to make good before his officers and fellow soldiers.'

Well, he certainly proved he was brave. He also proved he was reckless and perhaps the Army was right to demote him. Ironically, he was promoted back to Sergeant posthumously.

He could have been upset and angrily wanted to die – like 'suicide by cop' in today's world, where a man charges at armed police with a weapon, knowing what will happen. We just don't know.

He was seen as a tragic hero by German-Americans, and his body was exhumed in 1923 from Lorraine where he fell and given a hero's funeral back in Baltimore, plus a monumental plaque unveiled by the German Society of Maryland at 10.59 on 11/11 2010. There is also one in the village where he fell.

It is all too symbolic – a senseless death at the end of a senseless war, and very oddly, a German feted by Germans for killing and being killed by Germans, all absolutely pointlessly.

THE LAST BRIT WHO DIED in the Great War was George Ellison, a coal miner turned professional soldier from Leeds, shot on 11/11/18 at 9.30am while on patrol near Mons. He was old for the Army of the time – aged 40 and with a son James Cornelius, aged four. Indeed, his grandchildren survived into the 21st century.

Oddly, because the war started and ended at Mons for the British Army, his grave at St Symphorien Military Cemetery near Mons faces that of the *first* British soldier killed in the war, that of John Parr, who died at almost the same spot on August 21, 1914, aged just 17.

In fact that boy from 52 Lodge Lane, North Finchley – outside which house can be seen a plaque in the pavement – had lied about his age to join the Army in 1912, aged just 15. The Latin motto of Ellison's unit, *Quis Separabit,* means: who shall separate us? No one, now, not ever.

There is an awful, almost unbearable symbolism and symmetry about this. No one doubts the heroism and suffering of our men, once the war got going, or the atrocities on the other side – but for a war started for no discernible cause, the British fought from here, with the death of this man Parr (below, left), for four years to end back at the same spot and the death of this other man Ellison (right) lying opposite him, with 744,000 dead in the meantime. And it didn't even finish the matter with the Germans – the Armistice just turned out to be a 20-year ceasefire.

POINTLESS LAST DEATHS: The Armistice ending World War I was signed at 5am, and was to come into effect at 11am on 11/11/1918. But why wasn't an immediate ceasefire ordered? With Germany defeated, what was to be gained by carrying on killing?

It is suggested by historians that the Germans would have been willing to accept this but the French were not. Being convinced they should have the last word, as it were.

Some American generals – such as Pershing – did not agree with the concept of the Armistice. He argued that they should fight the Germans back to Berlin, so they would know they were defeated and would end the war, as he put it, on their knees, not standing up.

He argued – with some prescience – that the Germans would not really accept they had lost. If this was not done, he said, the war would have to be fought again over the same ground in 20 years' time.

But given that an Armistice *was* agreed in the early hours of November 11, and set for 11am that day, why on earth keep fighting?

Yet the Americans launched fresh attacks – as one bitterly pointed out later – to gain ground they could have peacefully walked into a few hours later. They suffered 3,000 casualties on the pointless last morning of the war, the British Commonwealth had 863 casualties of all kinds. French deaths? None, if you examine their graves. All those killed on the last day were dated November 10, perhaps to avoid giving the impression to their families that their boys' lives were just thrown away. But they were.

So in some areas, fighting continued pointlessly for six hours. In other artillery units – a British one for example – the sheer effort of lugging tons of ammunition through the muddy shell-torn landscape was such that they just fired off a load of ammo to get rid of it.

Not a very good reason for someone on the other side receiving a letter saying their son had died, you may think with today's hindsight.

SHELLED BY YOUR CHUM: Another pointless minor episode of a conflict was in the Indo-Pakistan War of 1971 when an unexpected artillery barrage made a Reuters journalist visiting the Indian front line throw himself into a trench, never mind the notebook and freshly ironed safari suit.

On getting back to his office at Delhi, he called his opposite number in the Reuters office in Karachi. 'The other fellow asked about the precise location, then said: "Sorry about that, old boy. I was visiting the Pakistani front line opposite you, and wanted a picture of artillery. The officer kindly offered to let off a few rounds. We didn't actually suggest it, but it made for a much better picture."'

The precise words may have been different – it was many years since I was told about that. He got his picture … but very nearly killed his friend and colleague.

HELL HATH NO FURY LIKE A WOMAN IN A TANK: Women are capable of a particular kind of fury, according to the common proverb. But even so, what were the chances of anyone taking any notice when a young Soviet telephone operator, Mariya Vasilyevna – after finding out the love of her life had been killed in the German blitzkrieg sweeping across Russia – wrote in anger to dictator Joseph Stalin with a very strange request?

She wrote enclosing her life savings, enough, she calculated correctly, to buy a new T-34 tank. She asked not only to buy one but also to drive it herself to take revenge on the Nazis who dared to ravage her beloved homeland.

The letter should have had a snowflake's chance in hell of being taken seriously in the melee of world war raging at the time. But it was. Stalin was moved by the request ... and was always open to a great propaganda idea in the Great Patriotic War, as the Russians called it. Perhaps the fact that she wasn't really Russian – Mariya (above) was from the Crimea – appealed to Stalin (below), who was also an outsider – born a Georgian, (and originally called Ioseb Besarionis dze Jughashvili).

You can also quite understand why Mariya Vasilyevna might have loved communism and the Soviet Union. She was born on August 16, 1905, as one of ten children, living in a Crimean hovel. Her family were dirt-poor serfs – in effect feudal slaves. They were their landlord's property and they could go nowhere and do nothing without his permission.

The Russian Orthodox Church backed this mediaeval arrangement, in a pyramid of privilege reaching from the grinding poverty of serfs right up through layers of aristocracy to the God-like Tsar. The penalty for rebelling against this order of things was death.

But the 1917 Russian Revolution had changed all his. People like her were allowed to have a home, to be educated, to have a job – in Mariya's case in a cannery, and later, as a telephone operator – to have some dignity and self-respect, and to fall in love as they wished. The fact that Stalin would turn out – for some people – to be more tyrannical than the Tsar and in some ways similar to Hitler was not yet obvious to her or millions of other Soviet citizens.

In 1925, just after Stalin succeeded Lenin as leader, she met a Red Army officer, Ilya Oktyabrskaya. Mariya became deeply involved in the military. She joined the Military Wives' Council, trained as a volunteer army nurse, learned how to drive Army vehicles, and even how to use different weapons. She wrote to her sister and enthused: 'Marry a serviceman and you serve in the army.'

Mariya in her T-34 tank emblazoned 'Fighting Girlfriend'

She believed in her country, the Red Army, and Stalin. Things were getting better and better, she thought, for herself and her country. All this was suddenly put in mortal danger when Hitler unleashed the largest invasion in history – *Operation Barbarossa*. It involved a staggering 3.8 million German troops, 3,350 tanks, 2,770 warplanes, and 7,200 pieces of artillery.

The onslaught was immense and conducted with ruthless barbarity. Though some Soviet tanks were as good as the German ones, they just didn't have enough of them. The Soviets also lacked logistical support – ammunition, radios, and supply lorries – giving the German Army a massive advantage.

Mariya – along with many other civilians in danger from the Nazis' murderous sweep through Russia – was sent east. The villages behind were burned and every useful thing or shred of food destroyed in a ruthless scorched-earth policy. Mariya ended up at Tomsk in Siberia. Two years would pass before she learned the fate of her beloved Ilya.

He had been killed by the Germans fighting outside Kiev in August 1941. Mariya went into a fury when she heard the news. Then she sold everything and wrote a letter to Stalin:

My husband was killed in action defending the motherland. I want revenge on the fascist dogs for his death and for the death of Soviet people tortured by the fascist barbarians. For this purpose, I've deposited all my personal savings – 50,000 roubles – to the National Bank in order to build a tank. I kindly ask to name the tank 'Fighting Girlfriend' and to send me to the frontline as a driver of said tank.

Troops repair a tank track: Mariya did it by herself, under fire

Against all the odds, she got her T-34 medium tank. She was then put through a five-month tank training programme, longer than the men who were thrown into the fight with far less preparation. Mariya joined the 26th Guards Tank Brigade as a driver/mechanic in September 1943 – and was laughed at by the regular troops. A *woman* driving a tank called *Fighting Girlfriend?* The whole idea was mocked. But they could not have been more wrong.

Mariya's own feelings were made clear in a letter to her sister, in which she wrote: 'I've had my baptism by fire… Sometimes, I'm so angry I can't even breathe.'

On October 21, 1943, in Smolensk, where the German invaders were being turned back, Mariya opened the throttle on *Fighting Girlfriend* and charged – taking out several anti-tank guns and machine gun nests before herself getting hit by a shell that stopped the tank with a track dislodged.

Against orders, she jumped out, and despite heavy enemy fire, fixed the damage, before jumping back in to continue the fight. Her fellow troops gave her new respect and called her 'mother' after that. She was promoted to sergeant.

On November 17, the Red Army recaptured the town of Novoye Selo. Mariya attacked German defensive positions till an artillery shell blew out her tracks. Under covering fire, she again jumped out to fix her beloved tank, before rejoining her unit. It was as if she had a charmed life – as well as immense courage.

But it could not last. On January 17, 1944, near the town of Shvedy, the fearless Mariya attacked several German trenches, machine-gun nests, and artillery, when yet again her tank was crippled by a German anti-tank shell.

As before, she fearlessly hopped out to fix the *Fighting Girlfriend*. She had just done so when another anti-tank shell burst just yards away, showering her with shrapnel – some of which slammed into her head.

Mariya never regained consciousness. She was taken to a hospital near Kiev and lay in a coma for two months, before dying on March 15, 1944, aged 38. They made her a posthumous Hero of the Soviet Union.

THE LAST SAMURAI: There's something very engaging, romantic even, about the famous story of the supposedly last Japanese soldier to surrender after the end of World War II, Onoda Hiroo, (pictured) the hold-out of all hold-outs, who kept his faith with his military mission for 29 lonely years after the atom bombs, unknown to him, ended Japan's war.

It's an amazing story, well worth revisiting, but the books, the film and the television programmes ignore one fact – he wasn't the last of these extraordinary men. Why is this ignored? And the further question arises – why do some Pacific islanders believe there could still be hold-outs? Is it possible there is still a very elderly soldier somewhere mistakenly doing his duty by the Emperor?

Onoda – the surname comes first in Japan – was born in March 1922 and an ordinary sort of kid by all accounts. But – and this turns out to be crucial – his family belonged to the ancient Samurai class of warriors driven by a strict honour code. His father was a sergeant fighting in China (where Japan had been waging a bitter war since 1937) and was indeed to be killed fighting there in 1943. By that time, the young Onoda had been enlisted in the Imperial Japanese Army infantry for three years, and had ended up in Intelligence.

Onoda was sent to Lubang island in the Philippines on December 26, 1944. He was ordered to do all he could to resist the anticipated Allied attack on the island, including destroying the airstrip and the pier. Onoda's orders also stated – and this was to prove of great relevance too – that under no circumstances could he surrender or take his own life.

His commanding officer said, with some prescience as it turned out: 'It may take three years, it may take five, but whatever happens, we'll come back for you.' A little out on the number of years, but basically correct.

The commander added: 'Until then, so long as you have one soldier, you are to continue to lead him. You may have to live on coconuts. If that's the case, live on coconuts! Under no circumstances are you [to] give up your life voluntarily."

Thirty-year war: Onoda Hiroo young and old, in the same patched-up uniform

The American and Philippine Commonwealth forces invaded on February 28, 1945. Within a short time of the landing, all but Onoda and three other soldiers had either been killed or had surrendered. Onoda, who had been promoted to lieutenant and was now the senior officer, ordered the men to take to the hills.

Onoda and his three comrades continued to fight – having occasional shoot-outs with police – but in October 1945 found a leaflet saying that the war was over and Japan had surrendered. It said: 'The war ended on August 15. Come down from the mountains!' But they decide that the leaflet was Allied propaganda. They could not easily imagine Japan surrendering, and why were the police still shooting at them if the war was really over? Late in 1945 leaflets were dropped from the air with a surrender order on it from a Japanese general. The group pored over them carefully, but decided this, too, was a trick.

One of the four walked away in late 1949 and eventually surrendered. This made the group even more suspicious – paranoid even – and when in 1952 family photographs and letters were dropped urging them to surrender, they concluded that their families had been forced to supply this by the enemy or tricked somehow.

In 1953, they had a shoot-out with local fishermen while attempting to steal food and commit further sabotage. In 1954, one of the four was killed in a gun battle with a search party and yet the last two carried on their mission of guerrilla attacks, sabotage and disruption into the 1960s and 1970s. In 1972, one more of the men was killed by farmers when they were burning their rice harvest as sabotage – so the authorities knew they were still active. The story became known in the world's media. But now Onoda was alone.

Enter into this amazing story on February 20, 1974, a completely different kind of young Japanese man. A hippie college drop-out no less, just 24 years old (in fact a bit older than when Onoda was sent to the island). Not, probably, someone Onoda would have understood, and wearing a garb the Second Lieutenant cannot have recognised – a printed T-shirt, blue trousers and (a crucial detail, this) rubber flip-flop sandals with socks.

The young man's name was Suzuki Norio. One of the baby boomers who had grown up in Japan's peacetime prosperity, he had freedoms and individuality it might have been hard for Onoda to comprehend. He was a bit of a non-conformist and an adventurer, and had decided, as he put it, to search for: 'Lieutenant Onoda, a panda, and the Abominable Snowman, in that order.'

Watching young Suzuki trying to make a fire that day beside a river was Onoda, still in his tattered uniform after nearly 30 years, clutching his still functioning rifle.

Onoda was puzzled by the young man and described what happened in his memoirs later:

If he had not been wearing socks, I might have shot him. But he had on these thick woollen socks, even though he was wearing sandals. The islanders would never do anything so incongruous.

He stood up and turned around. His eyes were round... he faced me and saluted. Then he saluted again. His hands were trembling, and I would have sworn his knees were too.

He asked, "Are you Onoda-san?"

"Yes, I'm Onoda."

"Really, Lieutenant Onoda?"

I nodded, and he went on.

"I know you've had a long, hard time. The war's over. Won't you come back to Japan with me?"

His use of polite Japanese expressions convinced me that he must have been brought up in Japan, but he was rushing things too much. Did he think he could just make the simple statement that the war was over and I would go running back to Japan with him? After all those years, it made me angry.

"No, I won't go back! For me, the war hasn't ended!"

Lt Onoda emerges from the jungle with Suzuki, left, who found him

Onoda and Suzuki became friends, but the Lieutenant still refused to surrender, saying that he was waiting for orders from a superior officer. Suzuki returned to Japan with photographs of himself and Onoda as proof of their encounter, and the Tokyo government tracked down Onoda's commanding officer, Major Yoshimi Taniguchi, who had become a bookseller. He flew to Lubang where on March 9, 1974, he met Onoda and fulfilled that promise made in 1944, 'whatever happens, we'll come back for you' by issuing orders including:

In accordance with the Imperial command, the Fourteenth Area Army has ceased all combat activity.

Onoda therefore surrendered. He handed over his sword, his functioning Arisaka Type 99 rifle, 500 rounds of ammunition and some hand grenades, plus a dagger his mother had given him in 1944 to kill himself with if he was captured.

Philippines President Ferdinand Marcos granted him a pardon for the killings, woundings and sabotage of the past 29 years. Onoda became a celebrity around the world and rather admired for his tenacity and Samurai-like honour code.

He became popular too in Japan, although not with everyone. For some, he was an unwelcome reminder of the country's brutal and embarrassing recent past. Not that he was that romantic a figure in the Philippines where he and his comrades had killed – murdered if you put it in a peacetime context – up to 29 people and wounded many more, plus destroyed or damaged much property in the three decades of guerrilla action.

That was the very end of Japan's war, the world was told when Onoda returned home at long last. But in fact Private Nakaruma Teruo, arrested on December 18, 1974 in Indonesia, held out longer.

His case received far less attention. Why? Because he was not an officer, not a Samurai Japanese – and in fact not racially Japanese at all, being from an ethnic minority in Taiwan. His uniform had gone, his rifle had rusted up.

No hero's welcome and ranks of flashbulbs for him on his return. In fact he was taken to Taiwan, not to Japan at all, and his back pay and pension – as a private and ethnic minority member – were a minimal ¥68,000 (US$227.59 at the time). Only after public outrage at the way he had been treated – compared to Lt Onoda – did the Japanese government increase this to about $100,000.

Onoda had a more successful retirement, writing his memoirs, the subject of TV documentaries – one of which detailed all the innocent people Onoda has killed in Lubang. In Japan, he came to stand for the old values – of imperialism, militarism and Samurai honour – and some urged him to run for political office. He refused money sent to him by well-wishers, and donated it to the Yasukuni Shrine to the Empire's war dead.

He became a beef farmer in Brazil, where he settled after getting married, and got involved in an old-fashioned Japanese community there. When he read about a Japanese teenager who had murdered his parents, Onoda returned to Japan in 1984 and set up the Onoda Nature School educational camp for young people, held at various places in Japan, designed to inculcate values of self-reliance, loyalty, survival in the wild, and self-discipline, all of which he was surely supremely well-equipped to provide.

Politically, he was affiliated to a right-wing organisation which advocates more power for the military and the monarchy. In all of these things, his views seem not to have moved on from Japan of the 1930s. Part of you wants to admire him, yet remember he was a mass killer and apologist for an unbelievably brutal fascist regime.

Onoda died in January 2014, aged 91, and that great age sort of answers those Pacific islanders who still believe there are Japanese soldiers out there, still holding out, rather in the same way people believe in yetis. It seems very, very unlikely that someone in their mid or late 90s could be surviving without any community support or health service, almost impossible – but not quite.

As for Suzuki, the hippie boy who vowed to find Onoda, a panda and a yeti in that order, he went on to meet a panda in 1975. In that same year, he claimed to have sighted a yeti. He never gave up on that quest and was killed aged 37 in November 1986 by an avalanche while still hoping to bring back a yeti, just as he had brought back Onoda.

'MAD' JACK CHURCHILL: Thud! The German soldier slumped forwards during the invasion of France in 1940, struck down by a silent attacker, and his puzzled sergeant pulled him up, lifeless, to find the feathered shaft of an arrow buried in his heart, as if he had been fighting in a war 500 years earlier. Before he had time to comprehend this, the Germans were cut down by a hail of rifle fire from the hidden British troops who had waited for the deadly arrow to find its mark as their signal.

Their leader, Colonel 'Mad' Jack Churchill was the bowman. The last British bowman to kill anyone in battle, it was apt that he was not so far from Agincourt and Crecy, where the English archers had met with more success than in this fighting retreat towards Dunkirk.

It wasn't surprising that Churchill was good with a longbow. He had been a top archer in the British team at the world championships the year before (pictured below).

But eccentric Mad Jack had others strings to his bow, as it were. He always attacked with a Scottish broadsword, and led commandos into action several times with only his medieval weapons. Once he used the sword to single-handedly capture dozens of terrified Germans.

And he had a great love of bagpipes – odd, given that he was about as Scottish as Omar Sharif's granny. But he viewed bagpipes – quite correctly – as more weapons of war than musical instruments, and believed the skirl of the pipes and the blood-thirsty yelling at the enemy during an attack did as much for victory as a few rounds of mortar fire.

Mind you, he did play them inappropriately on one occasion – when cut off and out of ammunition, last man standing and surrounded by wounded men – which led to the Germans blowing him up, though not fatally. Perhaps they couldn't stand the noise and wanted to shut him up. He was captured twice, and escaped twice.

Mad Jack, as he later came to be known, was born in Hong Kong in 1906, schooled in the Isle of Man, and after Sandhurst military academy was sent to the Manchester Regiment in Burma. While there he motorcycled right across India (when few roads were paved). He left the Army in 1936 and worked as a newspaper editor in Nairobi, Kenya, and as a male model, appeared in a few films, and represented Great Britain at the World Archery Championships in Oslo.

With war coming, he rejoined the Army, and was in France when the German blitzkrieg swept through. His aggressive rearguard against the Germans was a part of the miracle that let almost an entire British Army escape from the beaches in the famous *Operation Dynamo*, without their kit, but able to fight again another day.

During that campaign, Mad Jack was seen riding a motorbike with bow and arrow on his back, sword at his waist, a German officer's cap hanging from the handlebars. He stopped to ask a friend if he had any booze to fortify him, and the friend said no, but pointed out Churchill had blood down the side of his head. 'Jerry machine gunner!', Mad Jack said cheerfully, kick-started the bike and sped off. Whose blood it was is not entirely clear.

In 1941 Churchill was second in command of No. 3 Commando in the aptly named *Operation Archery*, a raid on the German garrison at Vågsøy, Norway, on December 27.

Churchill was responsible for taking out the artillery batteries on Maaloy Island. As the landing craft raced towards their landing spot, he belted out *The March of the Cameron Men* on the bagpipes to pump up his men. When the assault ramp went down, he fearlessly waded through knee-deep water at the head of his men, with his trusty sword blade lofted high in the air, screaming 'COOMMAAAAAAANNNNDOOOO!!!!!' at the top of his lungs and threw a grenade at the Germans with his other hand. Soon his commander received this signal:

Maaloy battery and island captured. Casualties slight. Demolitions in progress. Churchill.

The raiders took back with them some 100 prisoners and about 70 volunteers for the free Norwegian forces. The expedition had also sunk about 15,000 tons of shipping and destroyed not only docks and warehouses but the vital fish oil plants so important to German ammunition production and to dietary supplements for the German armed forces. And with another successful raid on the Lofoten islands (see following item), German occupation troops near any Norwegian coastline would not ever again sleep quite as well as they had before Vågsøy.

Churchill was wounded in the raid – by his own side and a wine bottle. Mad Jack was celebrating the raid's success with a bit of liberated Moselle wine leaning against a wall, unfortunately, of a building the British were supposed to blow up. The demolition charge went off and a chunk of broken bottle slashed into Churchill's forehead, the story goes.

Whatever happened, Churchill had another wound — or at least a sort of wound — to show for his successful leadership at Maaloy. As he himself joked later, 'I had to touch it up from time to time with (wife) Rosamund's lipstick to keep the wounded hero story going.'

Mad Jack Churchill leads his troops ashore from a landing craft, carrying a sword (on the far right). This was training, but he did so in action too

For his actions at Dunkirk and Vågsøy, Churchill received the Military Cross and Bar (that means getting it twice, non-military types might need to know). Quizzed by a senior officer about why on earth he chose to go into action bearing his basket-handled broadsword, he retorted crisply: 'In my opinion, sir, any officer who goes into action without his sword is improperly dressed.'

In July 1943 Mad Jack stormed ashore at Catania in Sicily with his sword around his waist, a longbow and arrows around his neck and his bagpipes under his arm, and repeated this at Salerno on the Italian mainland a few weeks later. Carrying his medieval weapons, he was ordered to deal with a German observation post on the edge of the town of Molina, which controlled a key pass leading down to the Salerno beach-head.

With the help of just a corporal, Churchill infiltrated the town and captured the post, taking 42 prisoners including a mortar squad by the ruse of taking one man first and holding his sword to his neck; a few men were dispatched in hand-to-hand combat. Churchill led the men and prisoners back down the pass, with the German wounded being carried on carts pushed by German prisoners. He commented that it was 'an image from the Napoleonic Wars.' He received the DSO for this action.

On his extraordinary success with capturing Germans, Mad Jack (pictured) explained that as long as you make it clear that you are a superior officer, and shout with authority at Germans, they will do what you say. But he made his extraordinary feat of capturing 42 men sound rather routine: 'I always bring my prisoners back with their weapons; it weighs them down. I just took their rifle bolts out and put them in a sack, which one of the prisoners carried. [They] also carried the mortar and all the bombs they could carry and also pulled a farm cart with five wounded in it....I maintain that, as long as you tell a German loudly and clearly what to do, if you are senior to him he will cry *Jawohl* and get on with it enthusiastically and efficiently whatever the ... situation. That's why they make such marvellous soldiers...'

Churchill later walked back to the town to retrieve his sword, which he had lost in hand-to-hand combat with the German regiment. On his way back, he encountered a disoriented American patrol, mistakenly walking toward enemy lines. When the NCO in command of the patrol refused to turn around, Churchill told them that he was going back to base and that he wouldn't 'come back for a bloody third time' to rescue them.

Not quite so successful was Mad Jack's attempt to lead an attack in Yugoslavia in 1944, through no fault of his or his men.

They were supporting Tito's partisans from the Adriatic island of Vis in an attack on the German-held island of Brac. Mad Jack had organised a 'motley army' of 1,500 partisans, 43 Commando and one troop from 40 Commando for the raid. The landing was unopposed but on seeing the eyries from which they later encountered German fire, the Partisans decided to defer the attack until the following day.

The following morning, one flanking attack was launched by 43 Commando with Churchill leading the elements from 40 Commando. The Partisans remained inexplicably at the landing area; only Churchill and six others managed to reach the objective. A mortar shell killed or wounded everyone but Churchill, who was playing *Will Ye No Come Back Again?* on his pipes as the Germans advanced. He was knocked unconscious by grenades and captured. Luckily he encountered a decent German officer who refused to carry out Hitler's orders to execute any captured commandos, and who said simply: 'You are soldiers, like I am a soldier.'

Churchill was later flown to Berlin for interrogation and then transferred to Sachsenhausen concentration camp. It may be that his famous surname delayed an execution at this terrible place.

In September 1944 Churchill and a RAF officer (Bertram James) crawled under the wire, through an abandoned drain and attempted to walk to the Baltic coast. They were recaptured near the German coastal city of Rostock, only a few miles from the sea. In late April 1945 Churchill and about 140 other prominent concentration camp inmates were transferred to the Tyrol in Austria, guarded by SS troops, known for their needless, ruthless and sadistic murders.

A delegation of prisoners told senior German army officers they feared they would be executed. A German army unit commanded by Captain Wichard von Alvensleben moved in to protect the prisoners. Outnumbered, the SS guards moved out, leaving the prisoners behind. The prisoners were released – the war was nearly over with Germany collapsing – and after the departure of the Germans, Churchill walked 93 miles to Verona, Italy, where he met an American armoured force and persuaded them that – despite his ragged appearance – he was a British colonel.

But the war was still raging in the Far East, with a particularly tough British campaign pushing the Japanese out of Burma. The much-vaunted Japanese army was finally being beaten at their own game, and Mad Jack wanted a bit of the action.

Perhaps sadly for him, by the time Churchill reached India, the atom bombs had been dropped on Japan and the war was over. As he himself put it: 'If it wasn't for those damn Yanks, we could have kept the war going another 10 years.' Churchill went on to have many more post-war adventures – saving an entire Jewish hospital including doctors, nurses and patients from being massacred by attacking Arabs in 1948 for example – and appearing in more films too. He died, rather surprisingly, of old age in 1996.

Clearly the family were cut from utterly extraordinary cloth. A brother led a commando unit, and a third went down fighting in the Navy. But neither of those two was as colourful as Mad Jack, striding along with his basket-handled sword and bow and arrow, playing his bagpipes at the height of danger.

As one bloodied, bruised, frightened, defeated soldier at Dunkirk, where German air raids were relentless and rescue seemed unlikely, recalled: 'The sight of Colonel Churchill striding up and down, unafraid and ready to fight, did wonders. That's the spirit, Sir!'

Lord Lovat, in his bizarre D-Day white jumper, with piper Bill Millin

LOVAT FIRST FIGHT: The previous item, about a swashbuckling, bagpipe-loving, pugnacious Commando leader might remind some people of Lord Lovat, who famously had his troops piped ashore under fire at D-Day – despite orders not to do anything so daft. He told his piper, Bill Millin, to play in direct defiance of specific orders not to allow such daft behaviour. When Millin queried it, Lovat said: 'Ah, but that's the *English* War Office. You and I are both Scottish, and that doesn't apply.'

'Les Britanniques débarquent sur Sword Beach au son de la cornemuse du piper Bill Millin' – as captioned in incredulous French, meaning the British landing on Sword Beach to the sound of the bagpipes of Bill Millin

Millin waded off the ramp, his kilt floating up to his waist, and continued playing *Hieland Laddie* even after the man behind him was hit and sank out of sight. On the beach he paraded fearlessly up and down, and Lovat shouted: 'Give us another' and Millin played *The Road to the Isles*. German snipers interrogated afterwards, asked why they didn't shoot the man parading up and down in a skirt, playing music, said they left him alone because they thought he had gone crazy. In the picture below, Millin is the large figure to the right. Lovat is seen to the left of his upper arm, wading towards the beach.

Like Mad Jack Churchill, Lovat had commanded a successful raid on Norway.

On March 3, 1941, Nos 3 and 4 Commando launched a raid on the German-held Lofoten Islands. In the highly successful raid, the commandos destroyed fish-oil factories, petrol dumps, and sank 11 ships. They also seized valuable codebooks and encryption machines. The commandos captured 216 German troops. Some 315 Norwegians chose to go with the commandos back to Britain to fight with their forces. It was a huge success and a major blow to German morale in Scandinavia.

Lovat also led a successful raid on the French village of Hardelot, and took part in the disastrous raid on Dieppe in August 1942.

Lord Lovat talks to exhausted troops at Newhaven after the raid on Dieppe

Simon Fraser was the 17th or 15th Lord Lovat – it depends how you count it and what is allowed for his ancestor, also called Simon Fraser, who was executed for siding with the rebels at Culloden (the last person to be beheaded in Britain).

The 17th Lord was also head of Clan Fraser of Lovat. His post-war years were not financially successful and he eventually had to sell the family castle, Beaufort Castle in Inverness. When he died in 1995, aged 83, his piper Bill Millin (statue, right) returned to play at the graveside. That's loyalty for you.

12 THE BRUTAL WAR OF BRAINBOXES

HOW A LAZY ITALIAN HELPED WIN THE WAR (FOR THE ALLIES): An Italian serviceman gave the British code-breakers at Bletchley Park an unexpected break one day. Ordered to send 1,000 characters as a system test on the brilliant German-built Enigma coding machine (one is pictured above), he pressed L. As he probably had a cigarette going, and – who knows? – an interesting magazine about glamorous girls to look at, he kept pressing L with one finger, not, as he should have done, a variety of keys. As the Enigma machine came up with a different letter each time for the L – this was why it was so much better than straightforward code letters – he doubtless thought he was doing his job adequately.

At RAF Chicksands in Bedfordshire, England, WRAF girls with headphones were jotting down the resulting stream of Morse code carefully. Two of them competed to get it down perfectly, so it could be cross-checked. It was rushed by the hourly motorcycle dispatch rider the 20 miles to Bletchley Park, the big country house with landscaped gardens that had been converted to a maze of huts into an intelligence hub filled with machines, meticulously careful clerical workers and outstanding brainboxes such as mathematics genius Alan Turing (pictured).

One thousand random letters. Where on earth to start? There were no Ls, someone realised! They knew the code would encrypt any letter as any other *except itself*. That meant some fool somewhere was pressing L 1,000 times.

It gave them the start to breaking that day's code settings in time for it to be of some use. A few hours later, perhaps signal lamps flashed across the grey Atlantic waves so a line of huge warships altered course to hunt down a German raider, or over the Western desert a lone Luftwaffe staff plane was perhaps bounced by Hurricanes and ruthlessly shot down, or perhaps in the moonlit Med a British submarine commander peering through a periscope at an Italian convoy ordered 'Fire One!' and a torpedo hissed away on a deadly mission. Or maybe not. Maybe the British cleverly did *nothing* (see next item).

THE HUMAN FACTOR: There was one German army signaller the listening Bletchley Park girls (see last item) felt they knew personally, because he tended to use the name Cilla, or the first three letters, in his own code settings. It was probably a girl he was sweet about. That was a clue, and other soldiers would do similar personal things, known as 'cillies' to the eavesdropping British. Towards the end of the war the German Navy realised the risks in allowing any human element of choice, and tried to remove this. Too late. The British had by then cracked the codes the Germans were certain could never be broken.

The resulting intelligence, known as 'Ultra', was very, very sensitive, for if the Germans ever suspected where it came from, this war-winning advantage would be lost. So before it left Bletchley Park, it would be disguised and made to look as it had come from elsewhere – spies for example.

Evil genius: Inside the Enigma machine were a set of stepped rotors or codewheels which changed every time a key pressed.

Only trusted commanders were allowed to see it. When it was acted upon, an apparent reason to act was often given – such as when a German warship's course was known, a spotter plane would fly over an hour before she was sunk.

Or sometimes, as was explained in the excellent 2014 film *The Imitation Game* about Bletchley Park – and also personally to me by the family of General Freyberg, the top Allied commander at the Battle of Crete – you had to *not* act on something that could only have come from Ultra, and – hard to believe – watch our own men die as a result of keeping quiet. That way the Germans never guessed the Enigma codes had been broken. It was a brutal war, this war of brainboxes in boring huts.

Dull-looking huts under grey skies with women toiling at desks: But they were fighting a thrilling new kind of war, and were winning it at Bletchley Park

An Enigma machine and Nazi paratroopers. The one thing was the key to the movements of the other Picture by courtesy of: DAILY EXPRESS

13 ALMOST TRUE: BRILLIANT FAKES, HOAXES AND CONSPIRACY THEORIES

GREAT WARTIME CONSPIRACY THEORY No 1: The case of the 'warning' in a mysterious small ad. When the Americans were remembering the shock they felt at history's worst sneak attack, the December 7, 1941 Japanese raid on Pearl Harbor, someone noticed something very odd in the run-up to that event which brought the USA into World War II.

In The *New Yorker* magazine of the previous month there seemed a clearly coded warning to the date 12-7, as Americans would put it, of the attack. After all, no dice have numbers 12 or seven on them, so what was going on?

The small ad pointed towards a main advertisement on a following page, which started off 'We hope you'll never have to spend a long winter's night in an air raid shelter …' adding 'it's only common sense to be prepared.'

> **Achtung**
> **WARNING!**
> **alerte**
>
> See Advertisement Page 86
>
> **MONARCH PUBLISHING CO.**
> New York

So it seemed to give the date, and being prepared for an air raid – as this main advert (left) showed. What was going on?

Roll on to the 48th anniversary of the raid, December 7, 1989, and someone called Joseph N. Bell wrote this compelling comment on the mystery:

But this year's anniversary reminded me of something quite different, a mystery I've carried around with me for more than four decades.

In 1944, I was flying Navy transport planes in the South Pacific. Along with the cargoes we delivered to combat areas, we often carried military passengers, and during the long hours between islands, I would often turn the plane over to the co-pilot and go back into the cabin to talk with the passengers. One of them was a young naval intelligence officer on his way to Okinawa.

We had some engine trouble on that trip and had to lay over unexpectedly in Guam. The trouble wasn't serious, and we were booked out the next morning. So my new intelligence friend and I went to the local officers' club to tip a few before we turned in. And there, over the third drink, he told me a story

---

Achtung
WARNING
alerte

We hope you'll never have to spend a long winter's night in an air-raid shelter, but we were just thinking . . . it's only common sense to be prepared. If you're not too busy between now and Christmas, why not sit down and plan a list of the things you'll want to have on hand. . . . Canned goods, of course, and candles, Sterno, bottled water, sugar, coffee or tea, brandy, and plenty of cigarettes, sweaters and blankets, books or magazines, vitamin capsules . . . and though it's no time, really, to be thinking of what's fashionable, we bet that most of your friends will remember to include those intriguing dice and chips which make Chicago's favorite game

THE DEADLY DOUBLE

that he probably shouldn't have that stayed with me until I was home after the war.

He told me that the Nov. 22, 1941, issue of the *New Yorker* magazine - two weeks before the attack on Pearl Harbor - carried an advertisement that in retrospect was full of double meanings and was considered by the intelligence community as a warning to someone about the timing of the upcoming Japanese offensive. He described the ad as best he could from memory and said it was accompanied by a pair of dice with the numbers 12 and 7 - the date of the Pearl Harbor attack- exposed.

He had been assigned to investigate the ad and ran into nothing but dead-ends. It had been placed across the counter in New York and paid for in cash. Both the main ad and the smaller lead-in ads had been set in type somewhere else and a matrix pulled for delivery to the New Yorker. The clerk who had accepted the ads had no recollection of who placed them, and neither the game that was offered in the double-entendre copy nor the company whose signature was on the ad existed. So my friend had drawn a total blank, and it was still eating at him. He was convinced that someone - for reasons he couldn't fathom- had been instructed to convey information about the upcoming attack in this manner.

I never forgot that conversation, and when I returned to college after the war, I went to the library and found bound editions of the *New Yorker*. Although it was only a one-column ad in a thick magazine, it was easy to spot. And it was every bit as mysterious as the intelligence officer had described it.

Thriller book stuff, eh? You could imagine the movie, Bruce Willis as the pilot, Matt Damon the young Intelligence officer. Except for one thing. It's 100 per cent pure horse poo. Like many things on the web, it's what people *want* to believe – but it's based on a gigantic coincidence.

Put it another way, how many publications around the world would have had 7 and 12 in them somewhere in that month? Yes, it's spooky, given the words that went with it.

But what would the Japanese gain by such an overt warning, and to whom? Why not make it an ad about farm equipment or something? The clincher in this case is on this page. I found an example of the supposedly fictional game made by a fictional company, recently for sale! The dice do indeed have such numbers on them. And then I found more ... sorry, Mr Bell, you don't quite ring true.

CONSPIRACY THEORY No 2, TELEGRAPH CROSSWORD: On August 18, 1942, the day before the Allied raid on German-occupied Dieppe, the name of the target port of the supposedly top-secret operation was the answer to a clue 'French port' in the ever popular crossword in Britain's *Daily Telegraph*.

The raid, which was trying out techniques for the invasion of France, was a terrible disaster because the Germans somehow knew the Brits were coming. More than 1,000 lives were lost, together with 94 aircraft, several warships, and tanks. Hundreds of men were taken prisoner. The harbour was left bobbing with the Allied dead– Canadians mostly – and the beaches with blown-up tanks, and all this was shown gleefully on German newsreels.

British prime minister Winston Churchill wanted to know what the hell had gone wrong, which meant the War Office wanted to know what the hell had gone wrong, which meant they instructed a Canadian Intelligence officer. Lord Tweedsmuir (aptly, son of John Buchan, author of spy thrillers such as *The 39 Steps*) to find out.

Grim aftermath: The beach at the Dieppe Raid

Tweedsmuir, after a few quick inquiries, took a train down from London Waterloo to Effingham Junction in Surrey and walked around to the Strand School, which had been evacuated there for the duration of the air raids on London.

He asked to see the headmaster, part-time crossword compiler Leonard Dawe, as a matter of urgency on War Office business. The two men retreated into the headmaster's study. Later, Tweedsmuir reported his conclusion: 'We'd noticed that the crossword contained the word "Dieppe", and there was an immediate and exhaustive inquiry which also involved MI5. But in the end it was concluded that it was just a remarkable coincidence – a complete fluke.' Case closed, you may think.

Then in the run-up to the June 1944 invasion of Normandy – the biggest amphibious battle in history, and one on which the fate of civilisation hinged – the remarkable 'coincidences' returned.

First 'Gold', 'Sword' and 'Juno' were given as *Daily Telegraph* crossword answers. They were codenames for the two British beaches, plus the Canadian beach. In May 1944, weeks before the invasion, 'Utah' and 'Omaha' – the American beach code-names – were given, which deeply alarmed the authorities. On May 27, there was 'Overlord' – code-name for the entire operation – and on May 30 'Mulberry' – the name for the prefabricated harbours to be towed in sections across the Channel – and on June 1, 'Neptune' – code for the naval operation.

No 5,775
ACROSS
1 A cause of postscripts (13)
10 Very attentive commonly (two words –3, 4)
11 A fool's weapon (7)
12 But this isn't to be bought at this shop (6)
15 Foils start thus (two words–3,3)
16 Definite (7)
17 One of the U.S. (4)
18 Achievement that the guardians of the Tower always have at heart (4)
19 Proper behaviour (7)
20 But cook has a practical use for this old weapon (4)
22 Part of one's last will and testament (4)
24 This knight of old had a fair start (7)
26 Little Samuel has got something from the pantry to make a boat (6)
27 The ceremonious tart (6)
30 Fifty fifty (7)
31 White wine (7)
33 "Intense matter"
DOWN
2 This probably has a lateen sail (7)
3 What all will be when the cease fire sounds (6)
4 Try the clue for 22 across (4)
5 Derby winner or preposition (4)
6 Systematically sorted (6)
7 When this loses its tail it doesn't grow another (7)
8 He rations the port among those who want it (15)
9 The ups and downs of business (three words –6, 3, 4)
13 Conference centre lately (7)
14 "Sleep rough" (7)

One of the many clues which seemed to give away codewords as answers

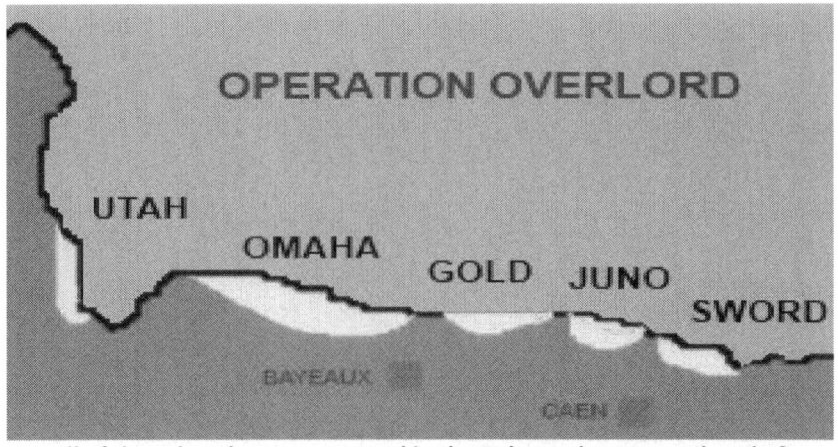

All of these beaches were named in the *Telegraph* crossword – why?

MI5 swooped on headmaster Dawe and arrested him, and also his fellow compiler Melville Jones in Bury St Edmunds, Suffolk. Both were interrogated extensively, and Dawe was threatened with at the very least losing his job, at worst the noose for treachery. The level of coincidence was extreme, but it was eventually accepted that no foul play had taken part. The headmaster kept his job. They were simply the sort of words that code-creators and crossword-setters both liked, it seemed.

Leap on 40 years, and in 1982, Britain was again mounting an amphibious invasion – of the Falklands, against Argentine opposition. A couple of years later, curious *Daily Telegraph* readers asked if it *had* all been coincidence back in 1944, then wouldn't analysis of the previous months' crosswords reveal similar supposed clues to codenames? They didn't. Not one.

GIs approaching Omaha Beach on D-Day: Their lives depended on the secrecy

At that point came a remarkable twist to the story. One of the then 14-year-old boys at the Strand School, Ronald French, by now a middle-aged property manager in Wolverhampton, felt he could tell the truth at long last, particularly as Leonard Dawe had been dead for 20 years.

Mr Dawe used to make his crossword task easier by involving the boys. He would write the letters on the blackboard with the gaps showing, and ask the boys to come up with words that fitted. He would then devise clues to fit those words. Harmless, you may think.

Except that some of the boys were in contact with soldiers,

including Canadians, waiting in nearby camps for the invasion. The boys had foolishly collected code-names these soldiers had been given to learn, and Ronald French, excited about the war, had a notebook full of them, in the same way that boys would collect shrapnel and bullets fallen in the streets from the air war overhead.

Dawes in turn interrogated French, and the shocking truth finally came out. He had been using his notebook to come up with words to fill in the crossword grid. Dawes was utterly appalled. His job and his reputation were at stake, and maybe his neck too.

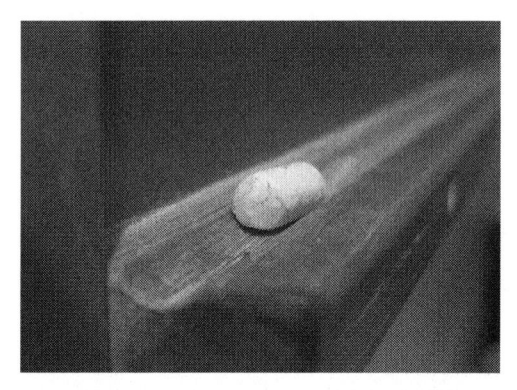

Scene of the crime: Chalk and a blackboard

He ordered French to burn his notebook and admonished him for his foolishness on a matter of national security. He demanded that French swore on the Bible never to reveal – during the headmaster's lifetime – what had happened, a vow which French kept.

History records, of course, that D-Day was a resounding success, changing the course of history. The sacrifice of all those Canadians at Dieppe two years before had shown the way to invade was not through a heavily defended port, but through landing on open beaches, and so perhaps those men did not all die in vain.

And the Germans, it transpired, were not fans of the *Daily Telegraph* crossword, so they were not ready for the invasion to come in Normandy, even though it did publish many of the key codewords as crossword answers and it was *not*, after all, a coincidence.

The Germans were repeatedly convinced the various invasions would come elsewhere, partly as a result of the following, most astonishingly brilliant masterpiece of deadly deception since the wooden horse at Troy, in fact far, far greater. This one would also be connected to a spy novel writer – the most famous one of all.

The greatest hoax of all time

THE key man in one astonishingly effective British operation against the Germans in World War II – indeed single-handedly sending whole divisions of panzers packing and making squadrons of Luftwaffe flee too, without ever receiving any official honour or even being named – was dead at the end of it. Not unusual in war, sadly. But he was dead at the beginning, and dead throughout.

Operation Mincemeat involved MI5 'recruiting' a dead Welsh tramp, Glyndwr Michael, who had died from eating rat poison. He was dressed in the uniform of a Captain of the Royal Marines and given an exhaustively detailed but fake life to match – even down to a fake fiancée and having completed fake shopping and theatre trips.

Why? Because he needed to be convincing in his role, which was to dupe the Germans into making the wrong preparations for the coming invasion of Italy. If this all seems a bit James Bond-ish, well the naval intelligence deputy in the department which produced the original idea was a certain Ian Fleming, who after the war would become famous as author of those 007 spy novels.

In the success of this scheme, Glyndwr Michael did more service to his country dead than most people ever do alive.

THE MILITARY BUILD-UP: The need for such an operation arose because the Allies had jointly been pondering at the end of 1942, with the Allied success in the North African Campaign after the Battle of El Alamein, what could be the next target. The British planners believed that a mass invasion of France from Britain – the vast operation which would become known as D-Day – could not take place until 1944. Prime Minister Winston Churchill therefore argued that the victorious British and Empire forces from North Africa should attack Europe's 'soft underbelly', joined by the Americans, who had landed in French North Africa.

There were two possible targets for the Allies to attack. The first option was Sicily; the narrow seas between there and the British island of Malta was the graveyard of too many Allied ships. It would re-open the Mediterranean to shipping from the Suez Canal, and would speed up supplies to and from India and the Far East without risking the submarine-infested trip round Africa.

The second option was to invade the Balkans through Greece, which would deprive the Germans of vital oil and mineral supplies and trap German forces between the Allied invaders and the Red Army, also now about to advance as the Battle of Stalingrad ground to its bloody conclusion.

At the Casablanca Conference in January 1943, the Allies agreed on Sicily and decided to undertake the invasion no later than July that year. It would be codenamed *Operation Husky*.

There was concern among the Allied planners that Sicily was an obvious choice – Churchill said 'Everyone but a bloody fool would know that it's Sicily' – and that the build-up of naval, air and army for the invasion would be detected. And if the Germans couldn't be persuaded to be 'bloody fools', then the amphibious assault could turn into a Dieppe-style humiliating massacre.

The Allies took two routes to persuade Hitler not to reinforce Sicily. One was *Operation Barclay*, a massive deception operation to play upon Hitler's known worries about the Balkans. To suggest Greece was the target, the British set up a special HQ in Cairo, Egypt for a non-existent formation, the Twelfth Army. Military manoeuvres were conducted in Syria, with numbers exaggerated by dummy tanks to deceive any observers.

Many Greek interpreters were recruited and the Allies took care to be seen to be obtaining Greek maps and currency. Fake radio traffic about its 12 divisions came to and from the Twelfth Army headquarters. Meanwhile the Allied command post in Tunis – the launch-pad for *Operation Husky* – reduced radio traffic by using land-lines or couriers wherever possible.

LOVE LETTER TO A DEAD MAN: The really clever bit, though, was *Operation Mincemeat*, the aim of which was to convince the Germans – once they had spotted the build-up in the Med – that Greece would still be the main target, with Sardinia a secondary.

The *Mincemeat* idea was to get key documents suggesting this to the Germans, but not in an obvious or direct way. It had to be credible. They would place the papers on Mr Michael's corpse, and then float it off the coast of Spain, as if it had been in an air crash. Spain's nominally neutral but fascist government was known to co-operate with German military intelligence, the *Abwehr*. After all, the Luftwaffe had perfected their techniques of merciless terror bombing of civilians during the recent Spanish Civil War.

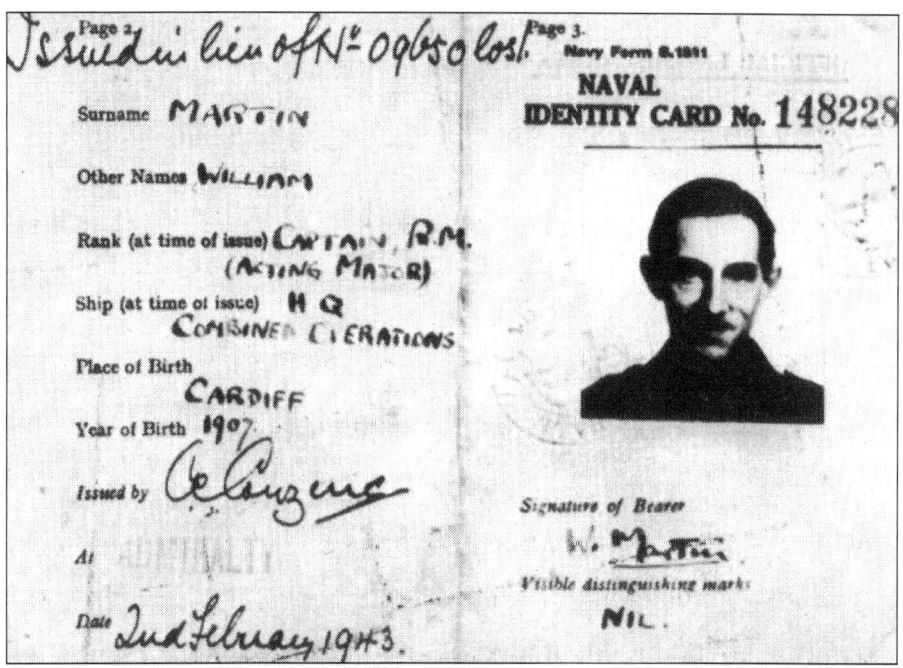

The beginning of a lot of lies: The false ID card. Note it was a replacement (top left) so it didn't seem oddly new

Lovely 'Pam': Theatre trips, bus rides, engagement ring...the Nazis lapped it up

So the MI5 officers had to create a convincing back-story for the body. Mr Michael was to become Captain (Acting Major) William Martin, of the Royal Marines, assigned to Combined Operations Headquarters. The surname Martin was chosen because there were several men with that name of about that rank in the Royal Marines. The rank would make him senior enough to be trusted with secret documents, but not so senior that German intelligence should have heard of him.

What is fascinating is the level of personal detail provided to make Martin convincing – known to spies as 'pocket litter'. This included a photo of his fictional fiancée named Pam (the image, previous page, was of an MI5 secretary, Jean Leslie), a pretty girl happy in a one-piece bathing suit (bikinis had not yet been invented).

Two love letters from 'Pam', written by female MI5 staff, were included in the pocket litter, as was a receipt for a diamond engagement ring costing a hefty £53 10s 6d from a Bond Street jewellers. There was a pompous letter from fictitious Martin's fictional father, and a letter from the family solicitor, and a note from Lloyds Bank, demanding payment of an overdraft of £79 19s 2d, hardly surprising given the lashing out on an engagement ring. All of these had to prepared using inks that would not readily wash away with sea water.

Also placed on Martin (right) were a book of stamps, cigarettes, matches, a silver cross and a St. Christopher's medallion, a pair of cufflinks, a pencil stub, keys and a receipt from Gieves & Co for a shirt. To prove Martin had been in London, ticket stubs from a West End theatre, a tuppeny bus ticket (for the right route, of course) and a bill for four nights' lodging at the Naval and Military Club were added. All of this gave him a detailed itinerary in London from 18 to 24 April.

The MI5 officers tried photographing the dead Michael

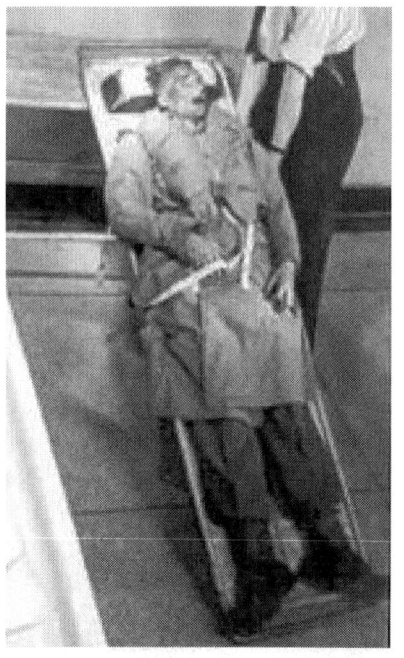

for the naval identity card Martin would have to carry, but it was too obvious that the images were of a corpse. Another MI5 officer stood in for the picture, wearing the correct uniform. Officers then spent a couple of weeks rubbing the three identity cards on their trousers to provide a used sheen to them, and wearing the uniform day and night so it did not look too new.

THE MINCEMEAT LETTERS: The way the false invasion targets were named was also cunningly indirect. The key document was a personal letter from Lieutenant General Sir Archibald Nye, Vice Chief of the Imperial General Staff to the commander of the 18th Army Group General Sir Harold Alexander, commander in Anglo-American Algeria and Tunisia under General Eisenhower. The letter covered several sensitive subjects, such as the annoyance of British military leaders at the needless award of American Purple Heart medals to British servicemen serving with them and various others points about staff appointments, etc. Only briefly did it touch on the invasion 'targets'. The key part of the letter read:

> **We have recent information that the Bosche have been reinforcing and strengthening their defences in Greece and Crete and C.I.G.S. [Chief of the Imperial General Staff] felt that our forces for the assault were insufficient. It was agreed by the Chiefs of Staff that the 5th Division should be reinforced by one Brigade Group for the assault on the beach south of CAPE ARAXOS and that a similar reinforcement should be made for the 56th division at KALAMATA [both suitable locations in southern Greece].**

That vital particular letter had one black eyelash put in it to test, if recovered, whether it had been opened and resealed.

One of the other letters had a corny joke about sardines in it – implying that one of the invasion targets might be Sardinia, the Italian island considerably to the north of Sicily.

The various documents were put in a briefcase which was connected to Martin by a leather-covered chain, as valuable couriers often carried such items. A study of tides, and where the Spanish co-operated with German spies, decide the best release point from a submarine – *HMS Seraph*.

MINCEMEAT GETS UNDERWAY: The special container, which contained dry ice, was marked 'Handle with care: optical instruments' and driven in an unmarked van through the night to the sub's base on the Clyde. The crew were told it was a secret meteorological device to be released near Spain.

Key men: Charles Cholmondeley and Ewen Montagu, with the van

At 4.30am on April 30, 1943, the submarine surfaced off Huelva, Spain, and the corpse was released from its container at the bow of the sub, which was facing towards the beaches. The captain read Psalm 39, which includes this oddly apt sentence for a man who was going to say nothing while being examined by fascists: **I will put a muzzle on my mouth while in the presence of the wicked.**

Then he ordered the boat to go full astern, so the propellers' wash pushed the body towards the shore.

The most explosive thing *HMS Seraph* launched was a dead body

The *Seraph* dived, then surfaced 12 miles out to get rid of the container. One hitch – it would not sink. They machine gunned it. It still wouldn't sink because of the insulating layer. It was blown up with explosives and the sub set course for home.

'Major Martin' didn't have to wait long to play his role – Spanish fishermen found him just five hours later and took him to Huelva, where the corpse was handed over to the custody of a naval judge.

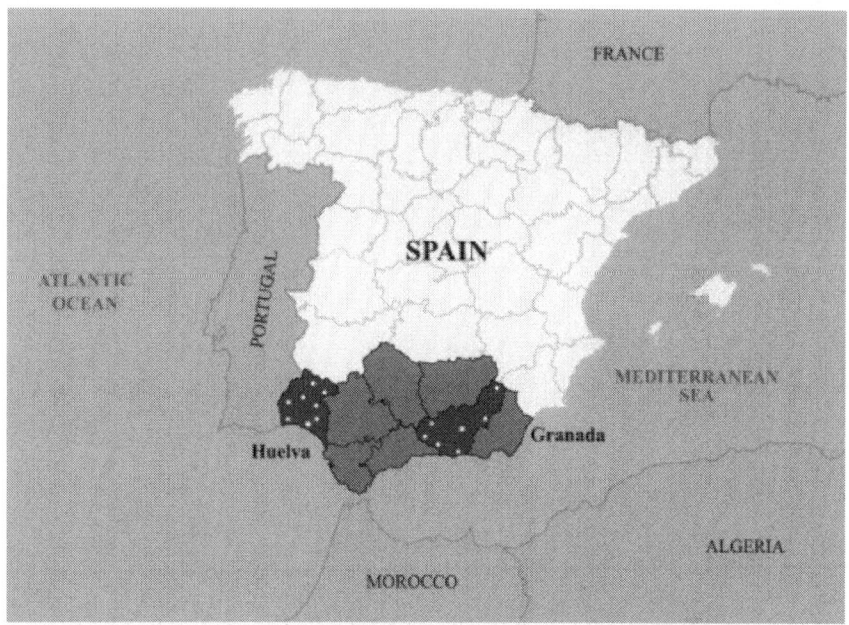

Target area: Huelva is in the middle of the big bay to the south-west

DOUBLE, DOUBLE DEALING IN SPAIN: The British Vice-Consul in Huelva, Francis Haselden, was notified and given a name by the Spaniards. Here's another cunning part. A series of scripted diplomatic cables were sent between Haselden and his superiors, which continued for several days. They were encrypted in code – but why? Because they were in a code the British knew had been broken and they also knew the Germans were getting these interceptions. The code was kept alive for less important traffic, so it could be used on an occasion such as this.

The gist of the telegrams was that it was vital that Haselden retrieve the briefcase and he must do everything he could to get it back unopened. In reality, this was the last thing the British wanted. Very odd – to be desperately begging for something and desperately hoping they wouldn't give it to you.

At noon on May 1 a post-mortem examination was conducted on Major Martin's body; Haselden was present and to make sure the autopsy was not too thorough – the body was really a three-month-old corpse – Haselden asked if, given the heat of the day and stench of the corpse, the doctors should bring it to a close and have a nice lunch. They agreed and signed a death certificate for Major William Martin for 'asphyxiation through immersion in the sea'. The Major's body was then released by the Spanish and was buried in the Nuestra Señora cemetery in Huelva, with military honours, on May 2. Job done, as far as the corpse was concerned.

Do dead men tell no lies? Oh, yes they do! (reconstruction)

Now it was up to the briefcase and its contents. It wasn't an easy ride. The Spanish navy kept the briefcase, knowing that if both the Germans and British were pestering them to get it, it might be important. They refused to hand it over. It was sent to a naval HQ near Cadiz, and on to Madrid. En route, a Spanish pro-Nazi took photos of the contents, without opening the letters.

In Madrid, the German *Abwehr* agents went into overdrive. They asked their chief, Admiral Canaris in Berlin, to push the Spanish into revealing the documents. This they did without breaking the seals by an extraordinary method. They removed the still-damp paper by tightly winding it around a probe into a cylindrical shape, and then pulling it out in the gap between the envelope flap – which was still closed by a wax seal – and the envelope. In the process the Spanish failed to spot the detector eyelash falling out of the key letter, but fall out it did.

The letters were dried, laid flat and photographed, and the pictures given to the Germans on May 8. Their top man in Madrid personally rushed them to Berlin.

The Spaniards then soaked the letters in sea-water for 24 hours, carefully reinserted them in the envelopes, then gave the briefcase back to Haselden on May 11, with apologies for the delay while nothing was done. Nothing was done!

It was forwarded to London in the diplomatic bag. MI5 experts analysed it forensically and found the key eyelash was missing, that the fibres in the paper had been changed by folding more than once, so the letters had been extracted and read. An outrageous bit of interference by the Spanish – luckily! How the Spanish had done this became obvious when the papers were dried out – they rolled themselves up just as the Spanish had.

A cable was sent to Haselden stating that the envelopes had been examined in London and that they had clearly not been opened. Encrypted, of course. In breakable code, of course. He also chatted about it in Spain to someone who, shall we say, had mixed loyalties.

The reward came on May 14, when at Bletchley Park, Bucks, experts reading the German's 'unbreakable' Enigma code – the super-top secret Ultra Intelligence source – saw German HQ warning commanders that the invasion would be in the Balkans. Churchill was told: '*Mincemeat* swallowed rod, line and sinker by the right people and from the best information they look like acting on it.'

MI5 continued the life – or rather death – of Major Martin, and he was included in the list of British casualties in *The Times* in London on June 4, along with two other officers who had died when their plane was lost at sea. On the facing page was a news story saying the popular film star Leslie Howard had been shot down in a civilian airliner by the Luftwaffe and killed, also off Spain. Total, horrible coincidences, all of them, but giving the Martin story some real, credible context.

> **ROYAL NAVY**
>
> The Board of Admiralty regrets to announce the following casualties which have been sustained in meeting the general hazards of war. Next-of-kin have been notified:—
>
> **OFFICERS**
> **KILLED**
> A/Capt. Sir T. L. Beevor, Bt;, R.N.; T/Lt. D. A. Burgess, R.N.V.R.; Lt. J. L. Fraser, R.N.V.R.; Lt. P. F. S. Gould, D.S.C., R.N.; T/Sub-Lt. (A) J. H. Hodgson, R.N.V.R.; T/Sub-Lt. (A) K. R. Joll, R.N.V.R.; Rear-Admiral P. J. Mack, D.S.O.; T/Lt (A) G. Muirie, R.N.V.R.; T/Lt. (A) G. Raynor, R.N.V.R.; T/Sub-Lt. J. N. Wisham, R.N.V.R.
> ROYAL MARINES.—T/Capt. (A/Major) W. Martin.
>
> **DIED FROM WOUNDS OR INJURIES**
> T/Sub-Lt. (A) J. Hall, R.N.V.R.; T/Lt. A. G. D. Heyburne, R.N.V.R.

From The Times, June 4, 1943:
See 4 lines up from bottom

THE GERMANS RESPOND: On May 14 German Navy chief Admiral Döenitz met Hitler to discuss the admiral's visit to Italy, his meeting with the Italian leader Mussolini and the progress of the war. His notes, later discovered, included this:

> The *Führer* does not agree with ... [the Italians] that the most likely invasion point is Sicily. Furthermore, he believes that the discovered Anglo-Saxon order [the Martin letter] confirms the assumption that the planned attacks will be directly mainly against Sardinia and the Peloponnese [Greece].

Hitler moved the battle-hardened 1st Panzer Division from France to Salonika, as Bletchley Park read on May 21. German troops and fighter aircraft were doubled on Sardinia, and two more panzer divisions were moved to the Balkans from the Eastern Front, thus helping the Russians advance.

German torpedo boats which could have wreaked havoc with the invasion fleet were moved from Sicily to the Greek islands in preparation. Seven more German divisions transferred to Greece, and ten were posted to the Balkans, raising the number present to eighteen.

The German commanders were no doubt rather pleased that they had outsmarted the *dummkopf* enemy and would be able to deal the Allies a devastating blow in Greece. Like Dieppe, but on a huge scale. It would be a fresh slaughter.

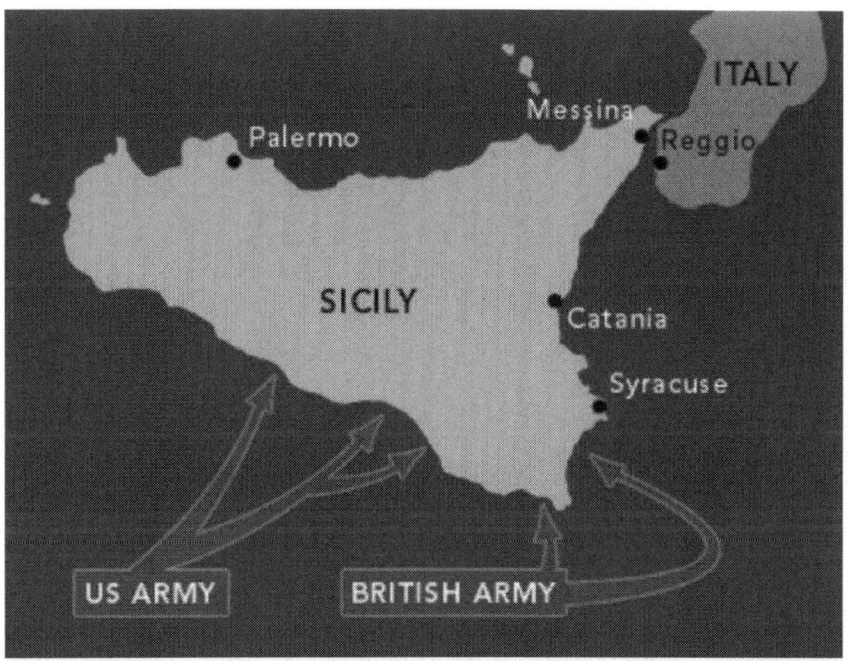

BRILLIANT FAKES, HOAXES AND CONSPIRACY THEORIES

Invasion of Sicily. Map: Anne Frank Foundation. Picture: Lt Longini, US Signals

On July 9, the Allies invaded Sicily. Hitler was not going to be fooled by a small diversionary attack (as he thought it was). Bletchley Park decoders showed that even four hours *after* the invasion of Sicily began, 21 aircraft left Sicily to reinforce Sardinia, where a real attack was expected.

Even in late July, Hitler sent his greatest soldier, Desert Fox Erwin Rommel, to take command of the coming struggle in Greece with all the forces mustered there. There they sat until the Germans realised that they had been bloody fools, judging by Churchill's dictum 'Everyone but a bloody fool would know that it's Sicily'. The fact is, they hadn't been. It was the Brits who had been bloody brilliant.

The invasion of Italy had begun, and the Germans were kicked out of Sicily by August 17. The Italians dropped out of the Axis, then changed sides. The long fight up Italy into Austria was on the way. The amphibious fleet that invaded Sicily would be re-used to attack the Italian mainland, then more than redoubled for the invasion of Normandy the following year.

THE VALUE OF A HOAX: The worth of *Operation Mincemeat* is hard to over-state. The Germans withdrew so many troops from Russia to deal with Greece, then Italy, that the Red Army regained the initiative and began its own long but unstoppable fight to Berlin. The Nazis never recovered their mastery on the Eastern Front, and this deception was part of that.

Just getting hundreds of enemy tanks, ships, planes and troop formations to flee the battle area before it starts is a massive achievement. Getting them to flee to an area which is almost impossible to return from quickly – you try getting a hundred tanks from the southern bays of Greece to Sicily through endless mountains in a hurry! – was a masterstroke.

Had *Operation Mincemeat* failed, things may have been far worse, and *Operation Husky* might have been a disaster. Look at the figures. In Sicily, the British had expected 10,000 casualties in the first week. Only a seventh of that number were killed or injured. They predicted 300 ships would be sunk, but lost only 12. They thought the campaign to clear the island of Axis forces would be over in three months – it took five weeks.

The story got global attention, here rendered in French

As far as 'Major Martin' was concerned, the deception continued. His grave was marked with a beautiful black stone, respectfully inscribed by a local stone mason:

BORN 29TH MARCH 1907
DIED 24TH APRIL 1943
BELOVED SON OF JOHN
GLYNDWYR MARTIN AND THE LATE ANTONIA MARTIN
OF CARDIFF, IN WALES

DULCE ET DECORUM EST PRO PATRIA MORI
R.I.P.

The last part, those who survived Latin O-level won't need reminding, means 'It is sweet and fitting to die for one's country' and 'May he rest in peace'. Except that every word on it was a lie –

although there's a hint in his supposed father's middle name. He wasn't called this, the dates were a fib, he didn't die for his country, and he certainly didn't rest in peace – far from it.

This was maintained by the Commonwealth War Graves Commission for decades without any knowledge on their part that no such man lay under the stone.

A more fitting epitaph might have been what an MI5 officer said at the time. 'He did more for his country dead than most of us do alive.' He defeated division after division without firing a shot. Or even lifting an ice-cold finger.

A book and film, *The Man Who Never Was*, made the story famous worldwide. Now most people accept that the man under the slab really is Glyndwr Michael.

The grave is never short of flowers left by some of the British visitors to that part of Spain.

Belatedly, a new part has been carved on this, surely the oddest of all graves. It now says at the bottom:

GLYNDWR MICHAEL SERVED AS MAJOR WILLIAM MARTIN, RM.

So that's it, settled by officials at long last. They wouldn't lie, would they?

14 THE SHAMEFUL HIDDEN WAR OF FRANCE v BRITAIN, 1940-42

CONTRARY to popular belief, the French fought hard almost throughout the Second World War. They fought fiercely, ruthlessly, they were certainly not quick to surrender, even when common sense would have dictated it, and they massacred the enemy most effectively when they could.

Unfortunately the enemies they were slaying so efficiently were the Allied forces. Yes, the young British, Americans, New Zealanders, South Africans, Canadians and Australians who were trying to free their homeland from the yoke of Nazi Germany, who were trying to stop French people being enslaved and shipped off to forced labour, or even torture and mass murder. The French were killing their would-be liberators. All this has been brushed under the carpet in the intervening decades, but it is, sadly, true.

French Vichy leader Petain meets Hitler, October 1940. Photo: Bundersarchiv

What happened between Britain and the France – more precisely the Vichy government of France that collaborated so enthusiastically with the fascist Germans after July 1940 – was a full-scale war, going on for years and killing thousands on each side. The fact that it was contained within the wider world war and so relentlessly covered up and rewritten afterwards doesn't make it any less of a war. And to make matters worse, it started with a slaughter of Frenchmen by the British. Consider the mainly Anglo-French battles in order:

1 BATTLE OF MERS-EL-KEBIR, July 3, 1940, Britain v France. *AIM:* Royal Navy reluctantly attacks Vichy fleet which was in danger of falling into the hands of the Nazis and was given many chances to flee or surrender without loss of life. *RESULT*: British victory. It also made clear to the world that despite the Battle of Dunkirk in the month before, with the defeated British feeling from the Continent, an apparently nearly beaten Britain fully intended to fight on. *FRENCH LOSSES:* 1 battleship sunk, 2 battleships damaged, 3 destroyers damaged, 1 destroyer grounded, 1 tug destroyed, 1,207 dead, 350 wounded. *BRITISH LOSSES:* 6 aircraft destroyed, 2 dead.

2 SEIZURE OF THE SURCOUF, July 3, 1940. Plymouth, England. *AIM:* Various French Navy ships which had fled the Nazi invasion of France were boarded early that morning by British forces, keen to prevent any chance of their falling into fascist hands via the new Vichy French collaborationist government, and make sure they join the Allied war effort as part of the Free French forces. This generally goes well, except on the extraordinary underwater cruiser/submarine *Surcouf*, where British boarding parties meet resistance. *RESULT:* British victory. *BRITISH LOSSES*: 3 killed. *FRENCH LOSSES:* 1 killed.

3 VICHY FRENCH AIR ATTACKS ON GIBRALTAR, July 18, September 24 and 25, 1940 – involving, respectively, 10, 120 and 83 aircraft. *AIM:* Revenge for No 1. *BRITISH LOSSES:* Slight damage to harbour and one ship sunk. *FRENCH LOSSES:* One French bomber shot down.

4 BATTLE OF DAKAR, 23-25 September 1940. France v Britain. *AIM:* To seize a vital West African naval base. *RESULT*: French victory. *BRITISH LOSSES*: 1 battleship crippled, 1 battleship damaged, 2 cruisers damaged, 1 armed trawler sunk, 6 aircraft downed, estimated 80 killed. *FRENCH LOSSES*: 2 Submarines sunk, 1 freighter sunk, 1 destroyer grounded, 1 battleship damaged. Estimated 100 killed.

5 BATTLE OF GABON, 7–12 November 1940, Free French (supported by British naval forces) v Vichy French. *AIM:* Making a colony change sides. *RESULT:* Free French victory. *VICHY FRENCH LOSSES:* 1 warship and a submarine. *CASUALTIES:* Unknown.

6 SYRIA-LEBANON CAMPAIGN, 8 June–14 July 1941, Britain/ Australians/Free French and Czechoslovakians troops v Vichy French supported by Germany. *AIM:* To frustrate a German-led plan to use Vichy French colonies to threaten the Suez Canal, undermine Iraq and grab its oil, and ultimately split the British Empire in half (as in World War I in this same part of the world, see next chapter) *RESULT:* British/Free French victory. *ALLIED LOSSES:* Australian: 1,552 dead. Free French: c. 1,300 British and Indian: 1,800, plus 3,500 sick or injured, 27 aircraft lost. *VICHY FRENCH LOSSES:* 8,912 men, 179 aircraft, 1 submarine, 5,668 defectors.

7 BATTLE OF MADAGASCAR, 5 May 1942–6 November 1942. British Empire v Vichy France (supported by Germany and Japan). *AIM:* To prevent fascist-backing Vichy offering a base to the Japanese and German navies in this vital ocean, crucial after the loss of Singapore to Japan, and move control to the Free French. *RESULT:* British victory. *BRITISH LOSSES:* 620 men, of which 107 killed in action, 108 by disease, rest wounded. 1 battleship damaged, 1 oil tanker sunk. *FRENCH VICHY LOSSES:* 159 killed, 500 injured, 1,000 taken prisoner. *JAPANESE LOSSES:* 2 midget submarine with crews.

8 OPERATION TORCH, 8–16 November 1942, Anglo-American invasion of Morocco and Algeria. *AIM:* To cut off the rear of Rommel's German troops retreating from British victories in Egypt and Libya and push them out of North Africa entirely. *RESULT:* Allied victory. *ALLIED LOSSES:* 479–500 dead, 720 wounded, 4 troopships sunk, *HMS Avenger* (D14) sunk with loss of 516 men. *VICHY FRENCH LOSSES:* 1,346 or more dead, 1,997 wounded, several shore batteries destroyed, all artillery pieces captured or destroyed, 1 light cruiser lost, 5 destroyers lost, 6 submarines lost. *GERMAN LOSSES:* 1 submarine sunk.

9 BATTLE OF RÉUNION, 28 November 1942, Free French v Vichy French. *AIM:* Change control of the Indian Ocean island. *RESULT:* Free French victory. Destroyer *Léopard* wins short battle with coastal artillery. *LOSSES:* 3 dead in total.

All in all, nine battles in which 30 ships were sunk, 219 aircraft destroyed, and more than 7,300 men killed – sounds like a war, doesn't it? If it was not within the Second World War, and politically rather inconvenient to remember, we would all have heard of the Anglo-French War of 1940-42, and it's all the more shocking that it took place between two countries that were Allies at the start and the end of World War II. And the real point is none of these tragic losses of men and *materiel* need to have happened. Not one of them. They were all desperately needed for the struggle *against* not for Nazi Germany, and to liberate France.

So what did happen and why exactly?

THE RUN-UP TO THE ANGLO-FRENCH WAR: The disastrous French role in World War II goes back to the start. After the German invasion of Poland, on September 1st, 1939, Britain and France declared war but neither did very much practical to help Poland. A massive French army just sat on its backside, letting the German army focus its full strength on Poland, crushing the much smaller Polish forces which were poorly equipped to resist.

This meant – and France and Britain knew this – that relatively few German troops manned the Siegfried Line, their defensive line along the French border.

At the French-built Maginot Line on the western side of the border, vast numbers of French faced them, and not quite so many British troops elsewhere. There was no significant fighting, yet the war could have been finished in a few weeks with the defeat of the Nazis – according not to me, but to top German sources.

There were some tiny local skirmishes, around the odd village or two, an incursion into undefended villages between the two lines, and an occasional isolated fight between small numbers of fighter planes. One large offensive was hesitant and quickly abandoned. A French soldier is pictured looking curiously at a Nazi emblem in the village of Lauterbach, Saarland.

At the Nuremberg Trials after the war, German military commander Alfred Jodl said: 'If we did not collapse already in the year 1939 that was due only to the fact that during the Polish campaign, the approximately 110 French and British divisions in the

West were held completely inactive against the 23 German divisions.' (Jodl, by the way, was convicted of war crimes and hanged in 1946.)

German General Siegfried Westphal, who testified at Nuremberg after surrendering to the Americans, stated that if the French had attacked in force in September 1939 the German army 'could only have held out for one or two weeks'. What years of terrible suffering and conflict would have been avoided!

As history records, the elaborately fortified Maginot Line just stopped when it reached the Belgian border with France. This is despite the obvious fact that the Germans had clearly demonstrated within recent memory – less than 30 years before – that they were quite ready to sweep through neutral Belgium with brutal barbarity. The Maginot Line – a sort of re-run First World War fixed line with knobs on – which the French complacently sat around in for eight months, from September 1939 to May 1940, while Poland was ruthlessly liquidated, turned out to be an 'Imaginot Line'. A comforting idea which excused inaction, not a proper plan to wage a modern war.

To fail to defend the area along the Belgian border after investing in the world's strongest and most expensive fortifications along the Maginot Line was an act of cretinous stupidity.

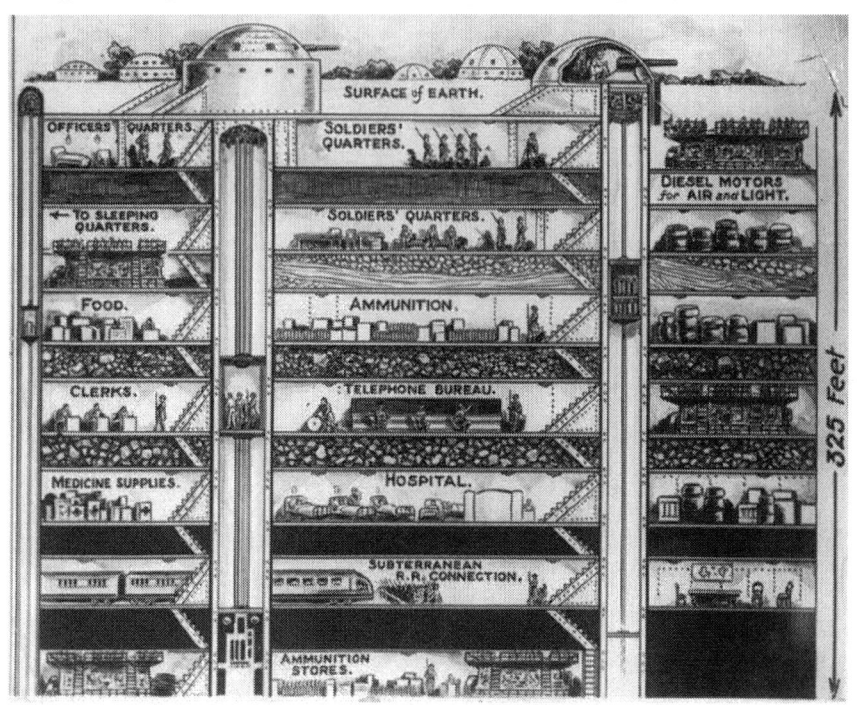

The amazing fortifications of France's Maginot Line: All utterly wasted

The Germans swept through Belgium, as a glance at a map would have suggested to them, and the fall of France rapidly followed.

The British weren't much better in that period of inaction, but were there in smaller numbers than in the First World War. The period was known as the 'Phoney War' in Britain, because very little happened outside of Poland and Norway. The RAF spent much effort bombing Germany with ineffective propaganda leaflets – 'the Confetti War' which was laughable with hindsight.

(A few attempted RAF raids on German naval targets on the North Sea Coast – the only targets the feeble bombers could easily reach – turned out to be tragic turkey shoots, with most RAF bombers shot down. They, in a gentlemanly way, tried to attack without endangering civilian housing – a bit bizarre when you think of later bombing campaigns by both sides – and would try to carry the bombs home if they could not do this safely. The bombs that were dropped mostly failed to explode anyway, the bombers' defensive guns did not work, nor did their radios – the RAF were hopeless, and slaughtered by German defences. Few made it home. The only plus side was that this taught the Germans that their home air defences were good enough and would always stop enemy raids, so little was done to strengthen them. A serious error, as the fiasco also taught the British their bombers had to be a lot better – as the Germans found faced with 1,000-bomber day and night raids a couple of years later.)

The Maginot stood ready - to fight the First World War better, not the Second

A French attack was made a few miles into a little defended Germany, but commanders called it off even before it came up against the Siegfried Line. The pretence was made to the Poles that they were in contact with the German army and fighting hard. This just was not true. It was virtually a sight-seeing outing.

Why the fatal error of inaction? One reason could be reluctance – or cowardice – arising from France's supreme sacrifice in World War I, when the nation lost more men than any other Allied power, in terrible, grinding battles such as Verdun. It was felt better to let the Germans attack their fortifications. Hence the Maginot Line concept.

Another reason could be incompetence and inertia at the top. And a third – more sinister – could be the number of fascist sympathisers and anti-Semitics that riddled the French establishment and military. The British had a few of these too, but only in France did they, sadly, come to dominate.

By the time the Vichy collaborationist government (whose flag is shown) had taken over south and central France – the Germans kept Paris and the Channel and Atlantic coasts to themselves – the anti-British and anti-Semitic feeling, both always strong in France, was to the fore. The Vichy leaders wanted Britain to fall to divert Hitler's attention from France, which they hoped that France would be the favoured province in a united Europe.

(And the hope for Britain's rapid defeat was shared in surprising quarters. In the Kennedy family, the Irish-American political dynasty, who saw it as revenge for British rule in Ireland. They were so blinded by this hatred that they could not see that Irish people would have been enslaved, would have been tortured and would have been gassed under a Nazi triumph, just like other Europeans – indeed in an oppression far worse than anything the British had ever inflicted. Nor could such people understand or respect that in both wars tens of thousands of brave, honourable Irishmen would recognise evil for what it was and join the Allied fight. And if even long after the war the charismatic Kennedys were still keen to be linked to continuing Irish terrorism against British civilians, it was deeply ironic that it was violence on the streets – which the Irish-Americans were financing and encouraging in Britain – which saw off the outwardly charming Kennedys.)

Churchill later reported to the Canadian Parliament how the French Cabinet had been advised by defeatist generals: 'In three weeks England will have her neck wrung like a chicken.' The great orator paused. 'Some chicken! Some neck!' Roars of support.

The one thing Hitler lacked in his fight with what he called the Anglo-Saxons – he included the British overseas and the Americans as potential enemies – was command of the seas. One or two German warships were powerful and modern, but it was a handful against the hundreds in the Royal Navy, the world's biggest by a long chalk. The coming Battle of the Atlantic to starve Britain into submission and deprive her of war *materiel* would be quicker done with warships, beyond the protection of air forces, than with submarines. Luckily, it seemed, the second biggest fleet in the world, and a very modern one too, was now within his reach – the French.

The biggest submarines. The fastest destroyers. Whole lines of battleships and cruisers – some virtually brand new. Undamaged, fuelled up and with thousands of shells in their magazines, with disciplined, trained crews at the ready. Seven battleships, 19 cruisers, 71 destroyers, 76 submarines – just think what havoc the Germans could wreak on the world with that lot!

The Vichy government, as part of the 1940 armistice – humiliatingly signed in the same railway carriage in the same spot in the forest of Compiègne as the Germans had been forced to do in 1918 – had for the time being left the bulk of the ships tied up in Toulon. This was in the South of France controlled by the Vichy government. It was held under strict German conditions, and their promises to leave it untouched were worth as much as all the other Nazi treaties and promises would turn out to be (the treaty vowing not to attack Russia, for example).

But a sizeable part of this huge fleet was overseas, in the French empire the Vichy government was trying to cling on to. And the biggest part of that was based in Mers el-Kebir, the port for Oran in France's main North African colony, Algeria.

Prime Minister Winston Churchill's scathing view of German assurances that the conquerors would leave the French fleet alone was clear. He told the War Cabinet that the addition of the French fleet to the German and Italian ones exposed Britain to mortal dangers. 'Who in his senses would trust the word of Hitler after his shameful record and the facts of the hour?' The fact remained that Hitler would need the French ships either to invade Britain against

Royal Navy opposition or to win to Battle of the Atlantic. And the fine ships were there for the plucking.

THE BATTLE OF MERS EL-KEBIR: This was the result of *Operation Catapult*, a British attempt to stop the French warships there being recruited for Hitler's war. Everything was done to try to avoid French blood being shed and get them to come to their senses.

The tragedy was that both sets of officers knew each other and had friends – even family – in common. The two navies had co-operated well in recent months – against the Italians in the Eastern Mediterranean, for example, and unlike the armies, worked rather well in liaison.

The British admiral, Sir James Somerville, was reluctant to use force, and queried his orders to do so, without effecting any change of heart among the Sea Lords at the Admiralty. He was to deliver a note to the French Admiral Marcel-Bruno Gensoul at Mers el-Kebir, explaining the need to 'to ensure that the best ships of the French Navy are not used against us by our common foe'.

This note suggested three possible peaceful outcomes, and threatened a fourth less peaceful one.

- **(a) Sail with us and continue to fight for victory against the Germans and Italians.**
- **(b) Sail with reduced crew to a British port. The reduced crews will be repatriated at the earliest moment. If either of these courses is adopted by you, we will restore your ships to France at the conclusion of the war, or pay full compensation if they are damaged.**
- **(c) ... or sail to some French port in the West Indies – Martinique for example... or perhaps be entrusted to the United States [then neutral]...**

If you refuse these fair offers, I must, with profound regret, require you to sink your ships [ie scuttle them themselves] within six hours. Finally, failing the above, I have the orders of His Majesty's Government to use whatever force may be necessary to prevent your ships falling into German or Italian hands.'

On the morning of the attack a lone British destroyer *Foxhound* anchored outside the harbour's anti-torpedo nets. Its captain, asked the purpose of his mission by the French using signal lamps, flashed his answer in uncoded French, knowing that all the ships in the fleet would read it.

It said that he was there to confer with Admiral Gensoul, that the Royal Navy hoped that the 'valiant and glorious French Navy' would be at their side, and that 'in these circumstances your ships would remain yours'. It added, perhaps with a hint of the underlying threat: 'A British fleet is off Oran waiting to welcome you.'

Two and a half hours of awkward negotiations ensued, on two motor launches meeting halfway. In the end the French officer agreed to take the three-option letter reproduced above to Gensoul.

Heated arguments ensued in the officers' messes of the French warships. The British started dropping sea-mines in the approaches to the harbour to show the French they meant business and to reduce their chances of escape.

The French admiral called the British back for more talks, playing for time – darkness would make an escape more feasible. The French fleet readied for actions, the coastal batteries and aircraft were armed. Admiral Somerville extended the deadline once again – very reluctant to start firing.

But Gensoul would not budge, and Somerville was ordered by the Admiralty in London: 'Act quickly or you will have reinforcements to deal with.' Ships were on their way from Toulon to intervene. And precious daylight was being wasted by prevarication.

The British left at 5.25pm and were about a mile out of the harbour in their motor launch when at 5.45pm they heard the first salvo from their own fleet. The British were firing from the north-west, across a spit of land so that over-shoots would land in the harbour and not endanger civilians in the town.

The shelling was devastating. In the end more than 1,200 Frenchmen lay dead, hundreds more wounded and several ships sunk. Yes, it knocked those ships out of war, but what a terrible way to do it! It must have strengthened the pro-Hitler element of French society considerably. None of it would have been necessary had the French acted in a reasonable way. But it *was* grimly necessary.

In the end, the rest of the magnificent French fleet, huge, modern, fast and well armed, sat out several years of the war at Toulon achieving nothing. In the end the British were proved right. Hitler, despite his promises to the contrary, did try to grab them in *Operation Lila* on November 27, 1942.

This provoked a mass scuttling and burning of the French ships by their own sailors, and an unlikely battle between a tank and moored warship.

The French losses that day were simply staggering in their size: 3 battleships (scuttled), 7 cruisers (scuttled), 15 destroyers (scuttled), 3 destroyers (seized by Germany), 13 torpedo boats (scuttled), 6 sloops (scuttled), 12 submarines (scuttled), 4 submarines (seized by Germany), 9 patrol boats (scuttled), 19 auxiliary ships (scuttled), 1 school ship (scuttled), 28 tugs (scuttled), 4 floating cranes (scuttled), 39 small ships (seized by Germany), 12 killed and 26 wounded. No other naval battle in European waters caused such losses – and this was done by the French, to the French, rather than fight. An absolute seagoing – or rather not seagoing – disgrace.

Ignominious end: Powerful French ships burn and sink at Toulon in 1942, having done absolutely nothing in the war. Picture: RAF

The rest of the hidden French war against Britain in the 1940s is too much to detail here. The best and only really comprehensive guide to this untold story is Colin Smith's book, *England's Last War Against France: Fighting Vichy 1940-1942* (Weidenfeld & Nicholson) which I recommend as a thorough yet compelling recreation of those battles and the pointless sacrifices therein. (In fact his similar book *Singapore Burning: Heroism and Surrender in World War II* is equally recommended as the best of all books on the subject for a blow-by-blow account of the British Empire's worst military humiliation at the hands of the Japanese.)

Here, with permission, are a few paragraphs of Smith's book on the Anglo-American invasion of French North Africa in November 1942. Two Allied ships, the *Walney* and the *Hartland*, with British naval officers aboard, are trying to land American troops in Oran harbour. The French are raining down shells and machine guns fire on the *Hartland*:

On deck the hoses needed to put [the fires] out were covered in mounds of dead and dying Americans. Engine room steam pipes cracked and hissed and scalded screaming stokers to death, while in the wardroom's makeshifts dressing station the wounded were being wounded again...

On the drifting *Walney* ... Lieutenant Duncan RN was letting them having it in what he fondly imagined was American French: 'Ne tiray pas! Noo sarmes vos armis. Noo sarmes Americaine. Ne tiray pas! Noo sarmes Americaine.'

The only response Duncan got was a burst of machine-gun fire, which killed him. He fell against [wounded war correspondent Leo] Disher who noticed how 'strangely soft' his friend's body felt, feeling nothing like the stiff muscles of the stiff muscles of a man merely thrown off balance. The next shell mortally wounded two doctors toiling in the wardroom dressing station, one American, the other British.

And so it went on. Even when the few, wounded survivors of the massacre crawled ashore, snipers wounded or killed them. Swimming helpless or wounded survivors were machine-gunned mercilessly by the French, they said.

Hundreds of Americans, and British sailors helping them, were killed and hundreds more wounded, completely pointlessly as it turned out, as the rest of the invasion of Vichy North Africa was going well enough so the French would soon be able to fight on the same side, to help liberate their homeland from fascists. Yet even while American troops mustered inland and took the various cities under control, French snipers killed or maimed their officers whenever they could.

All over America, officers were soon knocking on doors of parents who would be perplexed to hear their sons had lost their lives at the hands of the very people they were rescuing from Nazism.

The above was just one battle of many in North Africa, and Syria, where French forces gleefully massacred whoever they could, including Free French forces coming to liberate them.

But towards the end of the war, the contribution of the Free French to the defeat of the Nazis needed to be exaggerated for political reasons. In August 1944, the Free French leader Charles de Gaulle (pictured) entered Paris with his troops. He made a speech saying:

'Paris stood up to liberate Paris... Liberated by itself, liberated by its people with the help of the armies of France, with the support and the help of all France, of the France that fights, of the real France, of the eternal France!'

Well, of course he had to say something like that, but it was 100 per cent pompous poppycock, the start of a deceitful delusion that endures today. The French had not by themselves liberated France, the blood, courage, money and might of the Allies had done that. In fact, as we have just demonstrated the French had fought enthusiastically *for* fascism, not against it.

Contrary to de Gaulle's speech, the French had not by themselves liberated even Paris. The Germans had fled because they had been outflanked by the Allies, while the French units were almost led by the hand to make a rather symbolic entrance. The Parisians welcoming de Gaulle were cheering fascist quisling Petain on the same streets just four months before.

Even during the fighting after D-Day Petain's head of government Pierre Laval was broadcasting to the French people: 'We are not in the war. You must not take part in the fighting.'

French arrogance, inaccuracy and, frankly, ingratitude merely increased after the conflict was over. In Vietnam after World War II, (and French Indo-China in general), the French chose to ignore British advice that the best people to run those countries were probably the people who lived there, and insisted on resuming the glorious French empire. Result: 20 years of terrible conflict for France, and then the United States, and whole string of humiliating defeats for both countries. A similar disastrous failure to decolonise when it was clearly time to do so was to unfold in North Africa.

By 1966, the same Charles de Gaulle, now President of France, was leaving Nato in a fit of pique and demanding that all U.S. troops be removed from French soil, closing any bases there. U.S. President Lyndon Johnson, hearing this, ordered a reluctant Secretary of State Dean Rusk to ask de Gaulle at a forthcoming meeting about the Americans buried in France. Did they have to leave too?

So at the meeting, when de Gaulle repeated his demand for all American troops to leave France, Rusk duly asked if this included the more than 60,000 American soldiers buried in France following World Wars I and II. De Gaulle, flustered and embarrassed, got up and left without answering the question.

The strange French failure to be honest about World War II is a disgraceful, deceitful and demeaning delusion. The Germans, who by any measure have plenty of 20th century history to be ashamed of, are today admirably straightforward and honest about their nation's past crimes and mistakes. The French, on the other hand, are almost as bad as the Japanese, who try to avoid mentioned that anything nasty happened in the 1940s, whereas in fact the latter exhibited some of the most murderous, sadistic, barbaric aggression of the 20th century.

If you think this chapter's attitude to the French delusions about World War II is exaggerated, there are accounts and pictures available – which I would rather not republish here – of French women being hanged, often after torture, of distressed, thirsty and hungry French children, some as young as three or four, seen waving their little arms out of the bars of railway trucks wailing 'Maman!' as they were shipped unaccompanied to be murdered in Germany while their parents were being appallingly mistreated elsewhere (Jewish French children, that is). Who rounded them up for this appallingly evil treatment? Not, in many cases, the Germans, but their enthusiastic French followers, such as the paramilitary *Milice*. They even did the torturing of their fellow countrymen and women if required.

It is not the case, of course, that the French are always wrong. They couldn't have been more right about the Second Gulf War – they were right not to join in a fool's errand. Nor is it the case that a Britain over-run by fascists in World War II could not have found quislings and torturers. I am, sadly, sure they could have.

No, it's just that we should be honest about what happened. Actually if you want to take a serious subject lightly for a moment, go and see the French military museum at Les Invalides in Paris, one of Europe's biggest jokes. There you enjoy accounts of the Napoleonic Wars listing all the French triumphs with not a mention of the Battle of Waterloo (where they, of course, finally lost) that I noticed. Of the naval war with barely a mention of the Battle of Trafalgar (ditto). Of the brilliance of World War II's Maginot Line (with hardly a mention of the collapse of French morale at the same time).

Yes there was an honourable minority of French who fought courageously in the Resistance during World War II, and in the Free French forces, but it was a small minority. During the first part of the war, the French fought more strongly and effectively for fascism. Indeed, they *were* fascism to some extent.

Some French towns are very honest about the deportations, executions, etc. But as a nation, it's still one big Gallic shrug…

Lest we forget: De Gaulle inspects Free French troops in London in 1942, and the small but courageous force is rightly remembered. The other side of the story is not so openly discussed, however

15 MESOPOTAMIAN MAYHEM

YOU may recall the Chilcot Inquiry into the shambles of Britain's involvement in the 2003 Iraq War, published at long last in 2016, but for me – the author of this book, that is – it had a horrible sense of déjà vu. My grandfather fought from Basra to Baghdad a century before. That too had ill-defined aims, with the British unable to believe they were seen as occupiers, not liberators from a tyrant, and enduring constant guerrilla resistance. It ended with an inquiry, to learn lessons, so such a thing might not happen again. In fact because our leaders do not read history, it has happened *three times* since, over the same territory, making similar disastrous mistakes...

TO THE PEOPLE OF BAGHDAD: 'Our military operations have as their object the defeat of the enemy ... our armies do not come into your cities as conquerors or enemies, but as liberators ...

'Your sons have been carried off to wars not of your making, your wealth has been stripped from you by unjust men and squandered ...

'It is the hope and desire of the British people and their Allies that the Arab race may rise once more to greatness and renown among the peoples of the world ...'

THIS British message, which closely echoes some of the things Tony Blair said to Parliament in an emergency debate on Iraq in 2003, is not an extract from the leaflets dropped in Iraq in the First Gulf War campaign of the previous decade – nor even the similar Kuwait emergency of 1961 when Britain rushed troops (including one Paddy Ashdown, later a British MP) to defend Kuwait from Iraq.

It is from an extraordinary proclamation nailed up in Baghdad after the British Army finally fought its way into the city on March 11, 1917 in an appallingly bloody campaign, now almost completely and unjustly forgotten.

Mesopotamia, as Iraq was then called, was part of the Turkish empire stretching from the Balkans to the Gulf, and the Turks' Germans allies had long been intriguing to hamper Britain's influence in the region, with dreams of threatening India and routes to the Far East and Australia. A glance at a world map shows that if the

Germans and their Austro-Hungarian Empire and other allies controlled the Balkans, and then the Ottoman Empire, then a continuous swathe of Berlin-dominated territory would stretch from the North Sea to the Arabian Gulf, a daunting prospect. (Nor is this mere history. This decision – of those last two mentioned empires to throw their hats into the German ring – meant their total destruction within a few years and all the complicated consequences ever since of having dozens of new, free states across the Balkans and Middle East, still causing non-stop mayhem.)

The problem back then was how to halt the German land grab – or rather influence grab and oil grab – going ever southwards.

But looking back from around 2000, it all seemed rather like the series of modern conflicts. The modern map of Iraq shown here – of course Iraq and Iran did not yet exist – does show the key places of the earlier war: Basra, or Al Basrah, where the British landed and first attacked, Baghdad, their objective, about 280 miles away. About where it says Tigris was Ctesiphon, where the British were roundly defeated, and Al Kut, or simply Kut, where a British army was trapped, and then lost.

This first messy British involvement with this land started with the easy capture of Basra at the top of the Gulf – to protect oil interests and prevent, oh yes, a rumoured attack on Kuwait – in November 1914. So far, so familiar to us today. Then things got messier.

Riverboats are prepared on a slipway at Basra. Chinese craftsmen and labourers were imported, and dozens still lie there in unnamed graves

This limited objective – taking Basra and the oil fields – led to a ghastly drawn-out and needless campaign up to Baghdad – run from British India rather than London. Even by the appalling standards of World War I, the ill-starred adventure featured an extraordinary blend of bungling and bravery, leading to needless yet huge sacrifices for an aim that was never clearly expressed.

The initial campaign towards Baghdad was a logistical disaster, run with bewildering complacency and ineptitude from India. There was an out-of-date reliance on British and Indian cavalry's gallantry – still using sabres and lances – to overcome what were expected to be second-rate Turkish and Arab troops. Initially that seemed to work, and a series of easy victories took the British up towards Ctesiphon.

But it was winter. The ill-equipped British troops repeatedly ended up wading through mud in open ground towards Turkish trenches, barbed wire and machine-gunners, well trained by the Ottoman Empire's German allies. It was no walkover after all.

At Ctesiphon the British encountered well-prepared defences for the first time, and were shocked to lose 4,600 men in the attack, which – although the Turks lost perhaps 2,000 more men – was a catastrophic failure.

The men's bravery wasn't in doubt, but the slaughter on each attack was on a Crimean scale, particularly because of the failure to collect the wounded before scavenging Arab tribesmen could torture, murder and rob them in the battlefield. Even if the wounded were collected, they would as likely die en route back to British lines, being dragged over rough ground on unsprung carts, more suited to the Waterloo era of 100 years before. Then, if they were lucky, they faced a perilous journey down river to Basra.

An Indian army ambulance takes casualties to a river boat, from which the photo is taken. Soon such efforts would be over-whelmed by numbers

Military historians of the initial campaign have noted how when luck presented chances for a brilliant British breakthrough, these were repeatedly thrown away to stick to preconceived, and ill-conceived, plans.

Communications were stretched further and further up the

Tigris River, with only a few river boats and native craft for supply. Then the wounded who did make it back to improvised hospital ships on the river had to run the gauntlet of murderous enemy fire on both banks, and the riddled ships unloaded mostly dead at Basra.

The Army commanders were so incompetent they didn't even know what to ask for. When they did, it was straitjacketed by false economies. For example, desperate pleas for defensive wire, searchlights and Verey lights (flares, pictured being fired) from Major General Sir Charles Townshend at about the time of the first battle of Ctesiphon were refused by General Sir John Nixon back at the coast on the grounds of cost. Cost? Compared to what ensued?

When the government in India was stirred out of its complacency by the terrible setbacks, even then its actions were amazingly inept. There were no shallow draft boats left to navigate the rivers which were the only means of supply. The rivers of India and Burma were scoured for stern-wheel paddle craft, but only the oldest were released and they mostly sank en route, not being sea-going. Of one fleet of 21 sent, for example, only four reached Basra and these all turned out to be unsuitable. It was a fiasco.

A British firm, Lynch & Co., which knew full well from commercial experience how to navigate the Tigris, was approached to design, build, ship out and assemble suitable ships to save the campaign. They asked for a 10 per cent fee, then reduced this to a nominal fee 'for patriotic reasons' when the India Office balked at it, but their services were still refused.

The result was that alternative, hopeless designs of ships were built, taken out to Basra in crates where unskilled labour tried to assemble the unnumbered parts. On launching, they sank. All this while British and Indian troops were going through absolute hell up river.

Indian troops at Kut take aim with a Lewis gun at a Turkish aircraft

The retreat from Ctesiphon, which is near the 1991 Allied air forces' target of Sulaiman Pak, was only the beginning of the disaster. An entire British Army under Townshend was besieged in Kut, a name which should stand with Gallipoli and Singapore as the key humiliations of British arms in the 20th century, but which is now all but forgotten – except for a memorial in St Paul's Cathedral, London to the 5,746 of the garrison who died there or in brutal captivity.

Thousands of lives were spent on both banks of the Tigris fighting furiously and vainly to relieve the siege from December 5, 1915 to 29 April, 1916. The men in the little town died like flies while the Turks shelled everything, including the hospital, at their leisure.

While men were dying in the hell of Kut, the official bungling assumed a comic aspect worthy of a Carry On film. Signals from headquarters down at Basra asked: 'Advise attitude of enemy.' The besieged garrison replied: 'Angry.' The perplexed brasshats on the coast signalled back. 'Expand on angry.'

'Bloody angry,' came the reply.

The Entrenched Camp of Kut.

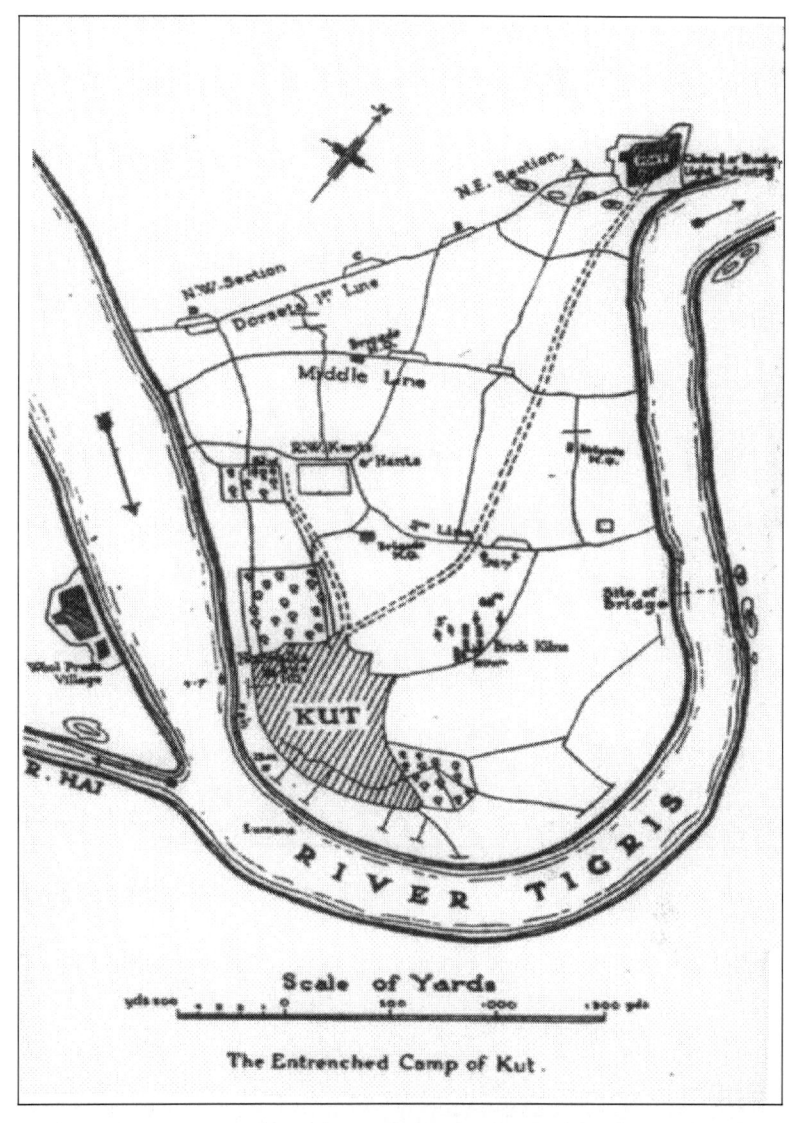

Then there was a long interchange of queries about the state of files – while the wounded were dying in droves! – which turned out to be all another ludicrous mistake. The signaller should have sent 'flies'- the Army had sent men desperately short of food and ammunition an ample supply of fly swats. Naturally, even the fly swats were the wrong sort. The Navy even armoured the steamer *Julnar* to attempt a breakthrough with food and ammunition, but it was caught in a Turkish obstruction, shot up and captured.

When the surrender of the army at Kut came, more than 13,000

British and Indian troops were exposed to a barbarity only matched in the 20th century by the Japanese on the Burma railway in World War II. The Indian troops, pictured, were in a shocking state of near-starvation after the siege, and the British troops too, although the officers seemed not to have suffered so much.

A death march of starving troops, many wounded, mercilessly beaten by their Arab tribesman guards, was started towards Turkey, which was to result in the deaths of 70 per cent of the British prisoners by the end of the war.

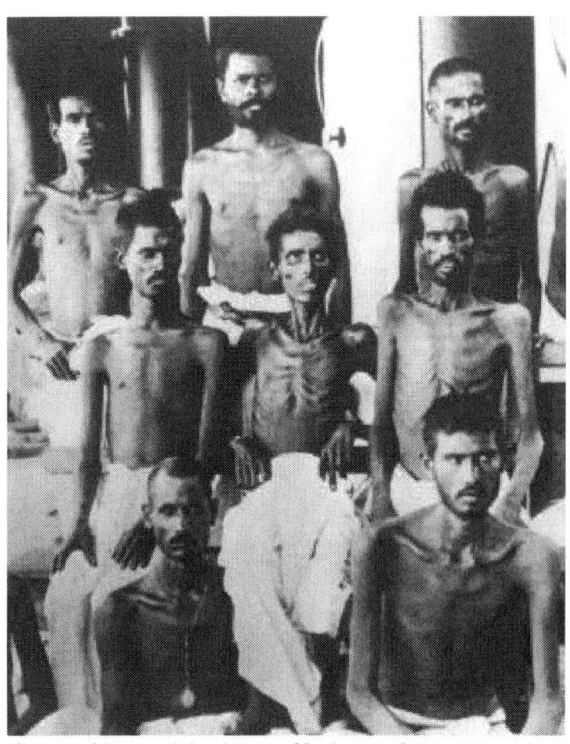

As Captain E. O. Mousley, one of the captured officers lucky enough to be taken by boat to Baghdad, wrote searingly in his memoirs: 'We tingled with anger and shame at seeing on the other bank a sad little column of troops who had marched up from Kut, driven by a wild crowd of Kurdish horsemen who brandished sticks and whips. The eyes of our men stared out from white faces, drawn long with the suffering of a too tardy death and they held out their hands towards our boat.' That was, for them, just the beginning of greater brutality.

After this humiliation, London finally took over the rest of the campaign and the effort needed to sustain a war hundreds of miles inland was made. The logistics were horrendous. There were no roads, no proper docks at Basra, no railway towards Baghdad. All these facilities, so carefully bombed by the RAF and the Americans in 1991, were built by the British after Whitehall, dismayed at the setbacks, poured resources into what had been a Cinderella of a campaign.

Not quite as starving as his men (previous page): Defeated General Townsend (centre) after the surrender at Kut, with his victor Khalil Pasha (right)

Army engineers – such as my grandfather, Major Frederick Cole sent from Lahore – beavered away at construction of roads, bridges and railways, the very targets of the RAF Tornados and their smart bombs in the 1990s campaign.

Those girder bridges so neatly blown in half by smart bombs, as shown in General Schwarzkopf's press conferences, would often have been assembled by British soldiers with girders from steel works at Middlesbrough and rails from Workington. You could see the British firms' names still stamped proudly on the twisted steelwork in the 1991 CNN film clips.

But it was not until the more recent conflict caused me to delve into the Imperial War Museum's fascinating collection of memoirs, letters, photographs and histories that I realised how lucky my grandfather was to have survived the ill-starred 1914 campaign at all. He was saved by being a railway engineer.

Family lore has it that he said to my grandmother on volunteering for duty in this conflict: 'Good! No more bloody railways, some proper soldiering at last.' When he arrived at Basra, he was greeted with: 'At last, Major Cole. There's a shipload of railway stuff over there. Get cracking.' Yet he was so fortunate not have joined the 'proper soldiering' up river at Kut.

At last things begin to go well for the British. Artillery crosses a pontoon bridge engineers had constructed near Baghdad in 1917

This war, which helped end German dreams of a place in the sun had, eventually, more British victories than defeats, although often at terrible cost, and had its comical side too. This is another echo down the years – the stoical, eternally bloody-minded humour of the British Tommy, or squaddie as we would call him today. I have to admit to liking their fatalistic black humour. My grandfather wrote rarely from the war zone, and talked of it little later. A letter home referring to being camped among the date palms had the word 'date' meticulously cut out because the censor had been told all references to dates was forbidden!

Later, in 1991 we see the Kurdish guerilla fighters called Pesh Mergas were naturally renamed the 'Peach Melbas' by the British squaddies. The objective of a town called Salman was naturally chalked up on a blackboard by officers as 'Rushdie'.

A victory, but at what cost and what for? The Hampshire Regiment march into Baghdad in March 1917. Britain had created a new country, Iraq

In 2003 we had a group of squaddies going through a grim Iraqi town and the conversation – recorded by a reporter – went something like this. Officer: 'This place is a dump, there's nothing to drink and the women are bloody ugly.'

'Just like Southampton, Sir.'

'And now they're bloody shooting at us.'

'Portsmouth, then, Sir.'

In 1991 we had the grim news of captured British airmen being abused and paraded. Yet again this was a re-run of 1914-17 when fliers who had staged a Lawrence of Arabia-style raid well behind enemy lines crashed their wooden biplane. They were captured, kicked, spat upon and paraded through Baghdad in contravention of international law, just as those Tornado crewmen were abused in 1991.

One thing *was* totally different back in 1914 – the lack of interest and complacency in Whitehall and Indian headquarters in Simla.

The Mesopotamia Commission was formed afterwards to investigate and the evidence of Major-General Sir George Gorringe was to the point: 'It was believed to be a side-show and "no man's child".' The cost had been 100,000 casualties and hundreds of millions of pounds. And as with that other disaster Gallipoli, this was part of a confused war with the Turkish empire that was not really necessary, had muddled objectives, but turned into a ghastly nightmare and didn't solve the underlying problems of the Middle East, and in fact made them worse. Sounds familiar?

As the 1914-17 war ground on, my grandfather (pictured) built his roads and railways, and conditions for the troops became more pleasant. There were even horse and camel races for the victorious troops in Baghdad, he wrote. A 'Mesopotamian picnic' as promised, at last came true for those who hadn't been cut down in their hundreds and thousands wading through the marshes towards machine guns.

With the end of the war it was back to India, where my grandfather was known for winning most of the shooting trophies going, despite having the same inherited slight tremble the whole family has. My mother's biggest teenage embarrassment was probably at her coming out ball in Lahore, where a young officer got down on the ground with an umbrella, waving the tip around wildly, to show how crackshot Major Cole did it.

He was also famed for having his own train, or at least a carriage complete with children and servants which he hooked on to trains steaming around India for his inspections. Sometimes the wilder frontier railways would have soldiers posted at the bridges to guard the line, he recalled.

The unbearably hot summers meant the family was sent away to lovely hill stations such as Simla and Darjeeling. The ghastly Mesopotamia adventure seems to have been little mentioned in those happy years.

When I was sent away to school years later I was given his thin Army blanket from the campaign and knew nothing of what it represented.

Independence for India had meant retiring to genteel Hove in Sussex. He had invested the earnings of generations serving British

India in British railway companies – 'You can't lose, it's all there in rolling stock and permanent way!' He lost the lot.

At least he didn't live to see the RAF bombing the hell out of all his beautiful bridges.

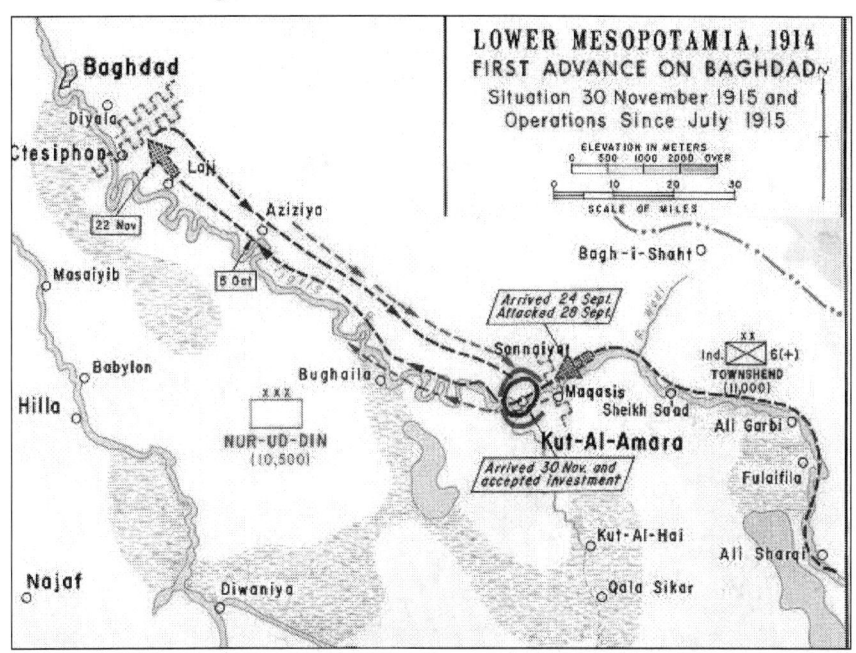

LOWER MESOPOTAMIA, 1914
FIRST ADVANCE ON BAGHDAD
Situation 30 November 1915 and Operations Since July 1915

POSTCRIPT: Britain's involvement in Iraq, as it had become, just went from bad to very bad. There was a stormy inter-war period, where a half-hearted colonial system achieved such disasters as bombing weddings (sounds familiar from the modern era, doesn't it?), and then in World War II we find the Germans – with precisely the same aim as in World War I of splitting the British empire in half, closing Suez, grabbing oil reserves, and creating a German-led empire from the North Sea to the Persian Gulf – fomenting a pretty good uprising in Iraq in league with their fascist French friends, the Vichy government who controlled Syria and Lebanon (see Chapter 13).

This had strange effects such as the siege of RAF Habbaniya in 1941. It was a sprawling base west of Baghdad, complete with schools, housing, cinema, green lawns using water from the Tigris, sailing school on Lake Habbaniya (where recently Empire flying boats had stopped en route to India), hospital, church, British shops, etc. When the Iraqis, with German assistance, surrounded it and started shelling the base from the overlooking plateau, things looked grim for a while. In a remarkable turnaround of fortunes, the British, using what were basically obsolete training aircraft and a few ancient armoured cars, managed to overcome the much larger and better equipped Iraqi army and regain control.

Then in 1961, the newly independent Iraqi republic threatened adjoining Kuwait and British forces were rushed to the area (including a young Paddy Ashdown, later Liberal leader, who was a Royal Marines officer). With the aid of troops and an aircraft carrier, Iraq was deterred for the time being.

Then in 1990, Iraqi dictator Saddam Hussain invaded Kuwait – he had one of the world's largest armies, and one of world's largest national debts – and a Western Coalition led by U.S. President George Bush (the father) pushed Iraqi forces out of Kuwait and half-way up Iraq. This seemed justified in stopping the naked grab of a neighbouring country by a torturing tyrant.

Then in 2003 British prime minister Tony Blair and U.S. President George W. Bush (the son) launched a second Gulf War (actually at least the fourth) for no fair or logical reason, based on a dodgy dossier of cooked-up exaggerations and lies, without United Nations authority. The Iraqis have been living with the legacy of this shameful war ever since, with tens of thousands of civilians killed. Hundreds of British and U.S. servicemen were killed too, all for no purpose than the deluded power complex of people like Blair.

As with the Mesopotamian War my grandad fought over the same route up from Basra to Baghdad, there was a long inquiry – the infamous Chilcot Report which conveniently for Blair took *seven years* and cost many millions of pounds to write. The report (Evening Standard headline below) concluded that the war was unnecessary, the intelligence wrong, and the legality of it doubtful.

Until that war, Britain's military track record had been mainly – not entirely – honourable. Going to Belgium's aid in World War I, to that of Norway and Greece and Poland in World War II, liberating Europe in 1945 and closing down the Nazi death camps.

Not any more. In any sane country, Blair and his spin doctors would be rotting in jail. Beware charisma in grinning politicians. And read history books.

ABOUT THE AUTHOR

Benedict le Vay is a London-born journalist, author and 'rather bad yachtsman and potter' who has worked as a newspaper sub-editor in major newspapers in Britain, Hong Kong and New Zealand. A father of two, his books have included the best-selling *Eccentric Britain, Eccentric London, Eccentric Oxford* and *Eccentric Cambridge* guides, and also *Britain From The Rails: A Window-Gazer's Guide*, all published by Bradt, and *Pearl Harbor, Still Shocking 75 Years On;* plus *The Secret History of Everyday Stuff: Astounding, Fascinating or Remarkable Facts About Your Daily Life* and *Weeping Waters: When Train Meets Volcano* (Amazon). Asked if he himself is eccentric, he says: 'Not at all, I'm afraid. The best I can do is being Honorary Secretary of the Friends of the A272, and asking for my ashes to be blasted from the chimney of my favourite steam loco at my funeral. But then hasn't everyone?' Picture: WENDY FULLER

BY THE SAME AUTHOR

The Bradt books above may be ordered through bookshops. All the books are available through Amazon.com and Amazon.co.uk

Printed in Great Britain
by Amazon